Domesday Economy

A New Approach to
Anglo-Norman History

JOHN McDONALD AND G. D. SNOOKS

CLARENDON PRESS · OXFORD
1986

Oxford University Press, Walton Street, Oxford OX2 6DP

Oxford New York Toronto
Delhi Bombay Calcutta Madras Karachi
Kuala Lumpur Singapore Hong Kong Tokyo
Nairobi Dar es Salaam Cape Town
Melbourne Auckland
and associated companies in
Beirut Berlin Ibadan Nicosia

Oxford is a trade mark of Oxford University Press

Published in the United States
by Oxford University Press, New York

British Library Cataloguing in Publication Data
McDonald, John
Domesday economy: a new approach to
Anglo-Norman history.
1. England—Economic conditions
I. Title   II. Snooks, G. D.
330.942'021   HC254
ISBN 0-19-828524-8

Library of Congress Cataloging in Publication Data
McDonald, John
Domesday economy.
1. Domesday book. 2. Great Britain—History—
William I, 1066-1087. 3. England—Economic conditions
—Medieval period, 1066-1485. 4. Normans—England—
Economic conditions. I. Snooks, G. D. (Graeme Donald)
II. Title.
DA190.D7M33 1986   330.942'021   86-5369
ISBN 0-19-828524-8

Set by Mid-County Press
Printed and bound in
Great Britain by Biddles Ltd,
Guildford and King's Lynn

To

Pamela　　　　　　　　　　　*Loma*
and Timothy　　　　　*Adrian and Roland*

Preface

An attempt has been made in this book to analyse aspects of the English economy in the late eleventh century. For this purpose we have employed contemporary economic and statistical methods to examine the remarkably detailed data in Domesday Book. By bringing new techniques to bear upon an ancient document, which is now 900 years old, we have crossed the boundaries of a number of disciplines. Fortunately we have been listened to with forbearance, and have received generous assistance and advice. Indeed, this has been one of the most rewarding aspects of our project.

Over the past few years we have accumulated many intellectual debts from colleagues who specialize in medieval history, economic history, political science, economics, and econometrics. While it is not possible to mention everyone, there are a number who should be named because of their valuable comments upon earlier drafts of one or more of the chapters in this book. Amongst the medievalists are J. Campbell, R. Fleming, J. Hatcher, P. D. A. Harvey, J. C. Holt, H. R. Loyn, and G. H. Martin; the economic historians and political scientists include P. A. David, S. Fenoaltea, C. H. Feinstein, G. R. Hawke, M. Levi, D. N. McCloskey, and D. C. North; and the economists and econometricians are J. Aldrich, D. Hendry, J. Hutton, R. Manning, T. Mills, G. Mizon, G. Phillips, P. Wagstaff, and A. Zellner. Many others provided helpful comments in seminars given in Australia, the United Kingdom, and North America.

Throughout the preparation of this book we were fortunate in receiving valuable research and typing assistance from a number of people. We are particularly grateful to Eva Aker, who assisted greatly in processing the data, proof-reading the various drafts, and offering helpful suggestions. Beverley Vickers also provided valuable research assistance. Special thanks go to Mary Cherin who, with remarkable cheerfulness and efficiency, coped with our illegible manuscript and unreasonable deadlines.

We are grateful to to the editors of the *Economic History Review*, the *Journal of Economic History*, and the *Journal of the Royal Statistical Society* for permission to use sections of our earlier articles on the Domesday economy. We thank Allen & Unwin for permission to reproduce (in Table 3.1) data from J. H. Round, *Feudal England*; Longman for permission to use (in Figure 2.1) material from F. Barlow, *The Feudal Kingdom of England*; and Cambridge University Press for permission to reprint (in Tables 3.2 and 3.3) data from H. C. Darby (ed.), *The Domesday Geography of England*, volumes v and vii. Finally we acknowledge the financial support provided by the Australian Research Grants Scheme and Flinders University.

JM   GDS

Contents

Contents

List of tables

List of figures

PART I
HISTORICAL STUDIES

1

Domesday Book re-examined

1.1 INTRODUCTION

An eminent scholar has claimed that 'Domesday Book is the most famous English public record, and it is probably the most remarkable statistical document in the history of Europe' (Darby 1979, ix). Domesday Book is remarkable because it includes detailed information on the 'ownership', income, resources, and fiscal responsibilities of virtually every manor in Norman England in 1086. From the wealth of manorial data it is possible to reconstruct, with considerable precision, the economic system of Domesday England. This is a unique opportunity, because no other document of any period or of any other country can match both the detail and the comprehensiveness of Domesday Book. It is possible, therefore, to obtain a clearer understanding of the economy of Domesday England than of any other until the twentieth century.

Not surprisingly, the importance of Domesday Book has attracted the attention of many distinguished scholars in the past, including F. W. Maitland, P. Vinogradoff, J. H. Round, J. Tait, F. M. Stenton, V. H. Galbraith, and H. C. Darby. Their imaginative studies of this document have added much to our understanding of Anglo-Norman society, and of the administrative processes that gave rise to, and that subsequently employed, Domesday Book. Although their achievement has been impressive, these scholars have not been able to analyse comprehensively the bewildering detail of the Domesday data. The richness of the data that attracted their attention remains largely untapped, because the theoretical and statistical methods required for this purpose were not available to them. As earlier scholars were forced to focus either upon small unrepresentative samples, or upon highly aggregated data that were stripped bare of their informative individual detail, the resulting traditional view of the Domesday economy is unnecessarily limited. In some instances, the interpretation of central economic relationships appears counter-intuitive and even fanciful. Now that the methods required to analyse the data comprehensively are available, it is time to undertake a major re-examination of Domesday Book.

1.2 AIMS AND METHODS

This study was undertaken with two major objectives in mind. The first was to test the existing interpretations of economic relationships in Domesday Book, because they appeared contrary to normal expectation. Modern statistical techniques have been employed to scrutinize traditional views concerning the determinants of tax assessments for danegeld, and of manorial income. As our conclusions (in Chapters 4 and 5) are radically different from earlier interpretations, we have attempted to explain the basis for the difference by examining (in Chapter 3) the empirical methods of previous Domesday scholarship. Secondly, as we were able to demonstrate that the relationships between the main Domesday variables do make sense when adequately tested, we proceeded further by using economic production functions to analyse the system of manorial production in Domesday England (in Chapter 6).

To achieve these objectives, two counties, selected on an economic rather than on a geographical basis, have been analysed in depth. There were three main reasons for adopting this strategy. First, the great volume of information in Domesday Book poses substantial problems in terms of transferring the data to the computer and in writing programs that can subject it to analysis. The cost involved in overcoming these problems had to be balanced against the possibility that, if the traditional interpretation were correct, then the data in Domesday Book would be meaningless. A modest beginning appeared to be the most sensible approach. Secondly, the units in which data are recorded in Domesday Book vary considerably between the seven or so Survey circuits, and it is even possible that the interpretation placed upon the responses of landholders by the Survey commissioners differed in a similar way. A county approach, at least in the first instance, appeared to be the wisest procedure. Thirdly, and most importantly, as there were considerable institutional differences both between and within counties, the ideal basis for statistical analysis appears to be the lay–ecclesiastical subdivision at the county level. To ignore these institutional differences is to squander the richness of the data in Domesday Book and, more seriously, to draw inappropriate conclusions from the statistical analysis. More aggregative work will be less hazardous and misleading at a later stage in the project.

Essex and Wiltshire were chosen for study because they appeared representative of 'normal' Domesday counties, and because their entries are clear and comprehensive. As our intention in this volume is to analyse the normal operation of the Domesday economy, counties relatively unscathed by natural and manmade disasters were selected.[1] A surprisingly large proportion of the other counties in 1086 were still suffering from devastation caused by the Conquest, savage Norman retribution following several English rebellions, attacks by Vikings and Celts, and outbreaks of disease. Essex was the most obvious starting point, because its entries are, together with the other two counties (Norfolk and Suffolk) in Little Domesday Book, more detailed than those for the remaining counties in Great Domesday Book (see 2.2.4). In addition, the Essex entries are far less ambiguous than those for Norfolk and Suffolk, both of which reflect the complicating influence of Danish settlement. Wiltshire, which is to be found in Great Domesday Book, was chosen because of a number of important contrasts it provided to Essex: it was from a different survey circuit (see 2.2.4), it had a different political and social background, it had a different manorial structure (see 2.1.2), and it did not have direct access to the sea. The Essex and Wiltshire data were obtained from translations in the Victoria County History, which were checked against the Farley text. The data are available on computer tape (McDonald and Snooks 1984).

Owing to the large number of observations available for Essex and Wiltshire, and the remarkable similarity of our statistical results despite the obvious differences between these counties, we are confident that the conclusions of this study provide a good guide to the normal operation of the Domesday economy. Later studies, however, will consider a wider range of counties, and will also be concerned with the Domesday economy in crisis.

1.3 SCOPE AND STRUCTURE OF INQUIRY

Basically this book is aimed at historians interested in the economics of Domesday England, but it should also be of value to the growing number of economists concerned with the medieval economic system. Among the historians we hope to interest are medievalists who are familiar with the social or political dimensions of eleventh-century England and may wish to discover more about economic motivation and processes at both the national and the manorial levels, and economic historians who are familiar with the method we have employed and wish to see what it can tell us about the English economy as early as the eleventh century.

While we are primarily interested in issues central to the Domesday economy, our results should be of assistance to scholars working on other aspects of medieval England. For example, political historians concerned with the relationship between wealth and power will be interested to learn whether our results confirm or reject the traditional view that the assessments and values are 'artificial'. If they are artificial they cannot be employed as indices of wealth. If they are not artificial, however, it will be possible to show which variable is the best index of wealth. Our results also provide information about the political and economic motivation of King William, together with his tenants-in-chief and other manorial lords. Did the Normans attempt to impose their authority in an arbitrary way, or were they more concerned to maximize their incomes for the purpose of military exploits and conspicuous consumption? Relevant information is provided on this question. Our results also throw some light upon the nature of territorial government in 1086. Something can be said about the relative importance of the vill and manor in the system of territorial, as opposed to feudal, administration. Our results also solve a number of longstanding problems concerning the interpretation of important entries in Domesday Book, and thereby help to clarify the intention of those who framed the great Survey.

Because of the wider relevance of our results, we have attempted to make them accessible to readers with backgrounds in a variety of disciplines. This objective is always difficult to achieve, but the importance of the issues make the exercise worth undertaking. In order to appeal to a wider readership, the book has been divided into two parts. Part I, 'Historical studies', outlines the state of existing knowledge on the economy and survey of 1086, reviews the traditional methods and interpretations, and introduces our methods and results in a non-technical way. The seven chapters in this part make up an integrated whole which, it is hoped, will be of interest to historians of all persuasions, and. to economists of broader vision. Part II, 'Economic and statistical methods', is concerned with the detailed methods employed in the first part of the book. While these three chapters will be of interest primarily to quantitative economic historians, economists, and econometricians, they have been written in an informal way (few proofs are given) so that interested medievalists will be able to satisfy themselves about our methods. Further, we hope that this Part will be of assistance to medievalists and other historians who wish to undertake quantitative work. We believe that an applied study of this type makes it easier for the practising historian to acquire the statistical knowledge necessary for analysing detailed data sources such as Domesday Book; and for this reason we have attempted to make the book as self-contained as possible.

1.4 THE TRADITIONAL INTERPRETATION OF DOMESDAY BOOK

It is important to distinguish between empirically based knowledge and pure speculation in the Domesday literature. Throughout this study the empirically derived conclusions will be referred to as the 'traditional interpretation' or 'conventional wisdom', which can be defined as the generally accepted view(s) about economic relationships in Domesday England that have arisen from a clearly definable empirical research strategy. Orbiting around this core of empirically based knowledge are a host of speculations, some of considerable interest and ingenuity, based upon intuition or logical reasoning but with little or no empirical underpinning.[2] In our view, it is necessary in an empirical discipline like history to do more than speculate about reality—it is essential to attempt some form of empirical verification or falsification. Only once the speculation has been convincingly verified, and the error in the traditional interpretation has been exposed, can it become the new interpretation. Normally this will result from the application of new and more suitable methods to existing data, or from the discovery of new evidence.

Sometimes, as in the case of the Domesday literature, the traditional intepretation of a particular issue may embrace contradictory explanations. It is possible for a contradiction of this nature to exist for a considerable time without detection (up to 100 years on the question of the determinants of Domesday tax assessment—see Chapter 4). The problem can arise if scholars, using different empirical tests and different data sources to test a particular hypothesis, are unable to evaluate the significance of their different approaches. The ability to distinguish between different testing procedures is, it will be argued in Chapter 3, an important strength of the new approach to Domesday Book adopted here.

An attempt has been made in this study to distinguish between speculation and empirical knowledge, to clarify contradictions within the latter, and to demonstrate which, if any, can be supported by a comprehensive examination of the data. This is a necessary prerequisite for the construction of a new interpretation of the Domesday economy.

1.5 HISTORICAL EVENTS SURROUNDING THE DOMESDAY SURVEY

The survey which gave rise to Domesday Book was ordered by William the Conqueror on Christmas Day 1085, and was completed before his death in September 1087. A brief discussion of the events which surrounded this survey may be helpful to readers unfamiliar with this period of history.[3]

William, Duke of Normandy, invaded England in September 1066. The land he won from Harold Godwineson, King of the Anglo-Saxons, had been gradually settled from the fifth century, at the expense of the Romano-British population, by Germanic tribes from north-western Europe. William's army was not the first invading force that the English had to face during these six centuries. The Vikings made successful inroads into England north of Watling Street (which joined London and Chester: see Figure 2.1, p. 18) in the ninth and tenth centuries and again in the early eleventh century, culminating in the rule of the Danish king Cnut (1016–35). Although Cnut ruthlessly removed much of the existing English aristocracy, he replaced it, not with a foreign elite as William was to do, but with a new class of English theigns (Mack 1984). One of the new English theigns was Godwine, father of Harold II who was to occupy the English throne for nine turbulent months in 1066.

Cnut was succeeded briefly by two sons (Harold and Harthacnut), but, as they left no male heirs, the throne went to Edward (later called the Confessor), a son of Ethelred the Unready and Emma of Normandy. Since Edward was half-Norman, and was given asylum in Normandy after Cnut seized power, it is not surprising that Norman influence at the English court increased during his reign (1043–66). At the same time, the Wessex house of Godwine grew stronger in the face of ineffective kingship (Fleming 1983). An ultimate conflict between these two growing influences in England was inevitable.

The occasion of a major conflict (a more minor one had led in 1051 to the expulsion of the Godwine family from England for a few months) was created by the death of Edward in January 1066. At the time, England faced a severe threat of invasion from Norway as well as from Normandy. As Harold was the most powerful and wealthy man in the country, Edward's Council (or at least, a section of it) hastily elected him as king. Harold's reign was both troubled and short. At the very beginning he had difficulty in persuading the northern earls to accept his rule, probably because he was not of royal blood (although his sister was married to Edward the Confessor), and because his family could trace its rise to power back only to the reign of Cnut. Throughout these months he also faced continual threats of invasion from Hardrada of Norway and William of Normandy. The first to land was Hardrada, in Yorkshire during September 1066, where he was joined by Tostig, one of Harold's younger brothers who had lost his earldom in Northumbria in 1065. Displaying the speed and decisiveness for which he was famous, Harold marched rapidly north, engaging the enemy at Stamfordbridge and winning a great victory. Before the excitement of his victory had subsided, Harold received news of William's landing in Kent, and with equal speed he marched south, staying in London only a few days to collect fresh forces before confronting William's army in Kent at a place later called Battle. Despite his lack of adequate preparation, Harold was drawn into battle with William's more balanced forces on 14 October 1066. The outcome was swift: Harold was defeated, and six centuries of Anglo-Saxon rule were brought to an end.

Who was William the Conqueror? William was born in 1027 or 1028 to Robert, Duke of Normandy, and Arlette, whose liaison was not consecrated by the Church. He succeeded his father (who died on a pilgrimage to Jerusalem) in 1035 at the age of seven or eight years, becoming heir to the small Norman duchy that had been carved out of Frankia (or France) in 911 by his Viking ancestor Rollo. Although Danish in origin, the duchy quickly became Frankish in speech and customs. William's succession, however, was disputed and civil war ensued, only to be finally decided in his favour in 1047, when he was about nineteen years old. His early training in war and intrigue stood him in good stead, as he was twice able to defeat the combined forces of the King of France and the Count of Anjou, in 1054 and 1057.

William's determination to extend his political influence was apparent from an early age. From 1049, when he was in his early twenties, William disputed with his neighbours until finally, in 1063, he was able to declare himself Count of Maine. His marriage in 1051 or 1052 to Matilda, daughter of Count Baldwin V of Flanders, also increased his influence on the Continent. But the most tempting prize of all was England, one of the wealthiest countries in eleventh-century Europe. He made claim to the English throne through Emma of Normandy, who had married Ethelred II of England, and had given birth to Edward, later to be called the Confessor. William also claimed that on a visit to England he had received a promise of the crown from Edward, and that Harold had later sworn allegiance to him.

In England, William's life continued as it had begun, in regular armed conflict. Although his progress from the victory at Battle in a great arc through Winchester to London, where he was crowned king on Christmas Day 1066, was surprisingly easy, the remainder of his long rule was plagued by war both in England and on the Continent. In England, William faced a series of rebellions and border skirmishes which continued until 1075: in 1068 there was a rebellion in Exeter; in 1069–70, very serious uprisings occurred in the north, which had the support of the Danes and which resulted in William's long-remembered campaign of infamy ('harrying the north'); in 1072 he successfully marched against Scotland; and in 1075 a final rebellion, which received some Danish assistance, was crushed. After 1072, William spent most of his time in Europe, where he pursued his ambitions against Maine (1073), Breton (1076), Anjou (1077–8 and 1081), and France (1087). By the time of his death at Rouen on 9 September 1087, at the age of sixty, William had spent more than half a century conducting regular warfare against his neighbours. His great political achievement, of uniting Normandy and England, was not without personal cost.

William was survived by three sons, Robert, William Rufus, and Henry. Being the eldest, Robert received Normandy, William was elected to the English throne, and Henry, the youngest, had to be content, for the time being, with private wealth.[4] The Conqueror's kingdom, however, did not remain divided for long. In 1096 Robert sold Normandy to William in order to finance the raising of a great host for the First Crusade, and in 1100, on the accidental death of William Rufus, both kingdom and duchy were seized by Henry, who captured Robert in 1106 and imprisoned him until Robert's death in 1134. Henry I, the youngest son of the Conqueror, finally became the major beneficiary of his father's remarkable achievements, ruling over the Norman empire from 1100 to 1135. During those thirty-five years, Henry consolidated Norman control over England, and presided over the emergence of two major instruments of state administration, the Exchequer and the Chancery. As Clanchy (1983, 67–8) has written: 'These institutions combined Anglo-Saxon governmental traditions with the most modern administrative expertise from the French schools.'

Domesday Book was not only a record of the Norman achievement in England, it was also essential to the success of a relatively sophisticated Norman administration (solidly based upon Anglo-Saxon foundations) in the period 1087–1135. The reason for its importance is that Domesday Book provided the information that was necessary to maximize net state revenue from feudal and non-feudal sources, to distribute estates more rationally, and to solve the pressing problems concerning disputed property. Even the name of this document reflects its importance. While the manuscript refers to itself only as the *Descriptio*, the name 'Domesday Book' was bestowed by those who saw it as the book of last judgement. In *Dialogus de Scaccario*, written almost 100 years after the Survey by a treasurer of Henry II (Richard fitz Nigel) about the Exchequer, it is claimed: 'we have called the book "The Book of Judgement" [i.e. Domesday Book] ... because its decisions, like those of the last judgement, are unalterable' (Johnson 1950, 64; Poole 1912, 3; Stenton 1951, 67).

It is clear from *Dialogus de Scaccario* that Domesday Book, which was held in the king's treasury, was in constant, some say daily, use during the first century after its compilation (Poole 1912, 36 and 61). A number of extracts dated as late as the first half of the thirteenth century are still extant, and can be viewed in the Public Record Office. It was even consulted as late as the fourteenth century by Edward III, and in the sixteenth century by Elizabeth I (Nicol 1981, 6).[5] Domesday Book, therefore, had a long and important career in English government, just as it will have a long and important role in attempts to reconstruct the economy and society of England in the late eleventh century. Provided that we ask the right questions and use appropriate methods, Domesday Book will repay careful re-examination.

Notes

1. It is true that Essex had been the victim of Viking raids in the past, but it appears to have recovered by 1086.
2. For examples of this speculation see 4.5.2.2 (final paragraph), 5.3 (fifth paragraph), and 5.3 (penultimate paragraph).
3. A more comprehensive account can be found in many works, including Stenton (1943), Stenton (1951), Loyn (1965), Clanchy (1983), Loyn (1983) and Brown (1984).
4. For a discussion of the traditions of Norman inheritance, see Holt (1972; 1982).
5. A book entitled *Domesday Book Through Nine Centuries*, which is being compiled by the Public Record Office for publication in 1986, should provide valuable information on the official use made of this document. Unfortunately we have been unable to consult it.

2

The economy and Survey of 1086

2.1 THE ECONOMY

2.1.1 Anglo-Scandinavian settlement

The decision of William, Duke of Normandy, to conquer the land of the English (*Angleland*) was a bold and dangerous gamble, but one which provided handsome returns. Together with his Norman and other French followers, William took possession of a systematically settled and relatively wealthy land. H. R. Loyn (1962, 384), evaluating the achievements of six centuries of Anglo-Saxon settlement, was able to conclude that, by the time of the Conquest, 'The foundations of the English economy were well laid'. But what exactly is known of the English economy at that time? To answer the question, this chapter outlines the conclusions reached by Anglo-Saxon and Domesday scholars. It is shown that while much has been written about economic institutions of the period, little is known of the way in which the economy worked. Economic processes, or in other words the causal relationships between key economic variables, are examined in subsequent chapters.

The economy inherited by the Normans in 1066 had emerged gradually during the previous six centuries of settlement by Anglo-Saxon and Scandinavian colonizers. These settlers came in a number of waves from the Germanic lands of north-western Europe. The first waves of raiding Germanic tribes—of Angles, Saxons, and Jutes—reached the eastern shores of Britain in the fifth century, and joined forces with others of their race who had been brought in by the British to fill the gap in their defences left by the departing Roman legions. As is well documented elsewhere (Stenton 1943; Loyn 1962), these warrior-settlers surged gradually, if unevenly, westward until, by the seventh century, they had occupied most of what we would recognize as England today. The success of this colonizing movement was well summed up by Loyn (1962, 42): 'By the seventh century the Anglo-Saxon had so tamed the land that it could support expanding and thriving communities capable of sustaining powerful kings, a prosperous aristocracy and a new Church that made heavy demands upon the faithful.' During the following two centuries, although further minor incursions were made into the lands of the Cornish, Welsh, and Scots, the Anglo-Saxons began to settle more intensively the land they had already occupied. This is reflected in the rapidly increasing number of settlements, which were achieved by clearing the forests, draining the fenland, and working the difficult clay soils with heavy iron ploughs pulled by large teams of oxen (Loyn 1962, 44–8). In this way the Anglo-Saxons provided the foundations upon which later generations, right down to the Industrial Revolution, built a prosperous agricultural superstructure.

The second wave of conquest and settlement had its origins in the Scandinavian countries of Denmark, southern Sweden, and Norway, and occurred in two distinct periods, 865–954 and 1016–35. In general the Danes, who were ultimately more successful, invaded England at various points along the central and northern parts of the east coast, while the Norwegians penetrated the country in the north-west from long-established bases in Ireland, the Isle of Man, and the islands to the north-west (Stenton 1943; Lyon 1962). The invading Scandinavians, in contrast to the early Anglo-Saxons, 'supplemented rather than superseded the existing community', even when one of their leaders, Cnut (1016–35), was able to secure the English throne (Loyn 1962, 52). Yet, as recent research has demonstrated (Fleming 1983; Mack 1984), Cnut was responsible for a major redistribution of property and power within the existing English community—a redistribution which sowed the seeds of political instability. Nevertheless, this eventual integration of the two communities had much to do with their similar social and economic institutions, although probably more to the existence of unused agricultural land. While the Scandinavian invaders appear to have settled easily into the Anglo-Saxon economy, they did impart a new character to the society of England north of Watling Street (appropriately known as Danelaw), which can be seen reflected in the different social and legal structure recorded in Domesday Book for this region. The basic economic effect of the Scandinavian invasions, therefore, was to accelerate the rate of closer settlement, particularly in the late ninth and early tenth centuries.

2.1.2 An outline of the economy in 1086

The central economic institution in the Domesday economy was the manor, which produced a range of agricultural products largely for internal consumption but also to exchange for luxury goods and military supplies.[1] Trade between manors within England, and between England and Europe, was facilitated by a network of markets ranging from local fairs to boroughs and large city-ports (like London and Southampton). The major shaping influence in this economy was a relatively strong central administration provided by the monarchy—whether Anglo-Saxon, Scandinavian, or Norman—which, if not the ultimate owner of land (the main source of income and wealth), certainly exacted a number of important services and taxes from landholders.

2.1.2.1 The manor

The manor in theory. Any description of the Domesday economic system must focus upon the manor which, unlike the modern firm, was the basic unit of consumption as well as of production. The process by which the manor emerged during the period of Anglo-Saxon rule, however, is difficult to determine with any precision, and as a consequence a number of different theories have been developed, both by historians and by economists. The traditional view, held by historians such as Vinogradoff (1908), Maitland (1897), Stenton (1943) and Loyn (1962), is that the main agency of colonization and agricultural production in the early Anglo-Saxon period consisted of communities of free warrior-peasants, who were bound by ties of kinship and who owed allegiance directly to the king. The free peasant, or ceorl, according to this interpretation, owned one hide of land (sufficient to maintain a family), lived in a lordless, nucleated village, and paid dues only to the king. It is claimed that power was gradually exerted over these free communities by the king's leading supporters. Although the reasons for this growing power of lordship have been the subject of much speculation, the consensus appears to be that it was largely associated with, or at least accelerated by, the threat of Scandinavian invasion in the late ninth and early tenth centuries. As Loyn (1962, 196) has so succinctly written: 'In an age of peril it was indeed natural for men to seek lords, and lords to seek men.' Accordingly, those leaders who demonstrated sufficient military strength increased their control over peasant communities and peasant land. Economic and social independence was traded for 'greater security in everyday living, in the law courts and in the fields' (Loyn 1962, 197). The nature of this exchange between lord and peasant, however, differed in different parts of England. Not surprisingly, peasant freedoms survived longest in areas settled by recent Scandinavian invaders, such as Danelaw. Other reasons have also been assembled under the banner of the traditional interpretation, including the crushing burden of geld, the growth of the state which found it more convenient to deal with a small number of lords rather than with a large number of freemen, the growing strength of the Church as a landlord, and the nature of the legal codes which encouraged the idea of allegiance to a lord (Maitland 1897; Stenton 1943; Loyn 1962).

A more recent interpretation of the emergence of the manor in Anglo-Saxon England was put forward by Aston (1958), and has been supported by most subsequent writers, including Postan (1972). Basically, Aston disagreed with the timing of the emergence of the manorial system suggested by the traditional interpretation, which regards this system as a late development coming shortly before and shortly after the Conquest. Aston (1958, 61) claimed: 'Almost all the detailed work on Domesday Book and the early estate surveys has emphasized that the Conquest did not interrupt the general continuity of agrarian and manorial life and that, for all the many changes in individual fortunes, there was no social revolution among the peasantry.' While acknowledging the problems of evidence, he wished to push the origins of the manor further back into Anglo-Saxon history: 'in its upper ranks', he claimed, 'Anglo-Saxon society was, from the very beginning, very aristocratic and organized by lordship ... and these lords, in their turn, had followers bound to them as closely as they themselves were to the king.' These bonds of lordship were, according to Aston (1958, 62), 'much more vital and effective than those ties of kinship'. According to this view, the economic aspects of the manorial system, of the demesne and its dependent cultivation, were established long before the Conquest, although they may have intensified as a result of the Scandinavian invasions. Only the legal definition of the manor and its dependent cultivation was in its infancy in Domesday England.

During the last decade a growing number of economists have turned their attention to the nature of the European manorial system. While they have focused largely upon the reasons for the decline of the manorial system and the emergence of the market economy, their economic models also have implications for the emergence of the manorial system. It is worth briefly introducing their arguments here, because they appear to have been ignored by historians, including Postan (1983) in a recent survey of approaches to the decline of feudalism.

Domar (1970), who was attracted to this subject by an interest in Russian history, developed a hypothesis to explain the emergence and decline of serfdom. Simply, his argument was that in a period when labour rather than land is scarce, the ruling class will attempt to impose property rights over labour. They do this by organizing an agricultural system in which labour is compelled to work for a lord in return for small plots of land. By keeping the peasants' share of their own product near the subsistence level, the ruling class is able to derive rent (or a surplus) from this scarce resource. According to Domar, this system will prevail until population growth has reduced the marginal product of labour (or wage rate) to the subsistence level. At this point it will be just as profitable (indeed more so, as hired labour will be more highly motivated) to employ workers at the market wage rate. Accordingly, ownership rights are transferred from labour to land.

North and Thomas (1971) expressed dissatisfaction with Domar's argument largely because it was based upon the experience of American slavery and Russian serfdom, and failed to take into account the contractual arrangement between lord and peasant under Western serfdom. They argued (1971, 778) that the manorial system was 'essentially a contractual arrangement where labour services were exchanged for the public good of protection and justice'.[2] According to this interpretation, which emphasizes the voluntary nature of such contracts, the manorial system owed its existence to the high transactions costs (i.e. costs of negotiation and enforcement of contracts) of the alternative forms of economic organization, such as fixed wage payments, fixed rents, and share cropping. The decline of this system results from population growth which creates a market economy, and which in turn lowers the transactions costs of alternative forms of organization to the point where they are more profitable than the manorial system.

While this argument is interesting and provides insights into a complex process, it is not without its critics. Fenoaltea (1975), for example, has rejected the North and Thomas argument on the grounds that they are mistaken about the relative transactions costs of the various possible forms of economic organization. He claims that the costs of supervision under the manorial system are much higher, and the costs of negotiating rents are much lower than North and Thomas were prepared to admit (for evidence on this debate, see 6.5.2.3 below). Fenoaltea's alternative hypothesis postulates that the manorial system arose in a period of insecurity, when warlords attempted to impose their authority to achieve social stability (and also a superior technology), and peasants were forced to accept dependence. 'Protection' was, in other words, a double-edged sword. This system eventually broke down, according to Fenoaltea, when the 'scale and scope of violence' was substantially reduced (and also when manorial lords lost their monopoly over technical knowledge). Clearly there are points of similarity between the hypotheses of Fenoaltea (excluding the question of technology) and those of the traditional historians.

The manor in history. It should not be thought that the manorial system was everywhere the same by 1086. The manor was most fully established in English England (as opposed to Scandinavian England), and particularly in the heart of the ancient kingdom of Wessex (Postan 1972, 90–4). Wiltshire, one of the counties chosen for study in this work, is an appropriate example of the fully developed manorial system. Not only was this county highly manorialized, with the vill and manor for the most part being coincident, but the manors were also relatively large. As shown in 5.4, the typical ecclesiastical and lay manors (measured by their modal values) in 1086 were worth 80 shillings and 40 shillings respectively. Some ecclesiastical manors were even recorded as producing as much as 2,120 shillings in the year of the Survey. By way of contrast the settlements in Danelaw, particularly those in East Anglia, were less tightly organized along manorial lines (Loyn 1962, 339–43). For example, in Essex, the other county chosen for detailed study, the village and the manor did not coincide quite so often, and indeed it was normal for a village to contain more than one manor. Further, the manors of Essex were somewhat smaller than those in Wiltshire. The typical manor (irrespective of whether it was ecclesiastical or lay) in 1086 was worth only 20 shillings, and the largest manor did not exceed a value of 1,800 shillings. Manorial structure also differed between these two counties. In Wiltshire, the manors usually consisted of single estates, whereas in Essex, composite estates, involving a manor together with a number of attached berewicks and other appendages, were more common.[3] Finally, there was considerable variation in the institutional nature of manors, particularly amongst those belonging to the Church (compare the Benedictine and episcopal holdings), even in the same locality (Postan 1972, 90–4).

What was the nature of the manorial economy? Arable farming was the central economic activity, and was based upon the cultivation of crops such as wheat, oats, barley, and rye, which provided both the basic food requirements of the manor and, sometimes, a surplus for the purchase of those luxury goods and military supplies that could not be produced locally. Supplementing this major activity was the raising of livestock including sheep, cows, pigs, and goats, which supplied milk, meat, hides, and wool. While manorial land was devoted largely to arable activities, other forms of land use were essential to maintain arable production (meadow was a vital source of hay to maintain the plough beasts in winter) and to supplement it (pasture and woodland were essential to the support of livestock).

The arable land of the manor was organized for production in large open fields. Loyn (1962, 161) claims: 'The evidence for the existence of open field farming in later Anglo-Saxon England is overwhelming and for early Anglo-Saxon England it is strong.'[4] While there was some regional variation, it is generally recognized that open fields predominated over a large part of England south of Yorkshire. Throughout much of this area, settlements took the form of nucleated villages, which in turn were the focus of one or more manors. Once again there was some regional variation in the form of settlement, which in Devon, for example, occurred mainly as isolated farmsteads (Postan 1966, 573–4).

Manorial production was organized typically into demesne and peasant tenancies, with the various classes of peasants—villeins, bordars, cottars, etc.—receiving small plots of land in exchange for labour services, customary dues, and even rents in money or kind (Lennard 1959). There were also freemen and sokemen who held their land directly from the king, but who were generally closely associated with a particular manor, often paying customary dues and even providing some services. While the peasants worked individually on their own plots, as well as on those of the demesne, the general organization of production of the open fields was undertaken corporately. Yet it is claimed that there was scope in this corporate system for the exercise of individual initiative and enterprise (Loyn 1962, 334). Freemen and sokemen, who constituted 14 per cent of the population in 1086 (a considerable decline from 1066), were recorded as living entirely in the east and north of England, corresponding approximately to the area of Danelaw. Of the dependent peasants, the villein was the most numerous, accounting for about 41 per cent of the population recorded in 1086. Typically a villein held a virgate of land (possibly thirty acres), although there was considerable variation around this average. While the villein was a substantial peasant farmer, the bordar (30 per cent of the population) and the cottar (2 per cent) held little land. The distinction is often blurred, but the bordar probably held in the vicinity of five acres while the cottar held little more than a cottage garden (Lennard 1959, 339–49).

Even so, these poorest dependent peasants possessed some freedoms which were denied to the *servi* or slaves, who in 1086 made up just over 10 per cent of the recorded population (and more in 1066). The importance of slaves varied considerably from county to county, being greatest in the west and south-west (over 20–5 per cent) and lowest in the south-east and Danelaw (under 5 per cent). It is claimed that the slaves of Domesday England worked on the demesne, where they were closely associated with the lords' plough teams (Darby 1977, 57–94). Our results in Chapter 6 (6.5.2.1), however, suggest that this is not correct.

Within this organizational structure, the techniques of agricultural production were fairly similar throughout much of England. While acknowledging certain exceptions in the fringe areas of the west and north of Cornwall, in the highlands of the Pennines, and the uplands of the highland spine of England, where the focus was on pastoral rather than arable activities, Loyn (1962, 334) claimed that 'over a great swathe of country from the Tees to the Tamar a general picture of uniformity in agrarian techniques is not too distorted and misleading'. Naturally, within this general technical framework there was local variation in some of the details, such as the balance between arable and pasture, the crop mix, and certain 'rules and institutions' of agriculture (Postan 1966, 573, Campbell 1983a; 1983b). It has already been noted that manorial arable land was organized on the basis of large open fields employing a two-field system of rotation, which was cultivated by co-operative groups of households (Loyn 1962, 334). These large fields were in turn divided into long narrow strips, the shape of which reflected the logistics of employing large plough teams of up to eight oxen pulling a heavy iron plough. While the Anglo-Saxons were not the first to use the heavy plough, they were responsible for its widespread use on the heavy lowland clay soils. This use of the 'co-operative plough' was, according to Postan (1972, 49), the great technical innovation introduced into England by the Anglo-Saxons. As is well known, the strips of arable land owned by individuals, including the lord, were scattered throughout the large open fields rather than being consolidated into compact holdings.[5] The fertility of these strips, a problem of critical importance in the eleventh century, was maintained by employing a two-field system of rotation whereby one was left fallow each year, and by the addition of animal manure, lime, marl, peat, and compost to the soil (Loyn 1962, 160). The latter measures were no doubt a valuable method of improving the structure of the soil, but they cannot have been applied on a very large scale, and appear to have been largely restricted to the demesne. Finally, other activities necessary for effective manorial production included the use of hurdle hedges to enclose arable and meadow, selection of stock for breeding and seed for sowing, draining of marshy land, and clearing of woodland (Miller and Hatcher 1978, 13–14).

2.1.2.2 The borough

Despite its predominantly rural nature, the Anglo-Norman economy supported a number of important boroughs or towns (see Figure 2.1). Although urban population figures are only approximate, they do provide a general idea of the

Figure 2.1. Main roads and boroughs of Domesday England

relative importance of boroughs. London, which was not recorded in Domesday Book, is thought to have had a population in excess of 10,000, possibly 12,000, at the time of the Survey. Of the other main boroughs, York had in the vicinity of 8,000 inhabitants; Winchester (also not recorded in Domesday Book), Norwich, and Lincoln had in excess of 6,000; Oxford and Thetford had about 5,000; Canterbury, Colchester, Dunwich, Exeter, Gloucester, Leicester, Lewes, Nottingham, Sandwich, Stanford, and Wallingford had more than 2,000; and Bath, Cambridge, Chester, Chichester,

Dover, Hastings, Huntingdon, Hythe, Northampton, Shaftesbury, Ipswich, Maldon, and Southampton had over 1,000 (Darby 1977, 302–9, 364–8). In addition, there were a further eighty smaller boroughs recorded in Domesday Book. By 1086, therefore, towns were clearly an integral part of the English economy. Yet their role should not be overrated. Although the population living and working in the thirty-one boroughs mentioned above constituted little more than 5 per cent of the total population of England, this would be a lower limit. Some scholars (Loyn 1962) put it as high as 10 per cent. Even so, urbanization in England had not proceeded very far before the Survey.

It is difficult to be very precise about the nature of Anglo-Norman boroughs, because the Domesday Survey appears to have been little concerned with them except in so far as they had some relationship with manors. In particular, no systematic attempt was made to record the industrial and commercial resources of even the major towns. Indeed, the Domesday commissioners appear to have been more concerned to record the agricultural rather than the industrial or commercial characteristics of boroughs. For some boroughs there are records of ploughs, arable land, villeins, and bordars, but not of artisans or their workshops (Darby 1977, 293; Miller and Hatcher 1978, 9). Towns were viewed, therefore, largely within a manorial rather than an industrial or commercial framework. No really satisfactory explanation is given for this in the literature. To point out, as Darby (1977, 289) and Harvey (1980, 127) have done, that no direction was given about boroughs in the otherwise comprehensive instructions contained in *Inquisitio Eliensis* is merely begging the question. It is possible, however, that the neglect of boroughs arose from an economic philosophy, not unlike that of the Physiocrats in the eighteenth century, which viewed land and its cultivation as the only true source of income and wealth. More pragmatically, rural land was the basis of Norman feudalism.

The origins of boroughs are usually traced directly to the *burhs* established by Alfred and his descendants in the ninth and tenth centuries. These burhs, which were fortified townships protected by walls and ditches, were established in response to military and political pressures.[6] While the earlier Anglo-Saxon history of these fortified towns is obscure, it is probable that on the whole they were centres of commerce and industry, because it is unlikely that substantial towns would have emerged from arbitrary administrative decisions. Indeed, only those burhs that were successful market towns developed into boroughs. Loyn (1962, 144) has written persuasively: 'The so called burghal policy of the late ninth and early tenth centuries ... did no more than create the conditions of defensibility in which it was possible for some favoured trading centres to grow into the typical medieval walled towns.' Postan, who supported this view, attempted to take the analysis further. He agreed that trade was an important factor in the growth of boroughs, but asked why those involved in trade congregated in towns rather than in villages. His answer was that towns not only provided security for those not closely associated with a powerful lord, but also enabled merchants to escape the feudal (or proto-feudal) restrictions of the manor and vill. Postan (1972, 212) wrote that medieval towns 'were non-feudal islands in the feudal seas; places in which merchants could not only live in each other's vicinity and defend themselves collectively but also places which enjoyed or were capable of developing systems of local government and principles of law and status exempting them from the sway of the feudal regime'. The public freedoms (or 'liberties') of the boroughs, which were listed in charters granted to them by the king or a great lord, concerned matters such as property rights, fiscal autonomy, and freedom from prohibitive taxes on trade. According to Postan (1972, 213): 'The charter and its liberties embodied the essential pre-conditions of urban development.' Villages, on the other hand, were private rather than public institutions, and were dominated by the local lords.

Evidence concerning the nature and role of boroughs in the Anglo-Norman economy is surprisingly deficient. It has been necessary for scholars to painstakingly build up a picture of the borough from a variety of sources, such as law codes, guild regulations, coins, and Domesday Book itself. But, as Darby (1977, 308) acknowledges, 'their [the boroughs'] economic activities never come clearly into focus'. Nevertheless, these sources confirm the importance of markets and mints in boroughs, and demonstrate that some were clearly ports for overseas trade (Darby 1977, 318–20). In addition, the borough entries in Domesday Book refer to castles, cathedrals, monasteries, administrative functions for hundred or county, fishing ports, a centre for salt production (Droitwich), and, in one rare instance (Bury St Edmunds), to 'bakers, ale-brewers, tailors, washerwomen, shoemakers, robe-makers, cooks, porters, [and] agents' (Darby 1977, 308–9, 313–17). While this picture is tantalizingly incomplete, there seems little doubt that boroughs owed much of their importance to their role as centres of trade. As Tait (1936, 130) has written:

Every borough had a market and every borough was a *port*, a place of trade. The early trade even of the more considerable of these ports must not be judged by the standard of the great cities of the Netherlands, which, with rare exceptions, they never reached. Yet by the end of the Anglo-Saxon period, many of them were evidently prosperous.

Despite the commercial, industrial, religious, and administrative nature of Anglo-Norman boroughs, together with the relative freedom from feudal restrictions of some of their inhabitants, these towns retained a close relationship with the surrounding manors. There are numerous references in Domesday Book to burgesses and town property belonging to the wealthier lords of nearby manors. Manors even had men working for them in far-distant salt-making boroughs, and claimed rights to salt produced in those centres (Darby 1977, 261, 309–10). The explanations in the literature for this close relationship between manor and borough include Maitland's 'garrison theory'—that those lords with borough connections were responsible for the maintenance of its fortifications—and the more generally accepted and compelling economic theory—that a rural lord purchased assets in the nearest town in order to reap the benefits of trading rights.[7] Whatever the relative merits of these arguments, it is clear that there was a tangible relationship between manor and borough in the Anglo-Norman economy.

2.1.2.3 Internal trade

While the Anglo-Norman manor was largely self-sufficient in the basic necessities of life (such as food, drink, and possibly the clothing and housing of peasants and slaves), it also had economic relationships with other manors, either directly or indirectly through borough markets, and with merchants from other countries. Therefore, while it is useful to consider the manor in isolation as the basic unit of production and consumption, it is also necessary to consider its interaction with other producer-consumers.

Those lords wishing to trade agricultural surpluses for luxury goods and military supplies had to contend with the considerable problems of transportation. The means of internal transport were slow and relatively costly, particularly by road (Miller and Hatcher 1978, 2). While there is considerable evidence of merchants travelling around the country by road, it is most likely that the nature of road surfaces, particularly during winter, made the transport of heavy and bulky commodities (such as grain) difficult. It seems to us that this could be an important reason for the constant movement of monarchy and nobility from estate to estate. It was easier and cheaper to transport one's household between estates than commodities like grain that had a low value per unit of weight. This, of course, would not have been an obstacle to the transport of luxury goods, military supplies, or staple commodities which had a high value–weight ratio, such as wool, salt, iron-ore, and lead. Also, while it was relatively costly to transport staples with a low value–weight ratio by road, they could be carried more cheaply by river. The major problem with river transport was that the direction of trade flows was limited. This would not unduly have restricted international trade, but would have made cross-country traffic difficult. Yet at least rivers provided a convenient method for transporting goods between manors and boroughs in the same river-valley system.

The evidence of internal trade is to be found largely in studies of the law codes, coins, and, as we have seen, boroughs. For example, the importance of highways in England—particularly of Watling Street, Ermine Street, the Fosse Way, and Icknield Way, which criss-crossed the country (see Figure 2.1)—is reflected in the laws of William I. Highways were declared to be under the king's peace, to enable their use by all who had legal business in England, including local and foreign traders. Laws of this nature appear to have had a long history in Anglo-Saxon England: there is evidence of their existence at least as early as the seventh century (Loyn 1962, 98–100). The kings of England were anxious to encourage and protect bona fide traders, probably largely because the former stood to gain revenue from borough markets that were directly under their control.

A glimpse of the type of goods involved in internal trade can be gained from legal evidence and the data in Domesday Book. It is known that there was a trade in textiles, metals (iron and lead), salt, horses, and agricultural goods such as dairy products and possibly grain. Domesday Book tells us of salt-making, a commodity vital for communities that needed to preserve fish and meat for the winter, which was undertaken at a number of inland centres (including Worcestershire and Cheshire) and at many places along the east and south coasts. A glimpse of what must have been a nationwide system of trade is provided by Domesday entries recording manorial involvement in far distant salt-making centres like Droitwich, together with tolls scaled according to distance that were imposed upon purchasers (Darby 1977, 260–5).

Another essential industry that provided the basis for a thriving trade was iron-making. The products of this industry, which included ploughshares, farm implements, horseshoes, and weaponry, were required on every manor. Centres of ironworking are mentioned in Domesday Book for Cheshire, Devonshire, Hampshire, Herefordshire, Lincolnshire, Northamptonshire, Surrey, Sussex, Warwickshire, Wiltshire, and Yorkshire. These numerous centres would have purchased from other regions those raw materials not found locally, and would have sold raw iron and iron products to manors throughout England and, as the reputation of English ironworkers increased, to Europe as well (Darby 1977, 266–8). Other metal crafts included leadworking in Derbyshire, the output of which was used in the building industry (particularly church and manor house roofing), and for making salt vats and other similar containers. These commodities would also have been an important item of internal trade, as may have been tin and tin products from Cornwall despite their omission from Domesday Book (Darby 1977, 268–9).

While Domesday Book maintains its silence about other secondary industries, it is possible to establish their existence from archaeological and legal sources. Traces of the manufacture of commodities such as pottery, glass, and textiles can be unearthed, but it is difficult to determine the extent to which manors were self-sufficient in their production (Loyn 1962, 109–16). The most reasonable conclusion would seem to be that the less sophisticated products were produced on the manor (with the exception of glass, which was largely imported into Anglo-Norman England), while finer items were purchased from specialized craftsmen in the major boroughs of England and Europe. Sufficient evidence is available, however, to demonstrate that extensive trade existed in industrial and agricultural commodities between the manors of England, and that this trade was facilitated by a network of boroughs throughout the country. The widespread establishment of mints and the resulting supply of adequate and acceptable coin provided the necessary medium for the development of an extensive system of internal trade.

2.1.2.4 International trade

Despite the tendency towards self-sufficiency on manors and the deficiencies of existing modes of transport, the English economy was not completely isolated from those of Europe. From various, although largely inadequate, sources, scholars have been able to sketch a picture of European trade, undertaken at first by Frisian and later by Scandinavian seamen and merchants, which by the time of the Conquest linked England with all parts of the continent. The late Anglo-Saxon economy had trading connections with Scandinavia, Flanders (and from there to Cologne and Bruges), southern Europe and the Mediterranean (Miller and Hatcher 1978, 79–83; Postan 1972, 185–90). In response to this commerce with Europe, a number of English coastal towns, such as London, Southampton, Dover, Hull, and Ipswich, developed into thriving ports, occupied by a rapidly emerging merchant class in the tenth and eleventh centuries. As the king imposed tolls upon ships entering these ports, he was keen to encourage this development.

What was the composition of this trade? The available evidence suggests that the main exports from England in the mid-eleventh century included both craft and agricultural products. Fine English craftwork, in the form of metalwork (particularly silver), embroidery, fine textiles, and manuscripts, appears to have been in considerable demand throughout Europe. In addition there were exports of agricultural products, including grain, cheese, butter, oil, honey, and salt. Imports, on the other hand, appear to have been mainly luxury goods that could not be produced on the manor or in the borough. These imports included silks, finely dyed textiles and garments, gold and precious stones, glass, wine, oil, ivory, tin, bronze, copper, and sulphur. Other less exotic imports included timber, furs, hides, and fish (Loyn 1962, 96; Miller and Hatcher 1978, 10, 79–80).

2.1.2.5 State intervention

Even before the Conquest the monarchy was profoundly involved in the English economy, and indeed was one of its major shaping influences. With the growth of the monarchy came the development of territorial organization which divided the country into shires (see Figure 2.2) and hundreds (or wapentakes). Under the control of the king's agents, these territorial units were used to implement royal laws and to collect the required dues. This was facilitated by a hierarchical social and economic structure within these territorial units (i.e. the manor), which, although appearing to have a long history, was probably intensified during the Scandinavian invasions. This organizational structure was fertile ground for William I, who was able to achieve an even greater concentration of power and control in the hands of the monarchy and a relatively small group of barons. In 1086, for example, thirty-two tenants-in-chief owned as much as 40 per cent of England's landed wealth (Lennard 1959, 25–6). The Conqueror's control of the economy was exercised

Figure 2.2. Counties of Domesday England

by his agent, the county sheriff, operating through the territorial structure of government which had been developed by Anglo-Saxon kings (Stenton 1943, 633).

The involvement of the monarchy in the manorial economy took a number of forms. In the late Anglo-Saxon period, the king exacted a number of onerous payments and services from his subjects (Stenton 1943). The first of these was the 'farm of one night', and involved the payment (in kind or money) required to support the king and his household for twenty-four hours. While the king's own estates bore the brunt of this burden, food rents were imposed upon the estates of others. It was probably for this purpose that the hidage system of assessment was developed (Stenton 1943, 647).[8] Secondly, landholders were also required to provide specific services, such as supplying men and weapons for the king's army, together with the necessary materials and labour to maintain bridges and fortresses in their locality. Thirdly, the king obtained revenue from rights over boroughs, particularly markets and mints, and from the profits of providing justice at both the national and local levels. Finally, from the year 991, geld was imposed by the king on landholders, using the pre-existing hidage system. Initially, geld was used to bribe raiding parties of Danes (and hence was called danegeld), and from 1012 to 1051 to finance a standing army (heregeld or army geld) together with a small fleet of warships (Lawson 1984).

The Normans adopted this system of economic intervention. William's economic power was even more clearly established than that of his predecessors, as his supporters received their estates directly from his hands In return for this land, tenants-in-chief were required to provide feudal services to the king in the form of knight service and attendance at court. The king also extracted feudal revenue from tenants-in-chief in the form of aids (arising from marriages, knighthoods, and wardships) and reliefs (paid on the inheritance of a fief) together with non-feudal revenue from various local and national courts, boroughs, mints, and the geld (Vinogradoff 1908; Mitchell 1914; Painter 1943). Of these the geld was particularly important, as it was one of the main sources of royal revenue in the Anglo-Norman period, and was a considerable burden on landholders. William I revived the geld, which had been allowed to lapse by Edward the Confessor, possibly as early as 1066/7, and, at least by the end of his reign, raised it on an annual basis. By the time of the Domesday Survey, therefore, the extent and effectiveness of royal involvement in the economy was well established, although there was a decline in the years after William's death (Warren 1984).

2.2 THE SURVEY

2.2.1 Historical background

The Norman Conquest brought about major changes in the social and political order of Anglo-Saxon England. So pervasive was this transformation that, twenty years after Harold's defeat at Battle, there remained only two English tenants-in-chief—Coleswain of Lincoln and Thurkill of Arden—of baronial status. The rest of the Anglo-Saxon aristocracy either had been killed in war or rebellion, had fled the country (to Scotland, Flanders, or Constantinople), had married into the Norman aristocracy, or had been considerably reduced in economic, social, and political circumstances. Further, by 1086 the English Church was ruled largely by Continentals, and all the main offices of the king's household, together with those at the county and hundred levels of territorial government, were filled by William's men. Yet, ironically, it would appear from the traditional account that William had originally intended to take his place merely as Edward the Confessor's legitimate successor, and had therefore attempted to base his rule upon a truly Anglo-Norman foundation (Stenton 1943, 622). A more cynical view, however, would be that William was merely waiting for the right moment to unleash his revolution.

The traditional explanation of this reversal of policy centres upon the tenacious opposition of the English, particularly in the north, to William's kingship. For the first three years of his reign, William made a determined effort to retain the structure of the Anglo-Saxon state, and to rule as Edward's rightful heir through those Englishmen prepared to make peace with him. In this early period, important Englishmen sat in the king's Council as the equals (or as aristocratic hostages?) of Norman barons, the major offices of territorial government remained in the hands of Anglo-Saxon sheriffs, the Church was governed by English bishops, the English language was the main medium of administrative and religious communication throughout the land, and English landlords who accepted William's rule continued to enjoy the fruits of their estates. Yet this experiment was short-lived. Following the great revolt of 1069 (cause or pretext?) came a major change in William's domestic policy.

The revolt, which began in Northumbria and Yorkshire, spread quickly to other parts of the country. As reports circulated of a Danish invasion in support of the rebels, Englishmen in Wessex and Mercia joined the uprising. So serious was the challenge to Norman rule that William found it necessary to lead personally the counter-attack. After defeating the English rebels in Mercia and Yorkshire, and forcing the Danes to withdraw, William ordered the devastation of the counties of Cheshire, Shropshire, Staffordshire, Derbyshire, and particularly Yorkshire, to ensure that they would never rebel again. This ruthless policy was responsible for the wholesale destruction of the means of production in the north and east of England (Stenton 1943, 601–5; Loyn 1965). So effective was this action that, even by the time of the Survey some seventeen years later, a number of these regions, particularly in Yorkshire, had failed to recover (Darby 1977, 232–59).

In the years that followed the 1069–70 rebellion and reprisal, the remaining political, social, and economic power of the English was, in the main, transferred to William's French followers. Further, less serious, rebellions (such as that in the north in 1075) and threats of invasion (by the Danes in 1085) accelerated this development. An interesting aspect of the massive redistribution of estates between 1070 and 1086 was the fact that it took place within the existing tenurial structure. When a Frenchman assumed control of an English estate, he not only came into possession of property scattered through a county or number of counties, but generally he also assumed all the associated traditional rights and responsibilities. William's control of this process of redistribution was remarkable. Inevitably problems were experienced, with some Frenchmen exceeding their authority by taking possession of property rightly belonging to others, even that of the king. As Domesday Book carefully records these disputed properties, which are occasionally listed separately under the heading 'encroachments', this problem was clearly of major concern to the Domesday commissioners.

During the great redistribution of estates, the hierarchical economic structure of England, which can be traced to the early Anglo-Saxon period, was shaped more precisely. In the first place, the economic power of the monarchy was more clearly defined. All tenants-in-chief in 1086 held their land directly of the king in return for a range of dues and services, of which the main one was the provision of knight service. Secondly, economic control passed into fewer hands, with twenty barons and twelve ecclesiastical tenants-in-chief holding 40 per cent of the land in England in 1086 (Lennard 1959, 25–6). This concentration of wealth was necessary to enable the king's most trusted followers to supply the large number of knights required of them. One estimate (Stenton 1943, 634) suggests that in the vicinity of 4,000 mounted knights had to be provided by little more than 180 of the king's barons. This number was supplemented by the knight service expected from an equally small number of bishops and religious houses. Thirdly, the degree of control over English peasants by their lords increased considerably. While the number of slaves declined dramatically during William's reign, the class of free peasants was everywhere greatly reduced in numbers and, throughout much of the country, may even have disappeared entirely (Darby 1977, 57–94). The precise nature of this more tightly controlled form of feudalism and manorialism, which emerged between the Conquest and the Survey, was apparently of great interest to the king, as its imprint is boldly stamped upon the structure of Domesday Book.

2.2.2 The purpose of the Survey

Over the last 900 years, many authors have speculated about the reasons for the Domesday Survey, the results of which were recorded in two volumes, Great and Little Domesday Book. Why did the Conqueror go to so much trouble and expense to record the economic resources and performance of every manor in England, especially as the magnitude and cost of the task was sufficient to deter other administrations for a further eight centuries from attempting to repeat the performance? The first to record an explanation of the Survey was the author(s) of the *Anglo-Saxon Chronicle*, and it is worth reproducing the relevant entry in full (Whitelock 1961, 161–2).

[At Christmas 1085] the king had much thought and very deep discussion with his council about this country—how it was occupied or with what sort of people. Then he sent his men over all England into every shire and had them find out how many hundred hides there were in the shire, or what land and cattle the king himself had in the country, or what dues he ought to have in twelve months from the shire. Also he had a record made of how much land his archbishops had, and his bishops and his abbots and his earls—and though I relate it at too great length—what or how much everybody had who was occupying land in England, in land or cattle, and how much money it was worth. So narrowly did he have it investigated, that there was no single hide nor virgate of land, nor indeed (it is a shame to relate but it seemed no shame to him to do) one ox nor one cow nor one pig which was there left out, and not put down in his record; and all these records were brought to him afterwards.

The explanation in this contemporary account is that the king wished to know the details not only of his own income and wealth but also that of his tenants-in-chief, both lay and ecclesiastical. That William wanted to know this right down to the last item appears to have shocked the chronicler, probably because he saw it as an attempt to squeeze the last penny out of the English. This was not the only occasion that outrage was expressed in this source about the king's 'greed' (Whitelock 1961, 163). The implication appears to be that the author of the *Chronicle* saw the purpose of the Survey as the basis for a new and more comprehensive tax for which no asset was to be overlooked. A reaction of this nature is not unusual among contemporary observers of income and wealth censuses, and should not be taken to exclude other, equally important, objectives.

It is interesting that the late Victorian scholars Round, Maitland, and Vinogradoff also assumed the purpose of Domesday Book to be entirely fiscal. It may be no coincidence that they also lived in an age which spawned official statistical inquiries (after eight dormant centuries), and which possessed governments that sought new sources of finance for their rapidly expanding activities. For example, Round's major publication *Feudal England* (1895) treats tax assessment as if it were the central issue in the Survey. In Part I, where Round analyses Domesday Book, his focus is almost entirely upon the different forms of assessment for geld and, in particular, the claim that they were entirely artificial. Maitland, who wrote *Domesday Book and Beyond* (1897) at the same time, but who generously delayed publication for two years to allow Round's views to circulate without competition, developed even further this view about the centrality of taxes in Domesday Book. Repeatedly Maitland (1897, 3–5) said: 'Domesday Book is no register of title, no register of all those rights and facts which constitute the system of land-holdership. One great purpose seems to mould both its form and its substance; it is a geld book.' This was a particularly strong claim for a complex document that has such an obvious feudal structure (with estates being recorded by tenant-in-chief), and which details the economic relationship between lords and men. Vinogradoff (1908, 141) was also persuaded to Round's point of view, but he expressed it more cautiously than did Maitland when he wrote: 'The Survey ... is mainly directed towards ascertaining the data for the imposition and repartition of geld.' It is not surprising that, under the influence of these major figures of

Domesday scholarship, the purpose of the Survey was assumed to be largely, if not entirely, fiscal.

Not until fifty years later was this view seriously challenged. In 1942, V. H. Galbraith, in reassessing the making of Domesday Book, claimed that the main objective of the Survey was feudal rather than fiscal. He wrote (1942, 177):

The plan of Domesday Book was neither 'curious', nor 'compromising', nor was its prime purpose a great reassessment of the geld. The object of the inquest of 1086 was a return by manors and by tenants-in-chief... Domesday Book was their supreme and successful effort to wrest the intractable material of O. E. [old English] tenures into the feudal form in which alone they could understand it.

Galbraith developed this basic idea further in both *The Making of Domesday Book* (1961) and *Domesday Book* (1974), and finally concluded that Domesday Book 'recorded the total wealth of each of the "king's men"—that is of the tenants-in-chief, which was valuable to the Crown in assessing the "incidents of feudal tenure" such as marriage, minorities, reliefs, fines, and forfeitures' (1974, 14). In other words, as well as a guide to the feudal structure of England, he saw it as a source of information about feudal dues. While Galbraith's interpretation gains strength from a more thorough examination of the way in which the Survey was conducted and Domesday Book compiled (see 2.2.3), his arguments lead not to a dismissal of the geld hypothesis, as he maintained, but rather to the possibility of a more complex purpose for the Survey. While the fiscal hypothesis still has its supporters in Prestwick (1954) and Aston (1962), more recent work by Loyn (1979) and Harvey (1971; 1975; 1980), advance convincing cases for a synthesis of the fiscal and feudal views. On the basis of a further and rewarding re-examination of the making of Domesday Book, Harvey argues that the Survey data were collected to enable a revision of the tax assessments, to provide a sounder basis for extracting feudal dues and services (particularly military), and to solve disputes over the right to hold land.

Much has been written about the purpose of the Domesday Survey. The current interpretation, which is based upon a detailed examination of evidence concerning the making of Domesday Book, is that this purpose was not one-dimensional as earlier scholars had thought, but rather complex and wide-ranging. In our view this position is supported by the economic circumstances underlying the period. As outlined in 2.2.1, major changes had occurred in both the economic control and the condition of the productive resources of England in the two decades following the Conquest. Consequently, William had no precise idea of what he could expect to exact in feudal dues and services on the one hand and in non-feudal taxes and revenues on the other. Such knowledge could have been critical to a newly established regime facing a continual threat of invasion. It would have been surprising, therefore, if the king had *not* been vitally concerned to define precisely his potential sources of 'income', whether in money, goods or services, whether feudal or fiscal. It is doubtful that any other motive could have justified the undertaking of such an expensive survey (see 2.2.4).

2.2.3 Interpretations concerning the making of Domesday Book

A number of estimates have been made of the time taken to conduct the Survey and to compile the *Descriptio*, but the majority view (including that in the *Anglo-Saxon Chronicle*) is that it occurred between Christmas 1085 and the death of William I in September 1087, a period of only twenty months. It has even been suggested that William was presented with a draft before he left England for the last time in September 1086, only nine months after the Survey was first mooted (Harvey 1971, 755). In view of the scope of the inquiry and the detailed information recorded, this was a remarkable achievement, indicating a high order of administrative efficiency. Yet all the credit should not go to the Norman administration. They were extremely fortunate to have had access to Anglo-Saxon hidage lists, which were arranged by landholder. It has been argued convincingly by Harvey (1971) that without these lists the Survey could not have been undertaken so quickly. Further, although the scale of the Survey was unparalleled in the Europe of its time, it has been suggested by Campbell (1975, 48–51) that the administrative processes employed were familiar in Francia between the reigns of Charlemagne and Charles the Bald, and were transmitted to England, probably through the Church, before the Conquest. In this sense Domesday Book was a product of both Anglo-Saxon and Norman administrations.

Our understanding of the making of Domesday Book has improved greatly over the past 100 years. The first major contribution was made by Round (1895), and was based largely upon the *Inquisitio Comitatus Cantabrigiensis*, one of several manuscripts contemporaneous with Domesday Book, which contained similar data. To Round (1895, 17) the *Inquisitio* was 'the true key to the Domesday Survey'. He saw the *Inquisitio*, in which the Survey data for Cambridgeshire were arranged by hundred and vill (rather than by tenant-in-chief and manor, as in Domesday Book), as a collection of hundred rolls that formed the returns from which Domesday Book was compiled. It was on this evidence that Round constructed his interpretation of the process of collecting and recording the Survey data: under supervision of the commissioners, the hundred courts were responsible for preparing the hundred rolls and returning them to Winchester, where they were reorganized, summarized, and consolidated into a single document. As these rolls would have been arranged on a territorial basis (hundreds and vills), and as Domesday Book is organized on a feudal basis (tenants-in-chief and manors), Round and Maitland were forced to conclude that the treasury officials in Winchester were responsible for completely restructuring the Survey data. This would have been a long and tedious task. It was this interpretation of the making of Domesday Book, therefore, that gave support to Round's belief that its main purpose was fiscal and not feudal.

Round's view prevailed unchallenged until the work of Galbraith (1942; 1961; 1974), which was based upon a detailed analysis not only of the *Inquisitio* but also of the Domesday 'satellites' of Exeter (or Exon.) Domesday (including the five south-western counties) and Little Domesday (including Norfolk, Suffolk, and Essex), which Round had largely ignored. Galbraith (1961, 35) claimed that the *Inquisitio* was not a return sent to Winchester, but rather a record of the proceedings of the Cambridgeshire county court. According to Galbraith's new hypothesis, information was presented to the county court by tenants-in-chief rather than by officials of the hundred court (i.e. on a feudal rather than a territorial basis), and it was compiled in this feudal form for each county in each of the seven survey circuits. These county documents formed the basis of the feudally arranged circuit returns, which, on being sent to Winchester, were merely summarized and consolidated (1974, 42–4). Examples of these circuit returns include Exeter Domesday (possibly a draft of the circuit return) and Little Domesday. In other words, Galbraith felt that the 'administrative process was a more complex one [than Round had envisaged], involving successive written drafts, the last of which alone, since it was sent to Winchester, became the "original returns" of the Inquest' (1961, 18). The *Inquisitio*, then, was merely part of the early stages of compilation, and as such provides an incomplete picture of the making of Domesday Book. As the Survey data were organized on a feudal basis from the beginning (according to this interpretation), Galbraith concluded that its purpose must be feudal rather than fiscal.

Since Galbraith's 1942 article, other scholars have confirmed the main features of his hypothesis, particularly concerning the relationship of Domesday Book to its 'satellites', and the role of tenants-in-chief in providing the initial returns to the county court (Sawyer 1955; Finn 1963; Loyn 1979). The main shift in focus since then has been the suggestion (Harvey 1971; 1980) that, because of the speed with which the Survey data were collected and compiled, a complex procedure involving numerous drafting stages is unlikely. As Harvey has written (1971, 755):

The majority of scholars think that something resembling Domesday Book was presented to King William in his lifetime, probably before he left England for Normandy, only months after the idea of the survey was first mooted. If we are to think likewise, such involved procedures are impossible.

From this starting-point, Harvey goes on to provide evidence for the existence of 'feudally arranged fiscal texts' of Anglo-Saxon origin which were compiled on a county basis and held by the treasury in Winchester, and probably also by the county courts. These hidage lists, which contained the names and fiscal liabilities of tenants-in-chief in each county, were employed both as a framework for collecting and compiling the data and as the 'chief source for Domesday's fiscal figures' (Harvey 1971, 759). In effect, Harvey was able to demonstrate the interconnection of both feudal (tenurial) and territorial-fiscal (county, hundred, vill) organization, together with the one-sidedness of emphasizing one or the other, as Round and Galbraith had done.

2.2.4 Survey methods and data accuracy

How was the Survey conducted? It has been suggested by a number of scholars that, for the purposes of the Survey, the counties of England were grouped into nine (Eyton 1878) or seven (Ballard 1906; Stephenson 1954) circuits, which were subsequently visited by different teams of commissioners who had no material interests in their circuit. These circuits are thought to be as follows (Stephenson 1954, 184–205):

I Kent, Sussex, Surrey, Hampshire, Berkshire
II Wiltshire, Dorsetshire, Somersetshire, Devonshire, Cornwall
III Middlesex, Hertford, Buckingham, Cambridge, Bedford
IV Oxford, Northampton, Leicester, Warwick
V Gloucester, Worcester, Hereford, Stafford, Shropshire, Cheshire
VI Huntingdon, Darby, Nottingham, Rutland, York, Lincoln
VII Essex, Norfolk, Sussex

The survey results for circuits I–VI were recorded in Great Domesday Book, and those for circuit VII were recorded, in greater detail, in Little Domesday Book.

Within each circuit, the procedures adopted are considered to be reasonably similar. A list of questions was supplied to the tenants-in-chief, who were identified by the hidage lists, in each county; the returns from the tenants-in-chief were reviewed in the county court by the hundred juries consisting of half Englishmen and half Frenchmen; the data verified in this way were recorded by tenant-in-chief for each county in the circuit; and the circuit returns were sent to Winchester, where they were summarized, edited, and compiled into volume I of Domesday Book.

It is generally agreed that the tenants-in-chief of each county were supplied with a set of questions similar to those contained in the text of *Inquisitio Eliensis*, which records the survey of the Abbey of Ely's estates in six eastern counties. The questions are (Hamilton 1876, 97):

What is the manor called? Who held it in the time of King Edward? Who holds it now? How many hides? How many ploughs on the demesne? How many men? How many villeins? How many cottars? How many slaves? How many freemen? How many socmen? How much wood? How much meadow? How much pasture? How many mills? How many fish ponds? How much has been added or taken away? How much, taken together, was it worth and how much now? How much each freeman or socman had or has? All this at three dates, to wit, in the time of King Edward and when King William gave it and as it is now. And if it is possible for more to be had than is had.

As can be seen from the sample entry in Figure 2.3, which is a manor at Woodham in the Essex hundred of Dengie, the recorded answers in Domesday

WDEHAM [Woodham (Walter)], which was held by Leveva as a manor and as 7 hides, is held of R[alf] by Pointel. Then 12 villeins; now 6. Then as now (*semper*) 4 bordars. Then 6 serfs; now 4. Then as now (*semper*) 3 ploughs on the demesne. Then 4 ploughs belonging to the men; now 1. (There are) 24 acres of meadow, (with) wood(land) for 500 swine. Then 1 mill; now 2. Then 2 beasts (*animalia*) and 7 swine, (and) 37 sheep; now 8 beasts, 21 swine, 6 asses, 130 sheep, (and) 13 hives of bees. It was then worth 8 pounds; and when received, 40 shillings; it is now worth 7 pounds.

Figure 2.3. Sample manor from Essex folios
Source: Domesday Book, vol. ii, fo. 69 (V.C.H. *Essex*, vol. i, 522).

Book appear to be responses to a remarkably similar set of questions. It is worthwhile examining more closely the data contained in this sample entry from the Essex folios. We are told that Leveva held the manor at Woodham at the end of the Confessor's reign (1066), when it was assessed for geld at seven hides, and that in 1086 it had passed to Pointel, who held it of Ralf Baignard, a prosperous lay tenant-in-chief (who controlled a further twenty-two manors in Essex). Following these details of ownership is a list of resources belonging to the manor in both 1066 and 1086. In 1066 there were 12 villeins, 4 bordars, 6 slaves, 7 ploughs (of which 3 belonged to the lord and 4 to the peasants), one water-driven mill, 2 beasts (or cows), 7 swine, and 37 sheep. By 1086 a number of important changes had occurred: the number of villeins had been halved to 6, bordars were unchanged at 4, slaves had declined to 4; plough-teams had almost halved to 4, due to a dramatic decline in peasant ploughs, probably due in turn to the halving of villein numbers; mills had doubled to 2; and the numbers of livestock, particularly sheep (from 37 to 130), had increased quite dramatically, which was probably a result of the decline in peasant agriculture. Additional information for 1086 includes 24 acres of meadow, woodland capable of supporting 500 swine, and 13 beehives. Finally, it is recorded that, although in 1066 Leveva's income (including demesne profits, rents, and other minor dues and fines) was £8, when Pointel came into possession it had fallen dramatically to £2 (probably because of the death or desertion of many of the peasants and their plough-teams), but that he had been able to build it up again (largely by increasing the manor's pastoral activities, possibly on the vacant peasants' land) to £7 in 1086. This entry is particularly interesting because it demonstrates how difficult it was to recover in the short term from a major loss of agricultural resources such as plough-teams. It appears to have been easier to switch to pastoral activities than to obtain additional plough beasts and peasant services. Agricultural resources appear, therefore, to have been highly inflexible in the short term.

Tenants-in-chief were circulated with a list of questions from the circuit commissioners, and were called upon to present their responses in the county court. Evidence in the *Inquisitio* suggests that these hearings were dealt with by an enlarged county court which, in addition to the circuit commissioners, consisted of the sheriff, the king's barons with fiefs in the county together with their French tenants, the court of each hundred with its hundred jury, and eight representatives—a priest, reeve, and six villeins—from each village (Stenton 1943, 652; Galbraith 1961, 36). Clearly this was a very large gathering, involving hundreds of people in each county throughout the land. Little is known of the identity of the main participants in these proceedings. It is thought, however, that the commissioners included bishops, lawyers, and the king's barons, none of whom had any material interest in the circuit for which they were responsible. More is known about the juries, as some are recorded in the *Inquisitio*. They consisted of eight people, of whom half were Englishmen and half were Frenchmen, and appear to have come from the rural middle class: Stenton (1943, 652) claimed 'none of them was of outstanding rank or wealth', and Galbraith (1961, 38) calls them 'small landholders'.

The involvement of so many people (possibly 10,000 throughout England) in the collection, verification, and compilation of the Domesday data suggests a number of conclusions. First, and most obviously, this was a very expensive survey in terms of both the official expenditures involved in invoking the necessary institutional procedures and the private opportunity costs (i.e. the time people were involved in the survey, valued by what they could have produced in their normal occupations) of the many who participated, from powerful baron to poor peasant. It is unlikely that such costs would have been undertaken unless the king were convinced that it would result in a higher future income. Secondly, it is clear that the manner in which the data were collected made it a very public event involving many people who had intimate local knowledge of all the manors under review. In these circumstances there would have been few occasions when falsification could have passed undetected. This evidence was also given under oath, and the penalties for perjury were probably severe, because falsification meant depriving the king of his rightful revenue. So concerned was William to ensure the accuracy of this record that he even sent out additional agents to ensure that the commissioners were carrying out his instructions carefully and impartially.

This is not to say that mistakes did not creep into Domesday Book, either deliberately or by accident, but the method of collection was such that they would have been minimized. While most scholars have been careful to outline the deficiencies of Domesday data, one has suggested recently that this approach has been taken too far. Harvey (1980, 130–1) sensibly pointed out that:

DB certainly contains deficiencies and gaps, but these are often due to its orientation to certain objectives, a consideration surely common to all sources... Certainly arguments from Domesday silence are invalid... But of the positive evidence, what is gratifying is that many curiosities, given enough further information, are found to be accurate and explicable... What *is* present in DB is highly reliable. About what may be absent there is still room for discussion and demonstration.

Even Round (1895, 30), who was 'able to detect a considerable number of inaccuracies and omissions', largely due to clerical error resulting from the use of roman numerals, stressed the overall reliability of Domesday statistics: 'if we find that a rule of interpretation can be established in an overwhelming majority of cases examined, we are justified ... in claiming that the apparent exceptions may be due to errors in the text.' His caution concerns the use of individual entries to support hypotheses (a method, as will be shown in Chapters 3, 4, and 5, often employed in the traditional approach). Finn (1971, 14, 245) also came to a similar conclusion in claiming: 'Long study of them [the values] convinces me that over the vast range of statistics serious misapprehension is unlikely', and again: 'The entries ... are so numerous that incorrect interpretation of the doubtful passages probably does not appreciably affect the results.' Other scholars (Darby 1977, 214–15; Maitland 1897, 473) also have noted 'minor errors' when comparing successive drafts of Domesday Book (such as the Exeter and Exchequer versions)—which, despite their words of caution, has not prevented them from drawing conclusions from a general examination of county-wide data.

While it is anticipated that, overall, Domesday data reliably measure values and resources on the recorded manors, there may be a few observations which produce inexplicable results because of clerical error. It is expected that the variable most prone to error will be the values, together with those few inputs which were measured subjectively (e.g. woodland which was measured in terms of the number of swine it could theoretically graze). In the main, however, inputs were measured in physical (e.g. numbers of labourers, or livestock) rather than conceptual terms. But it should be noted that, in many cases, Domesday Book data give the appearance of having been rounded, thereby introducing a further source of error, albeit minor and familiar to those who work with more recent data.

2.2.5 A comparison with modern rural surveys

Some of the more interesting features of Domesday Book can be highlighted by contrasting it with similar official data collected today. For example, *Agricultural Statistics for England*, published annually since 1866, provides on a county basis a breakdown of agricultural output and input quantities as well as prices. Although this agricultural survey has broadly similar features to Domesday Book, there are important differences. First, the purpose of this modern rural survey is to provide data on rural activities at an industry or commodity level, rather than at the individual farm level of Domesday Book.

Secondly, the nature of the output and input data differs between the two surveys. *Agricultural Statistics* provides output information (in quantities but not values) on a commodity basis, whereas Domesday Book records only the total value-added of manorial production. An important reason for the use of composite totals in Domesday Book could be that rural production was more of a monoculture than it is today. Finally, the major difference centres on the methods employed in the two surveys. Since 1866, the responsible government department has 'relied mainly on the postal service for both delivery of the forms to the farmers and their return to the Collecting Office' (*Agricultural Statistics*, 1968). It is candidly admitted that this method leads to major delays, as well as to some non-compliance (particularly in the first few decades of the survey). Also, as respondents are completely responsible for the information supplied, it is not easy to detect falsification. In particular, the confidentiality rules preclude the possibility of obtaining an assessment of the veracity of individual returns from people with local or expert knowledge. Only the most obvious discrepancies are, and indeed can be, checked by telephonic and postal inquiries. In the collection of modern agricultural statistics, therefore, it is not possible to evaluate systematically the accuracy of individual responses as was done in 1086. It is interesting that, while the methods of processing data have improved radically since 1086, in many respects the methods of data collection have deteriorated.

Notes

1. The term 'manor' has been used throughout this study as a matter of convenience. As recognized in 2.1.2.1, the manor only approached full development in English England.
2. A similar argument about the manorial lord providing protection was put forward earlier by an eminent economist (Hicks 1969, 102).
3. This can be observed from the Wiltshire and Essex folios of Domesday Book.
4. See also Postan (1966, 572).
5. There is a growing literature on the reasons for scattered strips. For a traditional account see Loyn (1962, 152), and for a neoclassical economic analysis see McCloskey (1972), with comment by Fenoaltea (1976) and rejoinder by McCloskey (1977).
6. There is a considerable literature on this question. See Maitland (1897, 172–219), Tait (1936, 1–29), and Loyn (1962, 133).
7. These hypotheses are discussed by Maitland (1897, 189–90), Tait (1936, 341–2), and Darby (1977, 310–12).
8. For an opposing view, see John (1960).

3

Old and new approaches

3.1 INTRODUCTION

Domesday Book literature has a long and distinguished history, particularly since the work of F. W. Maitland and J. H. Round in the closing decades of the nineteenth century. Over the last 100 years our understanding of the data in Domesday Book has grown considerably, due mainly to the large-scale study of H. C. Darby and his co-authors. This important achievement is based upon an empirical method, to be called the traditional approach, which experienced little change during these years. While large gains have been made in the past by employing the traditional approach, recent progress appears to have slowed appreciably. It will be argued that further major advances in the analysis of the vast quantity of Domesday data will require the adoption of a radically different approach. As a first step in this direction, a new approach based upon the application of modern economic and statistical methods has been employed in this study. To clarify the issues involved, the characteristics of the old and new approaches are outlined in this chapter.

3.2 THE TRADITIONAL APPROACH

3.2.1 A general outline

Our concern here is with the way in which previous scholars have analysed the statistical information in Domesday Book. There are two broad observations that can be made about the traditional approach: it is pragmatically rather than theoretically orientated, and it has experienced considerable difficulties in marshalling the detailed data for analytical purposes.

On the first point, Domesday scholars may have been influenced by the concerns of their disciplines, but they have not used the available theoretical models to develop specific hypotheses to be tested against the data. In the main the data have been extracted, assembled, and examined with little theoretical guidance. For example, Round (1895, 9), in expressing his aims, wrote: 'The object I have set before myself throughout [*Feudal England*] is either to add to or correct our existing knowledge of facts.' Darby, like Round, was also primarily interested in the facts. As he explained (Darby 1977, 375):

I became interested in Domesday Book while working on the medieval fenland in the early 1930s. The Domesday entries for the fenland villages yielded a harvest of information about such items as fisheries, salt-pans, ploughteams and population. I soon realised, however, that the individuality of fenland economy could only be appreciated by contrasting this information with that for the upland around. And this led to an examination of the complete Domesday texts for the surrounding counties.

Maitland differs from both scholars in this matter. He was more interested in wider intellectual and theoretical considerations, particularly concerning the legal structure of the society which gave rise to Domesday Book. For example, he wrote (Maitland 1897, 3):

If English history is to be understood, the law of Domesday Book must be mastered. We have here an absolutely unique account of feudalism in two different stages of its growth, the more trustworthy, though the more puzzling, because it gives us particulars and not generalities ... if we are to come by general rules, we must obtain them inductively by a comparison of many thousand particular instances.

Even so, the detailed questions which Maitland asked of the Domesday data arose from a pragmatic concern with that source, rather than from theoretical propositions. Because all these writers chose not to refer to an established body of generalized knowledge (or theory), the conclusions they arrived at were often highly subjective, idiosyncratic, and even fanciful.

Our second point concerns the statistical methods underlying the traditional approach, which can be classified into two broad groups: comprehensive description and selective analysis. Domesday data have been treated comprehensively only when they have been described rather than analysed. The most notable example is Darby's monumental geography of Domesday England. Darby's method involved the use of maps to display the spatial distribution of individual variables (such as peasants, slaves, plough-teams, livestock, land, industry, and towns) throughout Domesday England. In this way he provided an approximate visual impression of the variation in the use of these resources from county to county. On a few occasions, Darby was able to go a stage further by relating one variable to another to produce a composite measure, such as annual value per man (a measure of productivity), and to show how it varied across England. While this technique can pose a number of interesting questions—such as why productivity is higher in Wiltshire than Essex—it cannot answer them. Essentially, the method is descriptive rather than analytical. Nevertheless, work of this nature is very important, as it has provided a map of Domesday economy and society which is an essential guide for those attempting more analytical work.

When scholars have attempted, on the other hand, to analyse rather than describe the relationships in Domesday Book, they have been highly selective in their use of data. Most scholars (with the exception of Maitland) have based their analyses upon very small, non-random samples. And in all cases the observations appear to have been chosen because of the extreme characteristics they possess, probably to demonstrate the extent of the variation in the constituent variables. What has been overlooked, however, is that a relationship between two (or more) variables is determined by the vast majority of 'typical' observations rather than by a handful of deviant ones. It is, of course, useful to indicate that deviant observations do exist; but, if they are relatively few in number, they will not falsify the relationship.

There are a number of other reasons for traditional scholars overlooking or dismissing strong relationships between the key variables in Domesday Book. First, they generally expect to find an exact relationship between the two variables under examination. They expect to find, in other words, all observations conforming exactly to the relationship being tested. For example, if the traditional scholar expected a linear relationship between, say, tax assessments and annual values, then he would expect to find all manorial observations to be located exactly on the line fitted to a scatter diagram (as in Figure 8.6, p. 135). If instead, he found that the observations were scattered above and below the line (as in Figure 8.5, p. 133), he would dismiss the hypothesis of a relationship between assessments and values. While it is true that an *exact* relationship does not exist, this does not preclude a strong *non-exact* (or stochastic) relationship between the variables.[1] Most relationships in economics, and indeed in the social sciences as a whole, are of a non-exact nature. This possibility has not been considered in the Domesday literature.

Secondly, when the expected relationship involves more than one explanatory variable, the method of visual inspection becomes even more unreliable. The traditional scholar, in looking for a relationship between annual values and resources for, say, ten manors that have the same annual value, expects to find similar combinations of resources for each manor. If the resource combinations are not similar, he rejects the hypothesis of a relationship. What he has overlooked, however, is that a given output can be produced with a wide variety of resource combinations. Not only is this theoretically possible, it can also be demonstrated empirically for Domesday England by the estimation of production functions (see Chapter 6).

3.2.2 The traditional approach illustrated

The traditional approach can be illustrated by reference to the work of Round, Maitland, and Darby on two of the main issues analysed in this book: the relationships between tax assessments and annual values, and between annual values and resources. Our interest here is only with the methods employed by these scholars. In Chapters 4 and 5 we focus upon the interpretations arising from these empirical techniques.

3.2.2.1 J. H. Round to H. C. Darby: an enduring tradition

In the analysis of causal relationships, the traditional approach changed little between the work of Round (1895) and Darby (1979). The method developed by Round in the last decade of the nineteenth century is still employed by some scholars today. From casual observation of the entries in one of the famous Domesday satellites, *Inquisitio Comitatus Cantabrigiensis*, Round noticed that

Table 3.1. Sample entry from the *Inquisitio*: hundred of Staines

Vill	Hides	Ploughlands	Valets (TRE)
Bottisham	10	20	£16 0s. 0d.
Swaffham (1)	10	16	11 10 0
Swaffham (2)	10	$13\frac{1}{4}$	12 10 0
Wilbraham	10	17	20 0 0
Stow-cum-Quy	10	11	14 10 0
	50	$77\frac{1}{4}$	£74 10 0

Source: Round (1895, 48).

when manors were aggregated to the level of the vill (which is not done in Domesday Book), the tax assessment, in hides, appeared to be expressed in multiples of five. Having stated this hypothesis, he says: 'Let us now take a typical Hundred and test this theory in practice' (Round 1895, 48). Accordingly he presented a table (Table 3.1) containing five vills, each with the same number of hides, but with some variation in ploughlands and values. As the ploughlands and values for each village were not identical, Round dismissed the idea that they had any relationship with tax assessments. A further six tables showing hides and ploughlands were presented, and similar statements were made in respect of each after cursory visual inspection. This was sufficient for Round to conclude that assessments were not based upon an evaluation of capacity to pay, but rather were completely artificial or arbitrary—a result of administrative convenience. This evidence on values and ploughlands was marshalled merely in order to establish the importance of the five-hide unit, and from this point Round focused all his attention upon the pattern of hides he thought he had discovered. The remainder of the chapter consists of lists of hundreds, and their vills, which had a hidage expressed in multiples of five. All thought of a direct test of the relationship between capacity to pay and tax assessment was abandoned, in favour of an indirect test involving identification of the five-hide unit. The five-hide unit became the ultimate test of Round's hypothesis.

Darby and his co-authors accepted not only some of Round's conclusions (particularly the artificial nature of assessments) but also his statistical method. For example, when examining the tax assessments for Wiltshire, Darby's co-author R. W. Finn, set out a table (see Table 3.2) in which 'the variation among a representative selection of five-hide vills speaks for itself' (Darby and Finn 1967, 17). Finn concluded, from a visual inspection of this table, that 'assessment ... bore no constant relation to the agricultural resources of a vill'. This is the same procedure employed by Round over seventy years before, and it leads to the same conclusion. Finn even proceeded

Table 3.2. Sample holdings from Wiltshire Domesday

Manor	Ploughlands	Plough-teams	Population	Valuit	Valet
Beechingstoke	5	5	14	60s.	100s.
Chisbury	9	9	36	£8	£12
Smithcot	4	5	10	40s.	60s.
Surrendell	6	6	19	£7	£7
Westlecott	2	2	10	40s.	40s.

Source: Darby and Finn (1967, 17).

to search for evidence of the five-hide unit, claiming that 'a glance through the Wiltshire folios reveals many examples of the 5-hide unit'. Similarly, in the case of Essex, Darby (1952, 220) concluded, after an even more impressionistic examination of the entries, that no relationship existed between hides and resources. But, while he found some examples of the five-hide unit, he concluded that it was not so prominent as elsewhere.

Darby also employed Round's method as late as 1979, when examining the relationship between annual value and resources. He selected a handful of manors that had the same annual value, and presented them in tabular form (see Table 3.3). From visual inspection Darby (1977, 221) concluded that there was no systematic relationship between resources and values. This is Darby's analytical method in its most developed form. Almost a century after the appearance of *Feudal England*, therefore, Darby was still employing the impressionistic methods of Round when analysing (rather than describing) the Domesday data.

Table 3.3. Sample holdings worth £2 a year in 1086 from Exeter DB and Little DB

Place	Men	Teams	Demesne sheep	Other livestock	Other resources
Clatworthy (S)	23	7	100	59	M, P, W, mill
Redlynch (S)	14	2	20	21	M, W
Cheriton (D)	8	2	30	35	P, W
Feniton (D)	14	$\frac{1}{2}$	15	5	M, P, W
Banham (N)	11	$1\frac{1}{2}$	30	61	M, W
Lexham (N)	24	6	200	36	W, mill
Ilketshall (Sk)	18	$2\frac{1}{2}$	40	21	M, W, mill
Old Newton (Sk)	3	1	40	8	M
Bowers Gifford (E)	1	1	100	20	P
Bromley (E)	3	0	11	—	M, W

S = Somerset, D = Devon, N = Norfolk, Sk = Suffolk, E = Essex, M = meadow, P = pasture, W = wood

Source: Darby (1977, 222).

3.2.2.2 F. W. Maitland: a pioneer in the historical use of sampling methods

Unlike Round and Darby, Maitland did not attempt to isolate a small number of individual vills or manors. Instead, he gathered data on variables such as hides, values, and teamlands and aggregated them to the county level, in order to gain a perspective of the entire country. He explained this approach as follows: 'Now if we are ever to understand these matters, it is necessary that we should look at the whole of England' (Maitland 1897, 407). This aggregated (or macro) approach was both a strength and a weakness. On the positive side, it enabled Maitland to avoid the trap, into which Round and his followers fell, of focusing not upon the experience of the majority of manors but upon that of a few exceptional ones. Yet, in focusing upon county totals, Maitland lost touch with the richness of the individual data in Domesday Book: his was a rather blunt instrument of analysis. For Maitland's limited purposes, however, this approach was less likely to lead to major misinterpretations. Considerable development in statistical theory and electronic equipment was necessary before the individual data in Domesday Book could be effectively employed.

In examining the relationship between tax assessments and annual values, Maitland used both county aggregates and small samples from certain subgroups within each of these counties. While he began by making a number of impressionistic observations about the assessment–value relationship, Maitland realized the importance of substantiating his hypothesis. He wrote (Maitland 1897, 464–5):

In order that we may not trust to vague impressions, let us set down in one column the number of hides (carucates or sulungs) that we have given to twenty counties and in another column the annual value of those counties in the time of King Edward as calculated by Mr Pearson [1867]. No one can look along these lines of figures without fancying that some force, conscious, or unconscious, had made for one pound, one hide.

Hence Maitland came to his conclusion about the 1066 assessment–value relationship on the basis of a visual comparison of some twenty county totals.

Yet it worried Maitland that non-agricultural profits received by the king (from county courts and boroughs) were included in these county totals. He decided, therefore, to omit the king's manors. Probably because of the limited time he was able to devote to the exercise, Maitland drew samples from the lay and ecclesiastical manors in thirty Domesday counties for 1066. As he explained (Maitland 1897, 465):

from every county we will take eighty simple entries, some from the lands of the churches, some from the fiefs of the barons, and in a large county we will select our cases from many different pages. In each case we set down the number of gelding hides (carucates, sulungs), and the *valuit* given for the T.R.E. [in the time of King Edward].

Unfortunately Maitland did not discuss his sampling method in any further detail. It is impossible to determine whether he drew the sample observations from the lay and ecclesiastical subgroups in the same proportion as in the population, or whether he selected the manors randomly. The only hint he provides is a footnote in which he discusses the county of Stafford (Maitland 1897, 465): 'I have excluded (1) royal demesne, (2) cases in which there is any talk of "waste", (3) cases in which a particular manor is obviously privileged.' It would appear that Maitland was concerned to select manors that were normal or representative, and to exclude deviant or extreme observations. If this impression is correct, he was at the very opposite end of the methodological spectrum from Round and Darby, who focused upon extreme rather than representative variables. Yet, in exercising his judgement in the above manner, Maitland's samples may have been less than random.

While Maitland's selection of data was innovative, his analysis was more conventional. He merely aggregated the manorial data on both assessments and values to the county level, expressed them in terms of value per hide (or carucate or sulung), and from visual inspection concluded as before: 'Now "one pound, one hide" seems to be the central point of this series, the point of rest through which the pendulum swings', and, in an attempt to quantify this vague statement he continued: 'in some twenty out of thirty counties the aberration from the equivalence of pound and hide will not exceed twenty-five per cent: in other words, the value of the normal hide will not be less than 15 nor more than 25 shillings' (Maitland 1897, 465–6). This is interesting, as Maitland was attempting to determine the central value and dispersion of observations: his central value was £1 and the dispersion was plus and minus 5 shillings. As the mean, medium and mode of the totals for the thirty counties are £1.18, £0.99, and £0.99 and the standard deviation is £0.75, when recalculated by us, Maitland's impression of central value was correct, but he underestimated the degree of dispersion. The reason for underestimating the variation around the statistical average of £1 may have been that, like Round, he was searching for an attractive rule of thumb that Anglo-Saxon administrators could have employed in raising taxes. As will be demonstrated, both scholars appear to have underestimated the sophistication of Anglo-Saxon administration.

An interesting discovery to emerge from our study of Maitland's statistical methods is that he was a pioneer in the use of sampling techniques in social science research. In the early 1890s Maitland, faced with the overwhelming detail of data in Domesday Book, had little to guide him on how to employ it effectively. His use of samples of manors taken from each county was particularly enterprising. Only after Maitland had published *Domesday Book and Beyond* was the scientific method of sampling developed, and this occurred within the context of social survey work rather than of historical study. It is generally acknowledged that Booth (1889–1902) was 'the father of scientific social surveys', even though he did not employ random sampling techniques (Moser 1958, 18; Stephan 1948). Bowley and Burnett-Hurst (1915) are credited with the pioneering use of random sampling, first used in their survey of working-class households. It was as late as 1923 before random sampling was employed in an official British study (involving claimants for unemployment benefits), and not until 1937 that a large-scale government inquiry (into working-class expenditure) was conducted on this basis. By the late 1930s, random sampling techniques were being employed quite widely. For example, the BBC was sampling listener opinion, and private organizations were regularly sampling market attitudes (Moser 1958, 21 and 54).

In this light, Maitland's caution about his statistical work is understandable. He wrote in the preface to *Domesday Book and Beyond:* 'For my hastily compiled Domesday Statistics I have apologized in the proper place. Here I will only add that I had but one long vacation to give to a piece of work that would have been better performed had it been spread over many years.' Later, and 'in the proper place', Maitland (1897, 407) elaborated that statement:

Well would it be if the broad features of Domesday Book could be set out before us in a series of statistical tables. The task would be gigantic and could hardly be performed except by a body of men who had plenteous leisure and who would work together harmoniously. However, rather to suggest what might and some day must be done, than to parade what has been done rapidly and badly, some figures have been set forth... That they are extremely inaccurate can not be doubtful, for he who compiled them had other things to do and lacks many of the qualities which should be required of a good counter... What is here set before the reader is intended to be no more than a distant approach towards truth. It will serve its end if it states the sort of figures that would be obtained by careful and leisurely computers, and therefore the sort of problems that have to be solved.

Maitland here foreshadows the 'gigantic' effort of Darby and his team of co-workers, who became the 'careful and leisurely computers' he envisaged. He had no way of knowing, however, that their efforts would be followed so closely by computers of an electronic kind.

In discussing his sampling technique Maitland (1897, 465) deemed it 'rude', and warned that the 'method will not be delicate enough to detect slight differences; it will only suffice to display any general tendency that is at work throughout England and to stamp as exceptional any shires which widely depart from the common rule, if common rule there be'. And, when drawing conclusions from his sample data, he qualified them by adding: 'unless we have shamefully blundered'.

Maitland was a remarkable scholar in this, as in so many other ways. The pity is that other Domesday historians did not build upon the methodological foundations that he so skilfully laid, but chose instead to follow the lead of Round.

Only recently has an attempt been made to replicate Maitland's methods by using simple regression techniques. In an interesting paper concerned with military obligations on the eve of the Conquest, Abels (1985, 15–18) gives brief consideration to 'the meaning of hidage and its implications for the military organisation of late Anglo-Saxon England'.[2] Abels examines the 1066 relationship between hides and values using the county aggregates taken from Maitland, and a mixture of samples and total enumerations from a limited number of counties (eleven, rather than Maitland's thirty). To both sets of data Abels applies, without testing its applicability, a linear function, and comes to the same conclusion as Maitland, that 'prior to 1066 "one pound, one hide", was a general rule subject to local exceptions'. Also like Maitland, Abels accepts Round's claim, which is incompatible with Maitland's statistical results, that assessments were artificial (see 4.3). The confusion on this issue, therefore, continues to the very present.

There are two major problems with the way in which Abels has employed regression techniques. First, as shown in Chapters 4 and 5, the relationship between manorial values and assessments is not linear, as Ables has assumed. By imposing the wrong functional form upon the data, the results he obtains are inappropriate. It is important to use the data to estimate the correct functional form. Secondly, the analysis in our book shows that the Domesday data are difficult to handle using simple regression techniques, because a critical assumption upon which such techniques are based is often violated. It is important that the variance of the error disturbances be constant, a condition known as homoskedasticity. Instead, when the conventional functional forms are estimated using Domesday data, the disturbances are often heteroskedastic in such a way that their variances are related to the variable we wish to explain (see 8.10–8.14). Unless heteroskedasticity is allowed for, as we have done in Chapters 4, 5, 6, and 10, the estimated coefficients will be inefficient (or unreliable), and the tests of significance will be invalid. As Abels has not allowed for the problems inherent in the Domesday data, he has been unable to define the assessment–value relationship with much more precision than Maitland was able to do a century ago. While Abels does not solve the difficult problems inherent in the Domesday data, his work has nevertheless taken a step in the right direction.

3.3 A NEW APPROACH

Initially, the traditional approach appeared to offer major insights into the nature of the fiscal and economic systems in the late eleventh century; but as it does not embody a way of distinguishing between competing hypotheses, and as it is not able to handle the sheer volume of data available in Domesday Book, its usefulness is limited. It seems to be time for a new approach. We believe that an effective new approach should involve the use of economic theory, modern statistical method, and electronic computers. The use of economic theory makes it possible to challenge existing claims about economic relationships that appear counter-intuitive to the economist, and to replace them with less fanciful hypotheses. Modern statistical methods can be used to test the hypotheses rigorously, and electronic computers make it possible to analyse all the data. A modest beginning along the above lines has been made in this study.

3.3.1 The use of economic theory

Economic theory has been employed in this book in two ways. In the first place it was the basis of our initial doubt concerning the existing interpretation of economic relationships in Domesday Book. The two main economic interpretations of the traditional approach are that there is no systematic relationship between either tax assessments for geld and the capacity of manors to pay this impost, or manorial annual values (or income) and resources. While both hypotheses have been part of the conventional wisdom for the last century, neither makes any economic sense. For example, a tax which is arbitrary will not be an effective fiscal instrument. A head of state who wishes to maximize his net tax revenue will attempt to apply the principle of capacity to pay. If he does not, the taxpayers will resent the inequality and will resist the tax, even if the reason for its imposition (in this case defence) is basically acceptable. It is reasonable to suppose that public resistance, and hence the costs to the state of suppressing it, will increase as the inequity of assessment increases. The amount of net tax revenue, therefore, will be inversely related to the assessment system's degree of inequity. Accordingly, the head of state will be concerned not only with the concept of capacity to pay, but also with the best way of measuring it in practice.[3]

Also, it is hard to imagine a world in which there is no relationship between the income and resources of a firm (or farm). On the contrary, economic theory indicates that an increase in the resources of a firm (or farm) will normally lead to an increase in output. Obviously, if this were not true, no entrepreneur would bother to acquire and employ additional resources. It is curious that the conventional hypotheses could have persisted for so many years. Our starting point was that either the conventional wisdom on both these issues was wrong, or the data in Domesday Book were meaningless. These issues are analysed in Chapters 4 and 5.

In addition to redefining existing questions, economic theory has played an important role in our study by posing questions which have not been asked of the Domesday data before, and in analysing the answers we have obtained. This procedure is within the spirit of the fine intellectual tradition bequeathed to Domesday scholars by Maitland (1897, 2) who wrote: 'If only we can ask the right questions we shall have done something for a good end.'

One of the most well-developed and useful areas of economic theory is that concerning production. The theory of production has been of considerable assistance in framing questions about the manorial system: about the relationship between changes in resources and changes in output; about the way in which one resource, say villeins, can be substituted for another, say plough-teams, and still maintain a given output; about the existence of economies of scale. Similar questions are posed in Chapter 6, and are answered by estimating economic production functions. In the process, we believe, new light is thrown upon the system of manorial production in Domesday England.

3.3.2 Statistical method

The traditional approach, as we have suggested, involves the visual inspection of either a few individual manors (Round and Darby) or data aggregated to the county level (Maitland). In the first case it was not possible to achieve a representative perspective, and in the second a great deal of interesting information about individual manors was lost. Ideally a statistical method is required that will retain the information conveyed by individual manors, and that will also be capable of incorporating all the data, or at least a representative sample of it. Regression analysis can achieve both objectives.

An intuitive picture of the nature of regression analysis can be provided here by graphically illustrating our tax assessment–annual value results. A more formal, but simply stated, outline of this statistical technique is provided in Chapter 8. Basically, regression analysis involves summarizing a relationship between two variables (for the sake of simplicity), by fitting a line to a number of observations plotted on a diagram (called a scatter diagram), with one variable (say, assessments) measured on the vertical axis, and the other variable (say, annual value) measured on the horizontal axis. Figure 3.1 shows a line fitted to the assessment–value data (expressed in logarithms in this case) for 425 lay manors in Wiltshire in 1086.[4] This line could have been fitted to the data either impressionistically, and thereby approximately, or by the more objective principle of ordinary least squares, as in Figure 3.1. The strength of the relationship also can be gauged either impressionistically, by a judgement about how closely the plotted observations conform to the fitted line, or more objectively, from the estimation of the coefficient of determination, or R^2, which in this case is a remarkably high 0.79 (suggesting that 79 per cent of the variation in assessments can be 'explained' by the variation in annual values).

In addition, valuable information can be obtained about the relationship between two variables from this fitted line. For example, as this function is log-linear, we can discover by what percentage, on average, the assessment will increase with a 1 per cent increase in annual value. In the case of Wiltshire lay estates in 1086, a 1 per cent increase in annual value will lead to a 0.81 per cent increase in tax assessment. This information is summarized in the equation at the foot of the scatter diagram.

Had Maitland used a simple scatter diagram to graph his sample of individual manors from each county, not only would he have obtained a clearer visual impression of the strength and nature of the relationship between assessments and values, but he could have obtained valuable information from the individual data. While this would have been an unreasonable demand upon Maitland, as the theory of regression analysis was

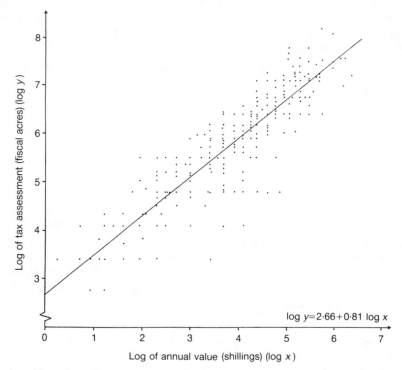

Figure 3.1. Scatter diagram showing the tax–value relationship for Wiltshire lay manors, 1086

developed only after his death,[5] it could have been achieved at any time in the last fifty years had someone decided to follow in Maitland's pioneering footsteps. Today it is desirable to proceed further than the simple scatter diagram, which allows for too much subjectivity. It is desirable to estimate not only the regression coefficients (the values of the intercept and the slope) and the coefficient of determination (R^2), but also to test for significance, and even to test the assumptions upon which this line-fitting procedure is based. Chapter 8 discusses these techniques.

The use of regression analysis also makes it possible, in certain circumstances, to distinguish between competing hypotheses. This is true, at least, of the competing hypotheses of Round and Maitland. For example, although Maitland thought there was a relationship between assessments and values, Round was adamant that no such relationship existed. The issue was complicated by the fact that Round's test of this relationship (the five-hide unit) was indirect and Maitland's was direct. In the absence of regression analysis, Maitland was unable to measure objectively the strength of this relationship, and, as he was aware of instances of the five-hide unit, he felt unable to distinguish between his hypothesis and that of Round. It is clear to us now, due to the development of statistical theory, that if there is a strong and significant relationship (even if it is non-exact or stochastic) between assessments and values, then Maitland is right and Round is wrong. Even if there are instances of the five-hide unit, these have nothing to do with the assessment–value relationship.

3.3.3 Data-processing techniques

More than a decade ago, one of the major scholars of Domesday Book, V. H. Galbraith, made an interesting prediction. He wrote (Galbraith 1974, 131):

There has since [the work of Ellis (1833)] been a great deal of further statistical research, notably in Professor Darby's giant *Domesday Geography*, but it is unlikely that Ellis's work will be superseded until, as now seems likely, the facts, in their entirety, are put through a computer; and this, of course, might revolutionize Domesday study.

The prediction is interesting, but not altogether accurate. Of course, it is true that the electronic computer is a powerful tool, which makes it possible to organize and analyse the massive detail of the Domesday data in a fraction of the time taken by Darby and his team of co-workers. Yet the computer will be neither the necessary not the sufficient cause of the revolution that Galbraith envisaged.

A major change in the interpretation of Domesday England could have occurred at any time over the last fifty years, even before the development of electronic computers. Galbraith's revolution depends not upon modern methods of data processing, but rather on the type of questions that are asked, and the statistical methods that are used to answer them. The computer can speed up this revolution, and make it more comprehensive, but is not essential to its occurrence. Indeed, as will be argued later, the computer may even slow down this process.

By the 1930s, most of the basic statistical techniques had been developed to enable a major new analysis of Domesday data. First, as we have seen, random sampling techniques were in widespread use in England before the Second World War. Maitland had even given the lead as early as 1897, although the statistical techniques required to handle individual data were not available. By careful use of random sampling techniques it would have been possible years ago to tame the overwhelming detail of Domesday Book. Secondly, regression analysis has been employed by economists since the 1930s, and by economic historians since the 1950s.[6] At any time over the last forty or fifty years, the combination of sampling techniques and regression analysis would have been sufficient to demolish a number of counter-intuitive hypotheses, particularly concerning economic relationships, and to reconstruct a more plausible picture of Domesday economy and society. In McDonald and Snooks (1985c), we demonstrated how this could be achieved by the use of simple calculators, which have been available since the 1950s.

It is necessary to labour this point because computers are now seen as the solution to all research problems. Certainly they can be extremely useful tools, as was the case in this study, but they can also create problems of their own. The availability of predigested statistical programs, which make it possible to apply all manner of sophisticated statistical tests at the touch of a keyboard, can create problems of interpretation. It is now possible for the sophistication of the statistical results to exceed the statistical knowledge of the researcher, in which case it is highly likely that the wrong conclusions will be drawn from the computerized analysis of Domesday Book data. If so, the resulting confusion, and necessary reworking of results, will slow down Galbraith's revolution. A possible source of such confusion concerns the violation of the assumptions upon which regression analysis is based. Attention has already been drawn to this problem in 3.2.2.2, and it is discussed in detail in Chapter 8 (especially 8.10–8.14).

3.4 CONCLUSIONS

The traditional approach to economic relationships in Domesday data involved neither the use of theoretical models nor adequate statistical techniques. Hence it gave rise to conclusions that were counter-intuitive and, as will be demonstrated in later chapters, that cannot be verified by a more thorough analysis of the Domesday data. The approach employed in this study, however, involves the use of both economic theory and modern statistical techniques. While modern data-processing techniques have also been extremely useful in this study, they were not essential. Similar, although less comprehensive, work could have been achieved at any time in the last fifty years.

Notes

1. The nature of non-exact, or stochastic, relationships is discussed in 8.2.
2. This discussion is based upon the galley proofs of a paper (Abels 1985) to be published later in 1985, which was kindly sent to us by the author. At the time of receipt, McDonald and Snooks (1985a; 1985b; 1985c) were in press, and the chapters of this book were in typescript.
3. Our argument is similar to, but independent of, that developed in the stimulating and wide-ranging work by Margaret Levi on the theory of predatory rule (Levi 1984a; 1984b).
4. The graph in Figure 3.1 is a rough computer plot that places the scatter points in approximately the correct location, and does not indicate multiple observations at a scatter point.
5. The techniques of regression analysis, although having earlier antecedents, were developed by R. A. Fisher, H. Hotelling, R. Frisch, and others from the early 1920s (see Frisch 1929; Shewhart 1933). An example of empirical work employing scatter diagrams is Tinbergen (1933).
6. See copies of *Econometrica* during the 1930s, and *Explorations in Economic History* during the 1960s. Earlier work (in the 1950s) in quantitative economic history (or cliometrics) was published in economics journals.

4

Tax assessments for the geld

4.1 INTRODUCTION

There is general agreement that the assessments for the geld were an important part of the data collected in 1086.[1] In particular, this data set is valuable as a detailed source of information concerning the manner in which Anglo-Norman kings raised a significant part of their revenue. In the literature, the prevailing interpretation, which has its origins in the work of the Victorian scholar J. H. Round, is that these assessments were 'artificial'. In other words, assessments for geld were imposed from above with little or no reference to the economic capacity of manors to pay this impost. Yet, despite the longevity of this interpretation, there are good a priori grounds for doubting its validity. In view of the inevitable opposition to an arbitrary tax system, it is hard to imagine such a system surviving for almost 200 years, as did the geld. Even if the suppression were effective, these costs would have drastically reduced the benefits to be gained from imposing the tax. It was this doubt which led us initially to investigate (McDonald and Snooks 1985a) the relationship between tax assessments and the capacity of manors to pay this tax (measured in terms of both their resource endowments and their revenues) for the county of Essex.

This issue is important because of its political as well as its economic implications. In the first place, our statistical analysis should provide insights into the motivation of the monarchy. Was the king attempting to impose his authority arbitrarily on his subjects, as Round's hypothesis suggests, or was he attempting to maximize his revenue, as the *Anglo-Saxon Chronicle* suggests?[2] Secondly, it should be possible to contribute to the debate about the role in territorial government of the hundred, village, and manor. A currently held view (Loyn 1962, reprinted 1981, 314), based upon Round's artificiality thesis, is that within the hundred framework the village, rather than the manor, was called upon to play the main administrative role: 'The village not the manor was the institution with which the Anglo-Saxon monarchy treated. Indeed it is the village which provided the fundamental unit of government in late Anglo-Saxon England.' If, however, Round's thesis is not correct, it may be necessary to alter our evaluation of the relative importance of village and manor in the territorial government of Domesday England. Finally, our analysis should throw light upon the ability of the Anglo-Saxon and Norman bureaucracies to assess and record the taxable capacity of English manors and, thereby, upon their administrative efficiency.

4.2 THE GELD: A NON-FEUDAL TAX

At the time of the Domesday survey, public revenue was raised from a variety
of feudal and non-feudal sources. As outlined in 2.1.2.5, this revenue was
required by the king in addition to feudal services such as knight service and
attendance at Court. Feudal revenue took the form of aids (arising from
marriages, knighthoods, and wardships) and reliefs (paid on the inheritance of
a fief), while non-feudal funds came from the royal demesne, various local and
national courts, rights over boroughs and minting, and finally the geld.[3]

In the provision of total public revenue the geld played an important part.
After an examination of the rights and obligations of Norman barons, Painter
(1943, 74–8) concluded: 'The most important public burden of the Norman
period was the tax known as danegeld.'[4] He showed that in 1162, the last year
in which the geld was levied, an amount of £3,132 was collected, which
compared more than favourably with the £2,408 raised from 'the most
profitable feudal aid of Henry's reign'. Postan (1972, 172) also claimed that at
this time the geld contributed between one-quarter and one-third of the king's
annual revenue. These conclusions are supported by our study of Essex: the
rate struck in 1083–4, of six shillings to the hide, implies that the average
manor was required to part with approximately 16 per cent of its annual
revenue to meet this impost.[5] The geld, therefore, was both an important
source of royal revenue and a considerable burden on landholders.

Yet what is known about the nature of the geld? Initially, geld was levied on
a national basis, as an extraordinary tax to bribe raiding parties of Danes to
direct their unwanted attentions elsewhere. During this early phase it was
known, rather appropriately, as danegeld. This impost, which has generally
been regarded as a land tax, was first levied in 991 by King Ethelred, and until
1012 was collected irregularly to meet the Danish threat.[6] From 1012 it
became an annual tax, employed to finance both a standing army (known as
royal housecarles) and a small fleet of warships, until it was discontinued by
Edward the Confessor in 1051. At this time the tax was known as heregeld (or
army geld). William I may have revived the geld as early as 1066–7, but little is
known about its incidence until the end of William's reign, by which time it
appears to have become an annual tax once more (Round 1895, 87–8;
Galbraith 1961, 42). From this time, more information is available. In 1083–4,
for example, the geld was levied at the rate of six shillings per hide, in 1096 at
four shillings per hide, during Henry I's reign at two shillings per hide (levied
annually), and during Henry II's reign at two shillings per hide for 1156 and
1162. Although the geld, as such, was not levied after 1162, owing to the
opposition it aroused, both Richard and John attempted to raise similar taxes
on five occasions (1194, 1198, 1200, 1217, and 1220) based upon hides and even
actual ploughlands. But renewed opposition from the king's barons meant
that even these irregular levies finally ceased in 1220 (Green 1981, 241–2).

4.3 INTERPRETATIONS OF DOMESDAY ASSESSMENTS

Even older than geld was the method of assessment upon which it was based. The underlying hidage system is thought to be linked 'to the more primitive tribute taken by Anglo-Saxon kings in early days, and also with the system whereby food-rents were extracted from dependent estates' (Loyn 1962, 305–6). From evidence contained in the eighth-century tax collectors' document known as the Tribal Hidage, it would appear that there was some continuity in the form of the hidage system both before and after the geld was first levied by Ethelred (Loyn 1962, 306–9). It is the nature of the assessment system in 1066 and 1086 that is the subject of this chapter.

Until a century ago, the general assumption among Domesday scholars was that the hide, being an areal measure, was directly related to a certain number of real acres. Although there was some debate over how many acres constituted a hide (or homestead), this area of land was generally regarded as being sufficient to maintain a peasant family at a subsistence level.[7] R. W. Eyton was the first successfully to challenge the idea that the hide was an areal measure. Eyton (1878, 10) claimed that the manor in Ethelred's reign (979–1016) had been 'assessed according to its value—according to its capacity to bear taxation', but that while 'values and capacities were liable to constant fluctuation, we cannot find a single instance where *hidation* appears to have been altered to suit the special circumstances of deterioration, or misfortunes, or neglect'. On this basis he argued that, by 1086, hides no longer corresponded closely to measures of area or value (revenue): the hide was solely a unit of tax assessment.

With the exception of J. H. Round, this new idea was resisted by other Domesday scholars. At the 1886 conference to mark the 800th anniversary of the Domesday Survey, most historians concerned with the hidage issue attempted to support the older view.[8] Only Round (1888, vol. i, 117) accepted Eyton's claim that the hide was a measure of tax assessment, which had come adrift from its economic origins. Even so, at this time there was little evidence in Round's work of the radical interpretation of Domesday assessments which was to grow from this seed. There were only two hints of what was to come. First, like W. Stubbs, Round (1888, vol. i, 117) believed that 'the hundred was the fiscal unit for the collection of Danegeld'. Secondly, in the same paper he made a brief reference to the regular occurrence of an assessment of five hides for Domesday *towns*. His only explanation of this was: 'Now five hides was the unit of assessment for the purpose of military service' (Round 1888, vol. i, 120). Over the following decade, these two separate observations were to coalesce and develop in Round's mind to produce a view of Domesday assessments which has prevailed unchallenged for the last century.

Round's revolutionary interpretation of geld assessment appeared in 1895 in his major work, *Feudal England*. From a study of *Inquisitio Comitatus*

Cantabrigiensis which, unlike Domesday Book, recorded the number of hides on a village as well as on a manorial basis, Round saw (or thought he saw) a pattern in the allocation of hides which suggested an arbitrary administrative game rather than economic reality.[9] As the method employed by Round has been examined in Chapter 3 (3.2.2.1), only his interpretation will be discussed here. After visual examination of only two hundreds (containing twelve observations) in *Inquisitio*, Round (1895, 48–9) asked rhetorically:

What is the meaning of it? Simply that ASSESSMENT BORE NO RATIO TO AREA OR TO VALUE in a Vill, and still less in a Manor.
    Assessment was not objective, but subjective; it was not fixed relatively to area or to value, but to the five-hide unit. The aim of the assessors was clearly to arrange the assessment in sums of five hides, ten hides, etc.

To this statement he added: 'The thing speaks for itself. Had the hidation in these two Hundreds been dependent on area or value, the assessment would have varied infinitely' (Round 1895, 49). In fact, ploughlands varied, somewhat less than infinitely, from $13\frac{1}{4}$ to 20. Round had overlooked the possibility of a non-exact relationship.

    Recognizing the narrow empirical base of his new interpretation Round sought support elsewhere. In this 'chase' for the five-hide unit, no further consideration was given to the relationship between hides and resources. In the first place, he extended his net to include other hundreds in *Inquisitio*. Unfortunately, this additional evidence is not only ambiguous but also damaging to his cause. In the case of the first two hundreds examined by Round, the hidage of *single* villages was divisible by five: hence the five-hide system. Round's additional evidence, however, was less accommodating, as it became necessary to group together varying numbers of vills to obtain a multiple of five. These village clusters ranged from two to five vills (and the number of resulting hides ranged from twenty to twenty-five), thereby implicitly allowing for variation in resource endowments. Despite this Round (1895, 51) concluded: 'The chase now becomes exciting: it can no longer be doubted that we are well on the track of a vast system of artificial hidation, of which the very existence has been hitherto unsuspected.' Secondly, Round gave brief and unconvincing attention to a number of isolated hundreds from other counties, including Bedfordshire, Huntingdonshire, Northamptonshire, Hertfordshire, Worcestershire, Somerset, and Devon. Once again, his search was for the illusive five-hide pattern, and not for the relationship between hides and other resources. In the course of this search, Round claimed to discover not only the five-hide system, but also the possibility that the hundred, rather than the village or manor, was the basis of the assessment. At the end of his ramble through a limited number of selected hundreds Round (1895, 62) concluded, with characteristic confidence:

Indeed, though I definitely advance the suggestion that the assessment was, in the first instance, laid upon the Hundred itself, and that the subsequent assessment of its Vills and Manors was arrived at by division and subdivision, the truth or falsehood of this theory in no way affects the indisputable phenomenon of the five-hide unit. On the prominence of that unit I take my stand as absolute proof that the hide assessment was fixed *independently of area or value* and that, consequently, all the attempts that have been made by ingenious men to discover and establish the relation which that assessment bore to area, whether in Vill or Manor, have proved not only contradictory among themselves, but, as was inevitable, vain.

It is little wonder that Round's contemporaries preferred not to contradict him. Certainly the gentlemanly F. W. Maitland had no desire to do so.

Maitland, in fact, played a significant role in propagating Round's views, not only on the fiscal purpose of Domesday Book, but also concerning the manner in which tax assessments were imposed upon landholders. A fascinating dimension of this process of the diffusion of intellectual ideas is that Maitland was responsible for propagating even those views of his contemporary which he did not accept. The reason is that, although much of the evidence Maitland assembled, together with the inferences he drew from it, contradicted the artificiality interpretation, he failed to confront Round's counter-intuitive claims,[10] and thus rendered Domesday scholarship a major disservice. As Round's views had the apparent support of the most accomplished of the late-Victorian Domesday historians, they were adopted by the leading scholars of following generations, such as Sir Frank Stenton and Professor H. C. Darby. These views have, therefore, remained the conventional wisdom on this issue up to the present time.

Maitland's view on the question of assessments is, at first sight, ambiguous. He presented two contradictory interpretations, together with the evidence upon which they were based, as if there were no difference between them. In the first place, Maitland examined the relationship between hides and teamlands in the counties of Buckinghamshire, Lincolnshire, Yorkshire, Leicestershire, Northamptonshire, Wiltshire, Dorset, Devon, Somerset, and Cornwall. By noting whether the number of hides was equal to ('equal rating'), greater than ('over-rating') or less than ('under-rating') the number of teamlands, Maitland (1897, 447) discovered that, while there was some variation, the equation of the two was 'a condition that we may call normal'. To explain the 'aberration of A [hides] from B [teamlands]' Maitland (1897, 448, 450) considered the effects of both privilege, or 'beneficial hidation', and 'the operation of natural and obvious causes [by which] an old rate-book will become antiquated'. But, after some consideration, he deemed their combined effect insufficient to explain the perceived variation, as the first of these could account only for 'exceptional cases', and the second only for slow changes, rather than those 'that take place suddenly at the boundaries of counties'. He turned, mistakenly, to Round to supply the complete answer:

A master hand has lately turned our thoughts to the right quarter. There can we think be no doubt that, as Mr Round has argued, the geld was imposed according to a method which we have called the method of subpartitioned provincial quotas. A sum cast upon a hundred has been divided among that hundred's vills; a sum cast upon a vill has been divided among the lands that the vill contains. (Maitland 1897, 450)

This was a method, he claimed, which was bound to produce 'inequitable results', and to lead to a system of patterned hides of the type discovered by Round. In order to 'emphasise the artificiality of the system', Maitland directed attention to the five-hide pattern apparent in a few hundreds in Cambridgeshire and Worcestershire.

Secondly, Maitland examined the relationship between hides and values (or revenue). He began, as before, by expressing the view that:

behind all the caprice and presumable jobbery, we can not help fancying that we see a certain equity principle ... Now we have formed no very high estimate of the justice or the statemanship of the English witan [council], and what we are going to say is wrung from us by figures which have dissipated some preconceived ideas; but they hardly allow us to doubt that the number of hides cast upon a county had been affected not only by the amount, but also by the value of its teamlands. (Maitland 1897, 463)

This is, of course, a contradiction of Round's hypothesis, to which Maitland had earlier deferred. Nevertheless, Maitland proceeded to test the relationship between hides and values using the two statistical procedures outlined in 3.2.2.2. According to Maitland, both statistical tests revealed a principle underlying the observed county variation: a principle of 'one pound, one hide'. But, characteristically, no sooner had he admitted the existence of a relationship between hides and values than he qualified his discovery.

We have spoken of a tendency on the part of the hide to be worth a pound. Now we have no wish to represent this equitable element as all powerful or very powerful; the case of Kent is sufficient to show that it may be overruled by favouritism or privilege ... Still that the kings and witan have considered the value as well as the number of teamlands seems fairly plain. Probably they have considered it in a rough, typical fashion. (Maitland 1897, 470).

Even this evaluation was further modified. Maitland (1897, 469–73) saw in some county totals (particularly Yorkshire, Lancashire, and Northampton-shire) 'the unreformed relics of an age when the distribution of fiscal units among the various provinces of England was the sport of wild guesswork'. And, once again under the influence of Round, he refers to the hide (and the teamland) as 'artificial and ... remote from real agrarian life'. And finally, he admits to being 'baffled by the make-believe of ancient finance'. Therefore, although claiming that 'we are endeavouring to loosen one of Domesday's worst knots', Maitland was, in fact, responsible for tightening it, both by endlessly qualifying his own interesting and pioneering statistical work, and by not taking issue with Round.

It is clear from this account that Maitland accepted without reservation Round's claim that the system of assessment was imposed from above on the hundred. Yet Maitland vacillated over the question of artificiality versus capacity to pay. While he admitted that there was some evidence for Round's discovery of the five-hide unit, he was reluctant to deny that there was a systematic relationship between hides and both teamlands and values. While these two views are essentially contradictory, Maitland provided not even a hint of this conflict in *Domesday Book and Beyond*. He just presented both views, together with the evidence upon which they were based, using one to qualify the other.[11] To present his own statistical work validly, it was necessary for Maitland to challenge and rebut the evidence and argument of Round. For some reason he chose not to do this. Why? While this remains one of the intriguing enigmas of Domesday historiography, there are a number of possibilities. It may have been due to an abnormal deference to the ideas of others, particularly when they were expressed as absolutely as Round's.[12] It may have been due to Maitland's lack of confidence about his pioneering statistical work on Domesday data, as expressed in the preface to *Domesday and Beyond*.[13] But most probably it was due to an inability to establish a method to determine which set of conflicting evidence was correct. Whatever the reason, those that followed Maitland appear to have regarded his failure to take issue with Round as unqualified support for the artificiality hypothesis.

A few notable illustrations—from the work of Vinogradoff, Stenton, and Darby—are sufficient to demonstrate the continued influence of Round and Maitland. Vinogradoff's method was similar to Maitland's. Vinogradoff (1908, 197–207) accepted that the system was artificial, as it was based upon a regular pattern of hides at the village and hundred levels. Similarly, he detected a relationship between assessment ('geld hides') and arable land ('field hides'), but, unlike Maitland, he drew attention to the conflict of evidence. Unfortunately, Vinogradoff attempted to resolve this conflict by a number of fanciful arguments about a peculiar relationship between 'geld hides' and 'numbered hides'. Once again Round triumphed over conflicting evidence.

Stenton, on the other hand, accepted without question Round's interpretation of danegeld. In *Anglo-Saxon England* (1943, 646–8) he wrote: 'The fact that assessment to gelds proceeded from above downwards—from king's court, through the county and hundred, to the village—was established long ago by scholars such as Round and Maitland.' And again: 'From a date which lies far back in English history a large round number of hides had been attributed by the king's ministers to each county in this region, without any but the most general reference to its true agricultural condition.' And most revealing of all: 'The intricate combinations of assessment-units into neat blocks of five hides or six carucates sometimes look like the result of a game with figures, played by clerks with no interest in realities.' In other words, Stenton accepted without qualification Round's view of the nature of the Domesday assessments.[14] That he did so probably accounts for a younger generation of historians (e.g. Loyn 1962, 341) continuing to advance the artificiality thesis.

More recently Darby, the pioneering geographer of Domesday Book, reiterated Round's artificial assessment thesis, in the five county volumes which first appeared between 1952 and 1967, and in the summary volume, *Domesday England*, first published in 1977. Of the Essex hidation, Darby (1952, 220) said: 'We cannot say to what extent the incidence of the hidage reflected the agricultural realities of the time. The figures certainly bear no relation to those of ploughteams.' And Darby's co-author Finn (Darby and Finn 1967, 17), who analysed Wiltshire, wrote: 'The assessment was largely artificial in character, and bore no constant relation to the agricultural resources of a vill.' Statements of this kind, with only minor variations, were repeated by Darby and his co-authors for county after county, thereby becoming formula-like.[15] In the case of Essex, Darby attempted to support this statement by examining the ratio between hides and ploughteams at the hundred level for only three hundreds; and for Wiltshire, Finn drew attention to only five 'representative' vills.

In his final Domesday volume, Darby (1977, 9) summed up his view of assessments for all England. In a section entitled 'Artificial assessments', he wrote that 'the assessment was essentially artificial in character ... We have no means of knowing how equitable the original assessment may have been, but by 1066 it was manifestly not so.' It is quite clear, therefore, that Darby accepted completely Round's artificiality hypothesis, and rejected that of capacity to pay. But what is surprising is that he did so despite being unable to find sufficient evidence in his county volumes to accept Round's supporting evidence concerning the five-hide pattern. As Darby (1977, 10) said: 'Not all counties display the five-hide system as clearly as Cambridgeshire, but whether they do or not, it is clear that villages with identical assessments had widely differing resources and populations.' In other words, while unable to accept Round's evidence of the five-hide (and six-carucate) system, Darby appears unwilling to reject Round's artificiality thesis which was based on this 'evidence'. Instead, Darby attempts to retain the longstanding conventional wisdom by claiming that there was no relationship between assessment and resources. Round was right, Darby claims, but for the wrong reasons.

Since Darby's work, medievalists interested in the geld have been concerned not with the relationship between tax assessments and the capacity to pay, but rather with matters such as its severity before 1066, a possible reassessment in 1086, and the nature of its exaction (including exemptions), together with reasons for its discontinuance in the twelfth century.[16] The most interesting of these is Harvey's hypothesis that the 'ploughlands' variable cannot be taken at face value. She claims that it is not a unit of arable land measured in terms of the teams required to work it, but rather a new and disguised assessment undertaken in 1086. While ploughlands are not recorded for Essex (nor for a number of other counties), they are available for Wiltshire, which allows some statistical analysis of this question.

4.4 THE INCIDENCE OF TAXATION IN 1086

The size distribution of assessments on a manorial basis in 1086 is illustrated in Figure 4.1. For lay manors the distributions are broadly similar in both Essex and Wiltshire, with both exhibiting a high degree of positive skewness. This reflects the fact that most lay manors were assessed at a few hides, with only a relatively small number having more than 5 or 6 hides and none with more

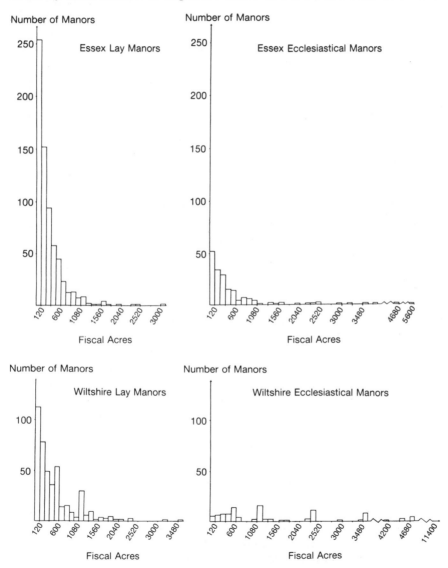

Figure 4.1. The size distribution of tax assessments, Essex and Wiltshire, 1086

than 26 hides in the case of Essex nor more than 30 hides for Wiltshire. To be more specific, the mean values were 2.5 hides for Essex and 4.1 hides for Wiltshire, with standard deviations of 2.8 and 4.1 respectively. The different vertical scales reflect the greater number of manors in Essex than in Wiltshire.

An interesting contrast is provided by the ecclesiastical manors. For example, Essex's ecclesiastical manors provide a profile of broadly similar shape to that of its lay manors, but with a much longer tail, due to some being assessed as highly as 47 hides. Wiltshire, however, is the real curiosity in this respect: it has a small number of manors in the 1–5 hide range, and a very long tail extending as far as 95 hides. More specifically, the mean values were 4.4 for Essex and 17.4 for Wiltshire, with standard deviations of 6.7 and 19 respectively. Given these marked differences in the size distributions of assessments between lay and ecclesiastical estates, and between Essex and Wiltshire, it will be of considerable interest to discover just how comparable are the statistical results for the major manorial subgroups.

4.5 STATISTICAL ANALYSIS OF TAX ASSESSMENTS

4.5.1 Domesday data on assessments and capacity to pay

The Domesday surveys of Essex and Wiltshire provide sufficient detail to test the relationship at the manorial level between tax assessments and the capacity to pay (measured both by a comprehensive list of resources and by annual values) for both 1086 and 1066. Data for both Essex and Wiltshire are available on a manorial basis for the following variables in 1086: the number of hides; the annual value (or income, consisting of rents and profits received by the lord); the number of plough-teams (consisting of a plough and up to eight oxen); the number of villeins, bordars (or cottars, coscets) and serfs (slaves); the amount of woodland, pasture, and meadow; and the numbers of mills, saltpans, fisheries, vineyards, and beehives.[17] In addition to this common set of resources, both Essex and Wiltshire are credited with variables not possessed by the other. For Essex, there is information on the number of additional plough-teams that could have been employed had they been available, the numbers of freemen and sokemen, and the numbers of cows, sheep, swine, goats, and horses; and for Wiltshire, the number of ploughlands is recorded. To reduce the number of explanatory variables to a manageable size for 1086, some—namely the components of labour and livestock—have been combined, and others—saltpans, fisheries, and vineyards—have been eliminated because they appeared incomplete or were minor resources.[18] The resulting sets of explanatory variables include: values (V) on the one hand, and the resource variables of plough-teams (Pl), livestock (Li), labour (N), slaves (S), woodland (W), meadow (Me), pasture (P), and mills (M) on the other.[19] There is, however, an ambiguity concerning the resource of meadow. Maitland (1897, 443) suggests that meadow was a very valuable resource because it was essential to the maintenance of the critically important plough-team (by producing hay), because it was highly fertile, and because it was scarce. Further, meadow was essential for the maintenance of horses, a key element of England's war machine after 1066. As it was vital that the area of meadow be maintained, it is possible that it was exempt from taxation, in which case meadow should not be included as an explanatory variable.

Domesday Book, data for 1066 is less comprehensive, particularly for the counties in Great Domesday. The Wiltshire folios, for example, include data for 1066 on assessments and values only. Little Domesday contains data on a wider range of variables, which for Essex include assessments, values, freemen, sokemen, villeins, bordars, and slaves.

4.5.2 An analysis of tax assessments in 1086

The statistical procedure adopted here is to test directly the relationship between tax assessments and the capacity of manors to pay this impost. This has important advantages over the indirect method employed by Round, as it eliminates unnecessary subjectivity and competing explanations of the alleged five-hide system. Further, by employing regression analysis it is possible to analyse all the data for a particular region, rather than focusing upon either a few observations (Darby) or larger, non-random samples (Maitland). For 1086 this involves, in the case of Essex, 678 lay and 179 ecclesiastical manors, and, for Wiltshire, 425 lay and 107 ecclesiastical manors. Each of these manorial categories has been analysed separately.

Before discussing the results, two statistical problems need to be considered, because they are critical to any evaluation of the data in Domesday Book. First, while we might expect the tax assessment to be an increasing function of resources, so that greater manorial resources are, on average, associated with a higher tax assessment, theoretical reasoning does not indicate the precise functional form of the relationship. Although researchers usually assume that the relationship is linear or log-linear, there is no a priori justification for either. It seems preferable, therefore, to allow the data to determine the choice of the functional form. This can be done by assuming that the appropriate function is a member of a broad class of functional forms, as defined by the Box–Cox extended model.[20] In this model the linear and log-linear forms are special cases. Secondly, a common problem with regression equations based on cross-sectional data is that the variance of the regression disturbance is not constant over the sample, but is related to the size of the unit of measurement: in this case, the size of the manor. When this occurs, the disturbances are heteroskedastic, and as a result the parameter estimates obtained from statistical methods that ignore the heteroskedasticity are inefficient, and the usual parameter standard errors and tests of significance are invalid. In order to overcome this problem, which plagues the Domesday data, the estimation method used here allows for the disturbances in the regression equation (which is linear in the transformed variables) to be heteroskedastic, with the variance of the disturbance depending upon the size of the manor as measured by the plough-teams variable.[21]

4.5.2.1 Lay manors in Essex

The regression results presented in Table 4.1 reflect the three alternative ways in which the capacity of manors to pay tax can be measured: total resources, arable land, and annual values (or income). If we focus initially upon Essex, it will be seen that regression 1 provides estimates of the relationship between tax assessment and the resources of plough-teams, livestock, labour, slaves, woodland, meadow, pasture, and mills for lay manors in 1086.[22] Before considering the detailed results, it is important to realize that this equation appears to be well-specified, and passes tests of the critical assumptions underlying regression analysis.[23] Indeed, unless otherwise stated, this is true of all results presented in this chapter.

A number of points about Essex regression 1 should be noted. First, the resource variables of ploughlands, livestock, peasant labour, and slaves are positive and significant (see *t*-ratios). In other words, an increase in any of these resources will result in an increase in tax assessments. The impact upon assessments of an increase in any one of these resource variables, holding all the others constant, can be measured by the partial elasticities (see line labelled *E*). For example a 1 per cent increase in the number of plough-teams is associated with approximately a 0.43 per cent increase in assessment (measured in fiscal acres), whereas a 1 per cent increase in the number of peasant labourers is associated with only a 0.18 per cent increase in assessment. A perusal of these partial elasticities shows that the main determinants of assessment were the number of plough-teams and, to a lesser extent, the number of peasant labourers.

Secondly, the estimated functional form in regression 1 is able to 'explain' a relatively high proportion of the variation in assessment.[24] The coefficient of determination adjusted for degrees of freedom is 0.626, which is a good fit for disaggregated cross-sectional data of this nature, particularly when the historical circumstances are taken into account. As the assessments for Essex were determined in the reign of Edward the Confessor, who discontinued the geld in 1051, they had not been revised for over thirty years at the time of the Domesday Survey. It is also known that tax concessions were granted to the king's favourites. Consequently an even better fit (higher $\bar{R}^2$) could have been anticipated had the tax been more recently revised.

Thirdly, while the literature led us to anticipate that the meadow variable may have been insignificant, it came as a surprise that it was both significant and negative. It is only possible to speculate about the reasons for this unexpected result at this stage. In 4.5.1 we suggested that, because of its importance to the Anglo-Norman community, meadow may not have been taxed. Our statistical results, however, suggest, not that meadow was free of tax, but that it was the basis of a tax deduction. A possible reason for the king

Table 4.1. Tax assessment–resources and tax assessment–income relationships for Essex and Wiltshire lay manors, 1086

		Const.	Pl	Li	N	S	W	Me	P	M	V	$\bar{R}^2$
I Essex												
regression 1	β	8.11	1.17	0.051	0.391	0.218	0.035	-0.206	0.111	0.048		0.626
	t	32.3	9.6	4.2	5.1	3.0	1.5	-4.6	4.5	0.3		
	E		0.43	0.06	0.18	0.07	0.03	-0.10	0.06	0.01		
regression 2	β	8.35	1.94									0.552
	t	71.9	28.9									
	E		0.72									
regression 3	β	2.41									0.709	0.642
	t	29.0									34.9	
	E										0.71	
II Wiltshire												
regression 1	β	14.07	2.12		0.734	0.630	-0.009	0.478	0.132	-0.366		0.737
	t	30.3	8.3		4.8	3.7	-0.3	6.1	4.4	-1.2		
	E		0.36		0.18	0.09	-0.01	0.13	0.07	-0.04		
regression 2	β	15.08	3.75									0.658
	t	73.0	28.5									
	E		0.71									
regression 3	β	2.66									0.808	0.794
	t	33.7									40.5	
	E										0.81	

Notes: The Essex regressions were based on 678 observations and the Wiltshire regressions on 425 observations. The Essex and Wiltshire regressions 1 and 2 are Box–Cox extended transformations, with $\lambda = 0.230$ for the Essex regressions, $\lambda = 0.340$ for Wiltshire regression 1, and $\lambda = 0.320$ for Wiltshire regression 2. The Essex and Wiltshire regressions 3 are of log-linear form.

The first row (labelled β) gives the parameter estimates of the intercept or constant and the following explanatory variables: plough-teams plus excess land for additional ploughs (Pl), livestock (Li), peasants (N), slaves (S), woodland (W), meadow (Me), pasture (P), and mills (M). (V refers to annual value.) The second row (labelled t) gives the conventional t-ratios and the third row gives the partial resource–tax assessment elasticities evaluated at the sample mean of tax assessment and the resource. For Wiltshire regressions 1 and 2, Pl refers to plough-teams only.

The Essex and Wiltshire regressions 3 appeared appropriate when a functional form test was performed, and for all regressions the hetero (a) and hetero (b) tests did not reveal significant heteroskedasticity in the disturbances. Details of the estimation procedure are given in Chapter 8.

granting a tax deduction on meadow could have been to encourage
landholders, who did not have permanent rights to this resource, to undertake
the investment (in clearing, drainage, and flood control) required to expand the
acreage of meadow, which was a critical resource for maintaining both plough-
teams and warhorses.[25] Needless to say, this explanation will remain highly
speculative until further corroborative evidence is forthcoming; but it is, at
least, an interesting starting-point for further research. Finally, to summarize
these results, Essex regression 1 indicates that there is a highly significant
relationship between tax assessment and the resources of the manor, with the
contribution of plough-teams being dominant. For all resources other than
meadow the relationship is, as expected, positive. It is also possible to provide
a persuasive explanation for the negative association between assessments and
meadowlands.

As some Domesday scholars have regarded the geld as a tax solely on arable
land, this question has been investigated. If manorial tax assessments depend
only upon the acreage of manorial arable land, the coefficients estimates (line β
in Table 4.1) on the other explanatory variables in regression 1 should be
insignificant from zero. We have already seen that this is not the case. It is also
possible to undertake a formal test that the tax assessments are not determined
by resource variables other than plough-teams: this hypothesis is rejected at all
conventional significance levels.[26] Further, it will be noted in Essex regression
2, which presents the results when assessment is related to plough-teams only,
that the coefficient of determination ($\bar{R}^2$) is considerably less than for
regression 1. The evidence is clear: in 1086 the geld was not simply a land tax,
but rather a tax based upon all the resources of the manor.

As the capacity of a manor to pay tax can be measured in terms of its revenue
as well as its resources, the relationship between tax assessments and annual
values is presented in Essex regression 3. First, the regression estimates (which
pass the diagnostic tests) suggest that there is a highly significant positive
relationship between the tax assessments and the annual values of manors.
Secondly, the elasticity estimate of 0.71 suggests that, on average, a 1 per cent
increase in manorial value is associated with a 0.71 per cent increase in
assessment. Thirdly, the value of the coefficient of determination ($\bar{R}^2$) is slightly
higher than in regression 1, reflecting a better fit of the estimated function to
the data. While this suggests that annual values may offer a slightly better
explanation than total resources of the variation in tax assessments, these two
regressions are not entirely comparable, as they are subject to different
transformations. Fourthly, the value-assessment elasticity in regression 3
(0.71) is similar to the sum of the partial resource-assessment elasticities in
regression 1 (0.74). In other words, similar results are obtained whether
capacity to pay is measured in input or in output terms.

Finally, the nature of the geld assessment can be illustrated by reference to
Figure 4.2, in which the average manorial tax assessment–value relationship
has been graphed. The average tax-assessment rate for a manor with an annual

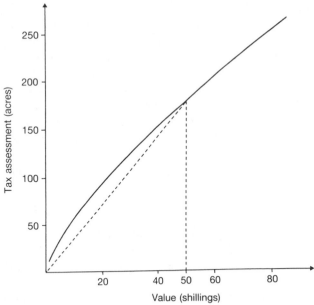

Figure 4.2. The tax assessment-manorial annual value relationship for Essex lay manors, 1086

value of, say, 50 shillings is given by the slope of a line from the origin to the point on the tax-assessment curve corresponding to a manorial value of that amount. For manors with an annual value of 50 shillings, the average tax-assessment rate is 3.6 fiscal acres per shilling, while for manors with annual values of 1, 5, 10, 20, 40, 60, 80, and 100 shillings the average tax-assessment rates are 11.1, 7.0, 5.7, 4.7, 3.8, 3.4, 3.1, and 2.9 fiscal acres per shilling respectively. As can be seen, the decline in the average assessment rate is quite marked at low annual values, but moderates as annual value increases. The marginal assessment rate when the manorial value is, say, 50 shillings is given by the tangent to the tax assessment curve at the point corresponding to that value. The marginal assessment rate also declines, but at a decreasing rate, as the annual value of the manor increases. These estimates suggest that the geld was a regressive tax levied on the economic capacity of manors. In other words, the holders of larger manors, who had greater influence with the king, paid geld at a lower rate than holders of smaller manors.

It may be thought that the log-linear relationship we have established between value and taxes must imply a complex tax-assessment system that would be difficult to administer. This need not be the case, for at least two reasons. First, our estimated relationship is between tax assessments and earned, rather than taxable, income. Because of differential tax allowances, a simple relationship between assessments and taxable income may correspond to a more complex relationship between assessments and earned income.

Secondly, even if tax deductions were unimportant, and taxable and earned income were similar, the log-linear function may be the closest approximation to a simple, linearly segmented relationship that can be obtained with the techniques employed. In other words, the true tax–income relationship in Figure 4.2 may not be a curve, but rather a series of straight lines that can be approximated by a curve. These linear segments would reflect a set of constant marginal tax rates consisting of, for example, x_1 hides per shilling for the first income interval, x_2 hides per shilling for the next income interval, and so on. A tax-assessment rule of this type (which is similar to that underlying modern tax systems) would not be difficult to administer, and would not have been beyond the demonstrated abilities of the Anglo-Norman administration.

4.5.2.2 Lay manors in Wiltshire

The statistical results for Wiltshire are presented in Table 4.1 and, despite the omission of livestock, are directly comparable with those for Essex.[27] It can be seen from Wiltshire regression 1 that, with the exception of woodland and mills, all coefficients are positive and highly significant. Once again, there is a close relationship between tax assessments and manorial resources, which disproves Round's artificiality thesis. Also, these results are sufficient to reject the idea that the geld was solely an arable tax. Not only are most of the resource coefficients significantly different from zero, but also the coefficient of determination ($\bar{R}^2$) is considerably greater for all resources (0.737) than for just plough-teams (0.658). The main difference between the two counties is that meadow, which is significant and negative for Essex, is significant and positive for Wiltshire. Although the manner in which taxes were applied could have differed between counties, this result does provide less confidence in our earlier suggestion that meadow was a tax deduction. Yet it does not disprove the hypothesis, which is clearly supported by the Essex data. This difference between Essex and Wiltshire could also have something to do with the more ambiguous way in which meadow is recorded (in both acres and linear terms) for Wiltshire. Resolution of this issue must await further evidence from other counties.

A further interesting result contained in regression 1, is that the coefficient of determination ($\bar{R}^2$) for Wiltshire (0.737) is considerably higher than that for Essex (0.626). In other words, manorial resources provide a better 'explanation' of the variation in tax assessments for Wiltshire than for Essex. There are a number of possible reasons for this. On the one hand, it could be that the tax assessment for Wiltshire is of more recent origin than that for Essex. While they are both recorded in Domesday Book as *Tempore Regis Edwardi*, and hence no later than 1051 (when Edward abandoned the raising of geld), the Wiltshire assessments may have been revised by the Confessor at a later date than those for Essex. On the other hand, the higher $\bar{R}^2$ for Wiltshire could merely reflect the higher level of aggregation of Wiltshire data.

Nevertheless the idea of a later revision for Wiltshire tax assessments is worth investigating.

The results of regressing tax assessments on annual values, the alternative measure of capacity to pay, are presented in Wiltshire regression 3. As with the other results discussed so far, the relationship is highly significant, and the coefficient of determination ($\bar{R}^2 = 0.794$) is unusually high for cross-sectional data of this nature. Once again, the results obtained from using either total resources or annual values for Wiltshire lay manors are very similar: the combined partial elasticities in the assessment–resources regression (0.78) is similar to the assessment–value elasticity (0.81), and the $\bar{R}^2$ are 0.737 and 0.794 respectively. If anything, the assessment–value relationship provides a better fit for the data. These results support the above analysis of Essex, thereby providing considerable confidence in our claim that assessments were based upon a careful examination of the economic capacity of manors in England. The main difference between these two counties is that the marginal tax rate for Wiltshire was considerably higher than that for Essex: a 1 per cent increase in value in Essex manors is associated, on average, with a 0.71 per cent increase in assessment, whereas in Wiltshire it is associated with a considerably larger 0.81 per cent increase in assessment. In other words, the landholders of Essex were receiving more favoured treatment than those in Wiltshire. It is difficult to explain why this was so, but it may have been owing to the influence over King Edward of Harold Godwineson (later King Harold) who became Earl of East Anglia in 1045.[28]

Finally, in order to throw some light on the suggestion made by Harvey (1975, 187) that the ploughlands variable in Domesday Book is not a measure of arable land, but rather a new assessment undertaken in some counties in 1086, we substituted ploughlands for plough-teams in Wiltshire regression 1. As Harvey's suggestion did not appear particularly likely, the results came as a surprise.[29] They were radically different from those of all our previous statistical analysis, thereby suggesting that, in ploughlands, we were not dealing with a normal resource variable. This led us to regress hidage on ploughlands, which resulted in a $\bar{R}^2$ of 0.796 and, surprisingly, an elasticity of 0.99. An elasticity of this value implies that a 1 per cent increase in ploughlands is associated, on average, with almost a 1 per cent increase in hidage, which is what we would expect if both hidage and ploughlands were alternative measures of the same variable—tax assessment. If this were true, then it would make sense to substitute ploughlands for hides in Wiltshire regressions 1 and 2. The re-estimation of regressions 1 and 2 produced very high $\bar{R}^2$ of 0.864 and 0.820, and elasticities of 0.84 and 0.74 respectively. Despite our initial scepticism, these results are indeed consistent with Harvey's suggestion that ploughlands were a measure of tax assessment of more recent origins than hidage. Yet this is not conclusive evidence, because it is not possible to test the Harvey hypothesis directly. Also, further statistical analysis of the data for other counties is required before anything more definite can be concluded.

4.5.2.3 Ecclesiastical manors in Essex

It seemed likely that some significant differences between the tax assessment experience of lay and ecclesiastical manors would emerge: it is well-known that the institutional structure of ecclesiastical manors differed from their lay counterparts (Postan 1972, ch. 6), and the contrast between their tax distribution profiles, as illustrated in 4.4, could not have been greater. Yet despite these structural differences, the main assessment–capacity to pay regression results are very similar. Generally speaking, the regression results for ecclesiastical manors show that there is a strong and significant relationship between assessments on the one hand and both manorial resources and values on the other. In fact our estimated functions provide a better fit (measured by $\bar{R}^2$) for the ecclesiastical than for lay data. Economic capacity, in other words, is a better explanation of the variation of assessments for ecclesiastical than for lay manors. The results are presented in Table 4.2.

Regression 1 for Essex indicates that the main resources of plough-teams, peasant labour, and pasture are all positive and significant determinants of tax assessment. In addition, the coefficient of determination ($\bar{R}^2$) is higher in regression 1 (0.729) than in regression 2 (0.682), where arable land is the only explanatory variable. This confirms the conclusion reached on the basis of the Essex lay data, that tax assessments were not based solely upon arable land. Yet despite the overall similarity of our regression results for ecclesiastical and lay manors, there are a number of differences of detail. First, the coefficients for livestock and slaves are no longer significantly different from zero. Secondly, meadow is negative as before, but is significant only at the 20 per cent level. Therefore, although meadow could be regarded as a tax deduction for Essex lay manors, it is difficult to support this hypothesis for Essex ecclesiastical manors.

Regression 3 for Essex indicates a strong and highly significant relationship between tax assessments and value. There are a number of points to be noted. First, the results are similar to those in regression 1 for Essex ecclesiastical manors, in terms of both $\bar{R}^2$ and elasticities (0.78 for total resources and 0.77 for annual value). Once again, it is difficult to determine which of these two methods may have been employed to arrive at the tax assessment figures presented in Domesday Book. Secondly, a comparison of regression 3 for Essex in both Tables 4.1 and 4.2 indicates very similar results in terms of the value of the constant term (or intercept), the annual value coefficient (or slope term), and the $\bar{R}^2$. If anything, the estimated function provides a better fit for the ecclesiastical data.

4.5.2.4 Ecclesiastical manors in Wiltshire

Once again, earlier results are confirmed by the data for Wiltshire ecclesiastical manors: tax assessments are closely related to economic capacity. It is only necessary to draw out the distinctive characteristics of the Wiltshire

Table 4.2. Tax assessment–resources and tax assessment–income relationships for Essex and Wiltshire ecclesiastical manors, 1086

		Const.	Pl	Li	N	S	W	Me	P	M	V	$\bar{R}^2$
I Essex												
regression 1	β	5.50	0.686	−0.003	0.290	0.093	−0.006	−0.053	0.073	−0.037		0.729
	t	27.4	6.4	−0.2	3.7	1.5	−0.2	−1.5	3.3	−0.4		
	E		0.50	−0.00	0.23	0.06	−0.01	−0.04	0.06	−0.02		
regression 2	β	6.20	1.21									0.682
	t	55.1	19.6									
	E		0.77									
regression 3	β	2.41									0.772	0.707
	t	15.1									20.8	
	E										0.77	
II Wiltshire												
regression 1	β	0.271	0.651		0.189	0.128	0.005	0.037	0.023	−0.059		0.879
	t	1.2	6.3		2.4	2.4	0.5	1.1	2.2	−0.7		
	E		0.58		0.22	0.09	0.01	0.04	0.06	−0.03		
regression 2	β	0.717	0.988									0.857
	t(w)	4.9	19.6									
	E		0.90									
regression 3	β	−2.37									0.899	0.887
	t	−14.3									28.8	
	E										0.90	

Notes: The Essex regressions were based on 179 observations and the Wiltshire regressions on 107 observations. The Essex and Wiltshire regressions 1 and 2 are Box–Cox extended transformations with $\lambda = 0.070$ for Essex regression 1, $\lambda = 0.100$ for Essex regression 2, $\lambda = 0.280$ for Wiltshire regression 1, and $\lambda = 0.230$ for Wiltshire regression 2. The Essex and Wiltshire regressions 3 are of log-linear form.

The first row (labelled β) gives the parameter estimates of the intercept or constant and the following explanatory variables: plough-teams plus excess ploughs (Pl), livestock (Li), peasants (N), slaves (S), woodland (W), meadow (Me), pasture (P), and mills (M). (V refers to annual value.) The second row (labelled t) gives the conventional t-ratios; and the third row gives the partial resource–tax assessment elasticities evaluated at the sample mean of tax assessment and the resource. For Wiltshire regressions 1 and 2, Pl refers to plough-teams only.

The Essex and Wiltshire regressions 3 appeared appropriate when a functional form test was performed, and for all regressions except Wiltshire regression 2 the hetero (a) and hetero (b) tests did not reveal significant heteroskedasticity in the disturbances. For Wiltshire regression 2 the hetero (b) (but not hetero (a)) test indicated significant heteroskedasticity at the 5 per cent significance level, so we give White's t-ratios (that allow for heteroskedasticity) for this regression. Details of the estimation procedure are given in Chapter 8.

ecclesiastical data. In the first place, the $\bar{R}^2$ in all regressions for Wiltshire ecclesiastical manors are considerably higher than those in comparable regressions for both Essex ecclesiastical manors and Wiltshire lay manors. This may reflect a more recent assessment, but is more likely to have been generated by more highly aggregated data. Secondly, the assessment–value elasticity for Wiltshire ecclesiastical manors (0.90) is markedly larger than that for either Essex ecclesiastical manors (0.77) or Wiltshire lay manors (0.81). In other words, the marginal tax rate for ecclesiastical manors in Wiltshire was not only higher than that of their counterparts in Essex, but also higher than that of lay manors in Wiltshire. The burden of the geld, therefore, was not only higher in some counties than in other counties, as is well-known, but also higher for certain broad classes of society within counties. Why did the clergy of Wiltshire deserve such unenviable distinction? This is an interesting starting point for more detailed research.

4.5.3 An analysis of tax assessments in 1066

There are considerably less data available for 1066 than 1086, particularly for the large majority of counties in Great Domesday. While data for Essex include tax assessments, annual value, peasant labour, and slaves, those for Wiltshire include only assessments and value. As the limited resource data for Essex involve specification problems when included in truncated assessment–resources regressions, it was decided to focus entirely upon the assessment–value relationship. This can be justified further by the statistical analysis for 1086, which suggested that, although the results for the assessment–resources and the assessment–value regressions are very similar, the latter provided a slightly closer fit to the data. Accordingly, it is possible with the data available in Domesday Book to undertake a useful intertemporal analysis.

4.5.3.1 Lay manors in Essex and Wiltshire

The 1066 results for the lay manors of Essex and Wiltshire are presented in the first half of Table 4.3. Once again it will be noticed that there is a strong and highly significant relationship between tax and value. In order to compare these results with those for 1086, it is necesary to rerun the 1086 results using the sample of manors employed in the 1066 calculations. These restricted 1086 results are presented in Table 4.4. A comparison reveals that the results for 1066 and 1086 are quite similar. There is, however, one curiosity. For Essex the estimated function exhibits a closer fit for the data in 1066 ($\bar{R}^2 = 0.580$) than in 1086 ($\bar{R}^2 = 0.510$), which is what we would expect if the assessment was made in the time of Edward, and became progressively out of date over the years between 1066 and 1086. The problem arises in the case of Wiltshire, for which the fit of the estimated function is better in 1086 ($\bar{R}^2 = 0.746$) than in 1066 ($\bar{R}^2 = 0.671$).

A possible interpretation of this result is that the hidage recorded in Domesday Book for Wiltshire was determined after 1066. Yet Domesday

Table 4.3. Tax assessment–income relationships for Essex and Wiltshire lay and ecclesiastical manors, 1066

		Lay manors			Ecclesiastical manors		
		Const.	V	$\bar{R}^2$	Const.	V	$\bar{R}^2$
Essex	β	2.25	0.769	0.580	2.36	0.799	0.668
	t	18.1	26.0		11.0	16.4	
	E		0.77			0.80	
Wiltshire	β	3.22	0.714	0.671	−2.17	0.910	0.774
	t	25.8	23.5		−7.7	16.2	
	E		0.71			0.91	

Notes: The Essex regressions were based on 491 observations for lay manors and 134 observations for ecclesiastical manors; the Wiltshire regressions were based on 271 observations for lay manors and 77 observations for ecclesiastical manors. All regressions are of log-linear form.

The first row (labelled β) gives the parameter estimates of the intercept or constant and annual value (V). The second row (labelled t) gives the conventional t-ratios; and the third row gives the value–tax assessment elasticities evaluated at the sample mean of tax assessment and value.

The Essex and Wiltshire regressions appeared appropriate when a functional form test was performed, and for all regressions the hetero (a) and hetero (b) tests did not reveal significant heteroskedasticity in the disturbances. Details of the estimation procedure are given in Chapter 8.

Table 4.4. Tax assessment–income relationships for Essex and Wiltshire lay and ecclesiastical manors, 1086, restricted sample

		Lay manors			Ecclesiastical manors		
		Const.	V	$\bar{R}^2$	Const.	V	$\bar{R}^?$
Essex	β	2.62	0.659	0.510	2.47	0.756	0.631
	t	20.4	22.6		10.9	15.1	
	E		0.66			0.76	
Wiltshire	β	2.58	0.830	0.746	−2.85	0.988	0.849
	t	20.4	28.1		−11.2	20.7	
	E		0.83			0.99	

Notes: The Essex regressions were based on 490 observations for lay manors and 134 observations for ecclesiastical manors; the Wiltshire regressions were based on 271 observations for lay manors and 77 observations for ecclesiastical manors. All regressions are of log-linear form.

The first row (labelled β) gives the parameter estimates of the intercept or constant and annual value (V). The second row (labelled t) gives the conventional t-ratios; and the third row gives the value–tax assessment elasticities evaluated at the sample mean of tax assessment and value.

The Essex and Wiltshire regressions appeared appropriate when a functional form test was performed, and for all regressions the hetero (a) and hetero (b) tests did not reveal significant heteroskedasticity in the disturbances. Details of the estimation procedure are given in Chapter 8.

Book appears quite clear on this point, that 'x held it [the manor] in the time of King Edward; it paid geld for y hides'. Only if the use of the past tense (it paid geld) is not, as it appears to be, attached to the time of King Edward, but rather to a date between 1066 and 1086, could the above interpretation be upheld. This matter of textual interpretation may repay further investigation. Alternatively, it is possible that the 1066 data for Wiltshire is less reliable (contains greater measurement error) than that for Essex, due to different survey procedures or to different manorial accounting procedures. A similar pattern can be discerned in the assessment–value elasticities, or marginal assessment rates: they decline for Essex between 1066 (0.77) and 1086 (0.66), but increase for Wiltshire over the same period (from 0.71 to 0.83). This is what we would expect if the Wiltshire assessments had been revised after 1066. Further investigation of this question, using non-statistical sources, is required.

4.5.3.2 *Ecclesiastical manors in Essex and Wiltshire*

The results for ecclesiastical manors, which are also presented in Table 4.3, bear out the above general remarks: there is a strong and highly significant relationship between tax assessments and annual value. There are only two matters which need detain us. First, both the $\bar{R}^2$ and the elasticities (or marginal assessment rates) in both regressions are markedly higher for ecclesiastical manors than for lay manors. The possible reasons for these results have been discussed above. Secondly, the $\bar{R}^2$ for Essex ecclesiastical manors declined between 1066 (0.668) and 1086 (0.631), whereas those for Wiltshire increased (from 0.774 to 0.849).

4.6 CONCLUSIONS

Contrary to the prevailing interpretation in the literature, which extends back to the Victorian scholar J. H. Round, it can be concluded that there was a strong and positive relationship between geld assessments and the capacity of manors to pay this impost. This is true for lay and ecclesiastical manors in the counties of Essex and Wiltshire for both years 1066 and 1086. It is, therefore, a particularly robust conclusion, because there existed marked institutional differences both between manors in Essex and Wiltshire and between those in the hands of lay and ecclesiastical tenants-in-chief, and because the period 1066–86 witnessed revolutionary political and social changes. It follows, therefore, that the assessments in Domesday Book cannot be regarded as artificial or simply based upon an arbitrary principle such as administrative convenience. Indeed, it supports the view that Anglo-Saxon and Norman kings were quite successful in attempting to maximize their net tax revenues. This conclusion is based upon the argument that the adoption of the equitable principle of capacity to pay would have minimized the opposition to this tax, which in turn would have minimized the costs of enforcement (or transactions costs) and hence maximized net tax revenue.

The existence of such a consistently strong relationship between assessments and the capacity of manors to pay, suggests that the former was not imposed from above, as Round asserted, but rather built up carefully from the manorial level. This evidence is not inconsistent with the claim that the hundred was the administrative unit for the collection of geld, but it does suggest that a reassessment of the administrative role of the manor, particularly in relation to the vill, should be undertaken. The manor should be brought into sharper focus in political histories of the period.

Our results also clarify a number of other aspects of Domesday geld. First, by 1066 the geld can no longer be thought of as a tax solely on arable land: it is either a total resources tax or, more likely, an income tax. This in turn suggests that the king's agents were attempting to take account of the growing sophistication of rural settlements when framing their non-feudal taxes. Secondly, there is no unambiguous trend between 1066 and 1086 in our results. The expected deterioration in the goodness of fit of our estimated function over these two decades, reflecting a growing obsolescence of a pre-1066 assessment, was evident for Essex, but not for Wiltshire. Is the Wiltshire assessment pre-1066 after all, or is there greater measurement error in 1066 for Wiltshire than for Essex? Thirdly, the geld was a regressive tax, in the sense that the marginal tax rate declined as the income of the manor increased. This reflected the Conqueror's need to placate his powerful barons, without whose support he could not have come to power in 1066. Fourthly, there is a strong possibility that for lay manors in the county of Essex, meadow was the basis of a tax deduction, possibly to encourage investment in this critically important resource. Yet this was not true for Wiltshire. Accordingly this hypothesis, which is suggestive but not conclusive, will need to be tested for other counties in future studies. Fifthly, the log-linear relationship between assessments and values could reflect a simple tax system in which the king's agents declared a set of tax rates expressed in terms of a number of hides per shilling for each designated income interval.

Finally, it is desirable to place our conclusions in a wider context by speculating briefly about the nature and development of the geld assessment system. As argued already, the fact that the geld assessment system was based upon the principle of capacity to pay is consistent with the hypothesis that the king attempted to maximize his net tax revenue, as claimed in contemporary literature. The effective application of capacity to pay, however, would have depended upon the employment of a good practical measure of this principle. This idea may be used to clarify the current ambiguity about the development of geld assessment from 991 to 1162. It can be argued that, in earlier Anglo-Saxon times, when population was small, land was abundant, and when production was of a subsistence nature resulting in similar mixes of inputs and outputs, a simple measure of arable land (such as the number of ploughlands required by a family for subsistence, i.e. the hide) would have sufficed as a measure of capacity to pay. As population grew, settlements expanded, less favourable land was brought into economic use, production became more specialized with varying input and output mixes, and trade became more common, a simple measure of arable land would not have reflected capacity to pay. Accordingly, it would have been necessary to adopt a more general measure of capacity to pay, such as manorial revenue or manorial resource endowments. The evidence suggests that this had been achieved by 1086.

By 1086, therefore, England was governed by a sophisticated and highly able administration. In this respect it was a worthy successor to the Anglo-Saxons regimes that it replaced.[30] William I's administration was able to accurately assess and record the taxable capacity of English manors, and it was at pains to employ this information (embodying the principle of capacity to pay) as the basis of its taxation policies. Domesday Book, therefore, is not only evidence of the serious and able intent of the Anglo-Norman regime, but is also a vital and remarkably rich source for the reconstruction of the English economy in the late eleventh century.

Notes

1. Harvey (1971) and Loyn (1979) provide good recent evaluations.
2. It was recorded in 1087 that: 'The king and the chief men loved gain much and over-much—gold and silver—and did not care how sinfully it was obtained provided it came to them. The king sold his land on very hard terms—as hard as he could. Then came somebody else, and offered more than the other had given, and the king let it go to the man who had offered him more. Then came the third, and offered still more, and the king gave it into the hands of the man who offered him most of all, and did not care how sinfully the reeves had got it, from poor men, nor how many unlawful things they did' (Whitelock 1961, 163). This may not describe the actions of a godly man, but it is a good description of an economic man (one who attempts to maximize his income).
3. See Painter (1943); Mitchell (1914); Postan (1972); Poole (1912); Loyn (1962).
4. A similar claim is made for this period by Campbell (1975, 52). Lawson (1984, 722–3) suggests that the burden of the geld prior to the Confessor's reign was even more severe than that after the Conquest.
5. This calculation is based upon the simplifying assumption that there were no exemptions from this tax. As there is some evidence that exemptions were granted, this estimate will form an upper limit.
6. Loyn (1962, 305) claims: 'The geld was a land-tax, the first regular and permanent land-tax known to the West in the Middle ages', which is supported more recently by Green (1981, 241). Both have accepted the interpretation of Stenton (1943, 645) in this matter.
7. On the size of the hide, see Eyton (1878, 14), who suggests 48 acres for Dorset, and Round (1895, 41–7), who claims that hides throughout England consisted of 120 acres. On the meaning of the hide, see Maitland (1897, 357–62), Stubbs (1874, vol. i, 79, 185), and Lennard (1944, 59). In order to add together hides and parts of hides (often expressed in acres), we have converted them to fiscal acres at the rate of 120

fiscal acres to the hide for both Essex and Wiltshire. For our purposes it does not matter if we use 48 acres or 120 acres, as it only affects the size of the intercept estimate (for Wiltshire, the former is 1.75 and the later is 2.66), leaving the slope coefficient estimate unaffected. In other words, the function will have the same slope but will just move slightly up and down the vertical axis as different hide sizes are used. When expressed in hides, predicted tax assessments for given manorial annual values are also very similar (if not identical) whatever size of hide is used.

8. See the chapters by Taylor and Poll in Dove (1888).

9. Round seems to have regarded most administrative arrangements of the Anglo-Norman regime as arbitrary impositions divorced from economic reality. He viewed, for example, knight service as an artificial system of military tenure, unrelated to the value of the property of those who were required to provide it. Professor Holt drew our attention to this matter, which we are currently analysing. See Round (1891; 1892); Holt (1894); Harvey (1970).

10. It is well known that Maitland and Round were working on their Domesday books at the same time, and that Maitland modestly and generously withheld publication of *Domesday Book and Beyond* for two years to allow Round's views to circulate without competition. This is acknowledged by both authors. Maitland said that it was done so that he and others might learn from Round. After reading *Feudal England*, Maitland (1897, v) said: 'In its light I have suppressed, corrected, added much.' Unfortunately he suppressed and 'corrected' too much, as his statistical work and historical insight were far superior to those of Round.

11. Very recently another writer (Abels 1985), in attempting to replicate Maitland's 1066 assessment–value results using simple regression techniques (see 3.2.2.2), has, like Maitland, accepted both mutually inconsistent interpretations. Abels also draws a number of further inconsistent inferences regarding the relative administrative roles of manor, vill, and shire from his analysis (compare his para. 2, p. 17, with footnote 84, p. 18).

12. Galbraith (1974, 9) made a similar suggestion on other issues.

13. Maitland (1897, vi). This has been discussed fully in 3.2.2.2.

14. It is interesting that Galbraith (1974, 16) complains that Stenton being 'a pupil of J. H. Round' accepted until his death Round's view of how the survey was conducted—on a hundred rather than a feudal basis. In discussion, Professor J. Holt suggested that Round played an important role in Stenton's early career.

15. For example see Darby and Maxwell (1962, 23, 106, 290, 339, etc.).

16. See respectively, Lawson (1984), Harvey (1975), and Green (1981).

17. The only problem of measurement concerns woodland, pasture, and meadow. Essex is comparatively simple: woodland is measured in terms of the swine it could theoretically support, pasture in terms of sheep, and meadow in acres. For Wiltshire, these non-arable variables are measured by a combination of acres and linear measurements. The latter includes a mixture of leagues and furlongs for both dimensions and sometimes for one dimension only. It has been assumed that there are twelve furlongs to the league, and that a single measurement implies two dimensions of the same length (see Darby 1977, 137–207).

18. The system of weights for combining livestock was: cows, 30; swine, 8; sheep, 5; and goats, 4. See Maitland (1897, 44); Ballard (1906, 27); Round (1903, 367); and Raftis (1957, 62).

19. Excluding horses which, as shown in McDonald and Snooks (1985*b*), were a

non-economic resource.

20. For a full discussion of the Box–Cox method, see 8.10.

21. The problem of heteroskedasticity, together with the method we have employed to overcome it, are discussed in 8.11, 8.12, and 8.13.

22. What has been called 'plough-teams' in the text (to avoid confusion with ploughlands) includes both actual plough-teams and additional plough-teams that could have been employed. It was thought that this composite variable would provide a more appropriate measure of arable land. In fact, these additions to plough-teams are small, and make no significant difference to the results in Table 4.1 whether included or excluded.

23. The diagnostic tests used in this chapter are discussed in 8.12.

24. The functional form of this estimated relationship is of interest. The Box–Cox Extended form ($\lambda = 0.230$) is intermediate between the linear ($\lambda = 1$) and log-linear ($\lambda = 0$) functional forms, lying somewhat closer to the log-linear form.

25. The scope for this can be seen in the case of Dorset, where in the 800 years after 1086 the area of meadow increased from 7,000 to 95,000 acres (Maitland 1897, 443).

26. The test is the likelihood ratio test of the null hypothesis that the coefficients on the above-mentioned variables are all zero against the alternative that at least one coefficient is non-zero, and is based on the result that $2(L_0 - L_A)$, where L_0 is the maximized log-likelihood under the null hypothesis and L_A the maximized log-likehood under the alternative hypothesis, is asymptotically distributed as a Chi-squared distribution with seven degrees of freedom. The test statistic has a value of 65.251 and the 5 per cent and 0.5 per cent critical values for this Chi-squared distribution are 14.067 and 20.278, respectively.

27. This is because the omission of livestock makes little difference to the Essex results.

28. For an excellent discussion of the growing power of the Godwine family over Edward the Confessor, see Fleming (1983).

29. If it is assumed for the moment that Harvey is correct, it is difficult to explain the fact that 'ploughlands' are not recorded, or recorded incompletely for a large number of counties. Why do the Essex folios record plough-teams together with the potential for additional plough-teams, but not ploughlands? Further, why are ploughlands recorded ambiguously for Norfolk and Suffolk, and incompletely for Kent, Sussex, Surrey, Hampshire, Berkshire, Gloucestershire, Herefordshire, Worcestershire, and some of the Midland counties?

30. For an evaluation of the administrative ability of the Anglo-Saxon monarchy using documentary evidence, see Campbell (1975).

5

Manorial income

5.1 INTRODUCTION

One of the central issues to emerge from an analysis of the data in Domesday Book is the nature of the relationship between manorial income (or annual value) and resources. Resolution of this issue is important for the study of both the economics and the politics of Domesday England. It can, for example, be expected to shed some light upon the important economic question of how the new Norman masters of England ran their estates: of just how effectively they were able to allocate resources for the production of a variety of rural commodities between a number of different regions. A good deal is known about the Normans as administrators of state and army, but very little about their role as economic managers.[1] Although this issue has attracted some attention from scholars in the past, it has been left largely unresolved, mainly owing to the bewildering detail and apparent ambiguities of the Domesday record.

The annual values are potentially important also for political studies of both Anglo-Saxon and Norman England, provided that they can be used validly as an index of income and wealth. The traditional interpretation, based upon the only large-scale study of Domesday data (Darby 1952–77), however, claims that no systematic relationship exists between manorial annual values and resources. The implication of this conclusion is that the annual values have no economic meaning and, therefore, cannot be used by political historians (such as Fleming 1983) as an index of economic wealth and power. Fortunately the results in this chapter, contrary to those of Darby and his Victorian precursors, demonstrate conclusively that there is a very strong relationship between manorial annual values and resources.

5.2 WHAT WERE THE ANNUAL VALUES?

In Domesday Book the annual values (or *valets*) constitute the incomes of landholders, in the form either of rents (or *reddits*) received from the leasing of land and other assets to subtenants, or of revenue gained from the direct exploitation of manorial resources.[2] A tenant-in-chief, who held land from the king, could deal with it in three alternative ways: make a grant of it to a feudal subtenant in return for feudal services; lease it to a subtenant for a negotiated rent; or work the manor directly for his own profit through a bailiff.[3] If a tenant-in-chief chose to grant a manor to someone else, he ceased to be the immediate lord, and accordingly surrendered his right to arrange or receive the rent or revenue accruing to the estate, whereas if he leased out the manor in question, he retained both the lordship and the power to negotiate its lease from time to time (Lennard 1959, ch. 7). It is those who held power over leases, rents, and manorial revenues that are the subject of this chapter.

It is important to realize that the annual values were data supplied by the manorial lords or their agents (see 2.2.4), and were not valuations made by those conducting the Survey. The role of the county courts was merely to assemble and verify the data supplied to them by landholders. Independent valuations by the hundred juries were only made when the rents appeared too high, or when a landholder did not appear before the county court. In the case of Essex, this occurred in less than 1 per cent of all manors. When the juries considered the rent paid for a manor to be too high, they recorded not only the actual rent but also their estimate of the 'true worth' of the property. Also, if a landholder did not report to the county court on the due data (DBi, fo. 66), an extremely rare event owing to the penalties (including confiscation of the property) that would be involved, the hundred jury would make its own estimate of the annual value. In the overwhelming majority of cases, therefore, the annual values are actual rents or manorial revenues, rather than valuations made by those conducting the Survey.

5.3   INTERPRETATIONS OF THE RELATIONSHIP BETWEEN VALUE AND RESOURCES

Victorian scholars, largely under the persuasive influence of J. H. Round and F. W. Maitland, saw Domesday Book as a geld book, and accordingly focused upon tax assessments rather than values as the central issue in their work. The consensus appears to have been that the annual values were not amenable to, or worthy of, economic interpretation. Round (1895), for example, ignored the values, largely because of his fascination with the novel view that assessments were artificial (in that they were imposed from above with no reference to the income-generating capacity of the manors or villages; see Chapter 5). Elsewhere Round (1903) expressed only fleeting curiosity about the apparent inconsistency between changes from 1066 to 1086 in values on the one hand and resources on the other. His main interest in this context was with the occasional excess of *reddit* over *valet*.[4] Maitland (1897, 5) also regarded tax assessments as the central issue of Domesday Book, although he made more systematic use of the values than Round had done. Yet, even in Maitland's work, values played a secondary role. For example, by examining visually the variation in both the assessment and value totals between counties, Maitland (1897, 464) was able to conclude: 'The *distribution* of fiscal hides has not been altogether independent of the varying value of land.' Yet he believed values were only one of a number of minor influences (including teamlands and privilege) on the Domesday assessments, which he ultimately regarded as largely artificial. Maitland (1897, 473) finally concluded that, for many manors, 'there are cases in which the *valuits* and *valets* look as artificial and systematic as the hides and the teamlands ... Everywhere we are baffled by the makebelieve of ancient finance.' Finally, Vinogradoff (1908), with his legal–political approach, also focused upon taxation, devoting two chapters to the subject in *English Society*, and gave only passing reference to values. Like his contemporaries he was attracted briefly to the difference between *valet* and *reddit*, although, unlike them, he regarded the latter as total revenue rather than rent. Also, while convinced that there should be a consistent relationship between values and land, he found its apparent absence throughout Domesday England impossible to explain. Round's hypothesis of assessment artificiality, therefore, had cast its long shadow over the annual values.

The attitude of the Victorian scholars to values (and also to assessments) has had considerable influence up to the present time. No Domesday scholar has yet systematically attempted to explain values in terms of economic resources. In fact, the values have been employed mainly for non-economic purposes. For example, Finn (1971) revived another Victorian preoccupation, when he examined the geographical distribution of estates suffering a fall in value between 1066 and 1086 to show the progress of William's armies of conquest, retribution, and defence around England.[5] Although Finn claimed to be interested in the economic effects of the Conquest, he developed a non-economic interpretation of variations in values between 1066 and 1086.

Only H. C. Darby, the pioneering geographer of Domesday Book, made more than passing reference to an economic interpretation of variations in the values and assessments. Yet even he was influenced by the Victorian scholars. Darby not only accepted Round's view concerning the artificial nature of tax assessments, but also, like Maitland, extrapolated this attitude to include the annual values.[6] For example, in the county volumes which appeared before the mid-1960s, Darby and his co-authors drew attention to the inherent difficulties of the values, presumably as justification for not mapping them, and usually concluded, as in the case of Essex (Darby 1952, 228–9): 'Generally speaking, the greater the number of plough-teams and men on a holding, the higher its value, but it is impossible to discern any consistent relation between resources and value.' This conclusion developed into a formula, repeated with little variation for county after county, often with the additional statement: 'It is clear that the values were not directly related to the number of working teams or to the recorded population. Nor does a consideration of other resources help us to understand the figures.'[7]

Darby's interpretation, which has its roots in the work of Victorian Domesday scholars, was only reconsidered after the astute critical review of P. H. Sawyer (1963, 155–7). In his review Sawyer said that the failure to give adequate consideration to the values was the 'critical weakness of this study' and even 'a fundamental flaw in the whole enterprise'. He went on to add, 'The compilers repeatedly assert that there is no correlation between values and other resources, but they are clearly thinking in terms of the resources noted in Domesday, such as woodland... There is indeed a perfectly reasonable explanation: sheep. [i.e. grazing of livestock].' This timely criticism encouraged Darby (1977, 208–31) to give the values more attention in his final volume, and to develop a more elaborate justification of his earlier interpretation.

Darby's final justification, which is easier to understand in the light of Sawyer's criticism, involves two steps. First, Darby (1977, 220) repeated his earlier formula: 'Generally speaking, the greater the number of teams and men on a holding, the higher its value; but there are wide variations and it is impossible to discern any consistent relationship.' For the purposes of illustration he selected seven estates from Warwickshire which were worth £2 per year in 1086, and from visual inspection claimed that there was a 'lack of correlation' between the values and such resources as teams, men, meadows, woods, and mills. Although slightly more formal, this test is similar to those employed in Darby's earlier volumes.

Secondly, and apparently to meet Sawyer's point about grazing activities, Darby suggested that a reason for this (alleged) lack of correlation could be the existence of 'unrecorded' resources such as livestock. He devised two tests for this. First, he examined a few estates in Little Domesday which had 'similar resources', except for livestock, in both 1066 and 1086. Holding resources constant in this way, he compared changes in values and livestock (mainly sheep) between these two years, and noted (Darby 1977, 221) that on some estates increases in values were associated with increases in livestock, but that 'Many other entries ... show no such correlations'. Darby gave but two examples, both from Essex, of this lack of correlation, and then, in order to buttress this slight empirical support, quoted Round on the 'incomprehensible advances' in the values of many Essex manors during this twenty-year period. Secondly, as discussed in 3.2.2.1, Darby selected ten estates with a value of £2 from Little Domesday and Exon. Domesday which record livestock as well as other assets and, on the basis of visual inspection, concluded (Darby 1977, 221) that 'no constant relationship between resources and values appears, although we must remember that it is only about demesne livestock that we are told'. He therefore appears to regard this test as refutation of Sawyer's point about the need to include livestock, and therefore as support for his original conclusion about the lack of a systematic relationship between values and resources.

The implications of Darby's view, the ancestry of which extends back to the late nineteenth century, are difficult to accept: that the Normans were either unable to arrive at and clearly document sensible estimates of income, or lacked either the desire or the ability to manage their estates efficiently, or a combination of both. None of these possibilities fits the usual picture of the Normans as efficient administrators in what has been described (Hollister 1965, 13) as a 'community organized for war'. In the first place, is it reasonable to conclude that an administration which was able to conduct such an impressive survey in so short a time would collect meaningless data on income (yet meaningful data on the other main variables), or compile it in such a way that its meaning could not be reconstructed? And secondly, if the Normans possessed the desire and ability to be effective administrators of state and army, why should they lack these qualities when it came to managing their own estates?[8] Finally, there is a further and disturbing implication that arises from Darby's conclusion about the values. Of the various combinations of resources in his chosen sample, Darby (1977, 223) wrote:

Their variety can only lead us to suppose that many considerations now lost to us entered into manorial valuations. We can however plot the valuations if only with the idea of marshalling the information of Domesday Book rather than with the hope of penetrating through that information to the geographical reality of eleventh-century England.

This is a pessimistic conclusion, because it rejects the central objective of the social scientist: of using the available evidence to reconstruct something of reality. Our interest in Domesday Book is not in its inherent value as a document—remarkable as it undeniably is in this respect—but rather in what it can tell us of English economy and society in 1066 and 1086. This document had an important meaning for those who compiled it, otherwise they would not have gone to such expense and effort (see 2.2.4) to do so. It was a summary of a reality in which they were vitally interested. If this summary could be used by the Normans to recall that reality, then it should be possible for us to do the same even 900 years later.[9] Indeed our results support the contention that it is possible to penetrate to the economic reality which gave rise to Domesday Book.

Darby's monumental work has intimidated, or at least made life difficult for, those Domesday scholars interested in both the economic and political history of eleventh-century England. If it could be demonstrated that Darby was wrong about the annual values, much more could be said about this period. The response of scholars to Darby's work has been either to repeat the litany of supposed shortcomings of the values in order to sidestep them entirely (Galbraith 1974), or to ignore Darby's conclusions about the artificiality of the values and to proceed as if they contained some meaning (Fleming 1983; Harvey 1983).

The size of the first group of scholars cannot be determined, because only the tip of the iceberg can be seen. A notable example of one who rejected the values is Galbraith (1974, 143), who wrote: 'worst of all are the uncertainties regarding the annual values (*valet, valuit*) of the separate manors, which are at times manifestly bogus.' Clearly other students and scholars have been completely intimidated by Darby's work, and if they seriously considered working with the values at all, have rejected the idea.

There are, however, a few scholars who have been unable to refute Darby's interpretation, but whose intuition tells them that there should be some meaning in the values. It is not surprising that the chief of these have had some contact with economics or economic history (which tells us that there is a positive relationship between resources and income), and include P. H. Sawyer and S. P. J. Harvey. Of Sawyer we have already written: he was critical of Darby's claim that there was no relationship between resources and value in Domesday Book, but made no attempt to test the relationship. Harvey, on the other hand, has refused to confront Darby directly but has, on a number of occasions (Harvey 1980; 1983), expressed her faith in the reliability and meaningfulness of the Domesday data, including the values.

For example, in a review of the most recent works of Galbraith (1974) and Darby (1977), Harvey (1980, 130–1) wrote: 'Rightly, in the cause of careful research, the deficiencies of the Domesday texts have been minutely rehearsed by commentators in the last two decades or so; but there is a danger of their being over-stressed'; and again: 'Domesday values were useful guides to contemporaries in their transactions and so ought to be of use to us.' While this was asserted in a review of Darby's work, Harvey did not draw attention to differences in their points of view, let alone attempt directly to confront Darby's interpretation. Further, when Harvey (1983) used the values as an index of profitability, she did not attempt to show that Darby was wrong, but merely implicitly *assumed* that the values were meaningful. It is as if Harvey believes that both views can coexist. This is, of course, logically impossible. Maitland also mistakenly attempted to handle the differences between Round and himself over tax assessments in this way (see 4.3). If Darby is correct then Harvey must be wrong, just as Maitland would have been wrong had Round been correct. It is essential to confront and refute an established interpretation before further progress can be made. This is what we have attempted to do in this chapter.

Other scholars, who are not economic historians, have chosen to ignore the unpalatable conclusions of Darby, taking their lead from Harvey's commonsensical, but non-empirical, declarations of faith. For example, Fleming (1983), when discussing the values as an index of wealth, refers not to Darby but to Harvey (1980). Yet Darby's influence is obvious when Fleming (1983, 990) warns of the need to approach the values 'cautiously', to regard them as 'approximate rather than exact', and concludes that they 'can, at least roughly, be compared'. Of course, if Darby is correct, the values cannot be used even as rough indices of wealth, and, if he is not correct, there is no need to hedge one's conclusions in this way. Indeed, a more confident approach could be taken to the whole question of the relationship between economic wealth and political power, if only Darby could be shown to be wrong about the values.

5.4 THE DISTRIBUTION OF MANORIAL INCOME

A wider context for the experience of Essex and Wiltshire is provided by the important work of Darby (1977, 220–31) in which he has mapped and described the geographical distribution of income on a county basis. He also wisely cautions the reader about the problems involved in mapping the values, which include the variety of ways that the values are expressed in Domesday Book, the occasional occurrence of composite entries, and the difficulty of making a distinction between the values of boroughs and rural properties. Yet, despite these difficulties, the maps showing distribution of values by county provide a convenient, if approximate, overview. Darby's results show that Wiltshire and Essex rate highly in terms of both values per square mile, which will be called yields, and values per man, which will be called productivity.[10] First, in the case of comparative yields, the Wiltshire (69 shillings per square mile) and Essex (67) figures were more than twice as great as the average (32) for all English counties, and were exceeded only by Oxfordshire (78), and equalled merely by Dorset (68). Clearly Wiltshire and Essex were productive counties, and were largely untouched by the ravages of invasion, revolt, and royal reprisal.[11] Secondly, the level of labour productivity in Wiltshire (11 shillings per man) was higher than that in any other county, and even that of the highly populated Essex (8 shillings per man) was exceeded by only five other counties—Dorset (10), Gloucestershire (10), Oxfordshire (10), Buckinghamshire (9), and Kent (9)—and equalled by a further four—Cambridgeshire, Surrey, Hampshire, and Somerset. Both counties, but particularly Wiltshire, were productive counties in terms of yields and labour productivity.

The size distribution of income is illustrated in Figure 5.1, which presents a set of histograms showing the manorial values for Essex and Wiltshire in 1086. For lay manors the distributions are broadly similar for both counties, with each exhibiting a high degree of positive skewness. This reflects the fact that most manors produced an income of less than 100 shillings per annum, with a few producing as much as 600 shillings in Wiltshire and 1,200 shillings in Essex. More specifically, the mean, median, and modal values, in shillings, were respectively 77.8, 49.9, and 40.0 for Wiltshire, and 94.6, 60.0, and 20.0 for Essex, with standard deviations of 85.5 and 126.0. Although the mean and median values were greater for Essex, they were unduly affected by a few very large manors; indeed, the typical manor for Wiltshire (measured by the modal value), was twice as large as that for Essex.

A significant contrast is provided by the ecclesiastical manors. The ecclesiastical manors for Essex provide a profile broadly similar to that of the county's lay manors, but with a longer tail, owing to some manors producing up to 1,800 shillings per annum. Wiltshire, however, exhibits a radically different pattern: it has a small number of manors producing under 200 shillings, some manors producing as much as 2,120 shillings, and a thin scattering of manors in between. More precisely the mean, median, and modal values, in shillings, were respectively 128.7, 60, and 20 for Essex, and 327.3, 179.7, and 80.0 for Wiltshire, with standard deviations of 215.7 and 393.5.

It is interesting to note that the really large manors in Wiltshire were held by ecclesiastical rather than by lay barons. In Essex the distinction between the

Manorial income

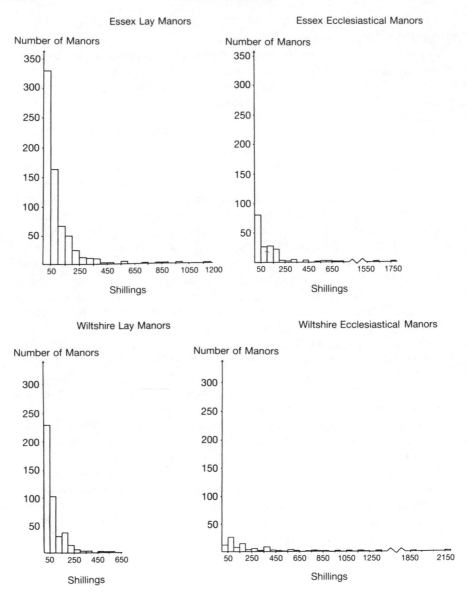

Figure 5.1. The size distribution of annual values, Essex and Wiltshire, 1086

size of lay and ecclesiastical manors was not so marked. As was the case with tax assessments, it will be interesting to discover just how comparable are the statistical results for the major subgroups, because of the marked difference in the size distributions of their annual values.

5.5 STATISTICAL ANALYSIS OF MANORIAL INCOME

5.5.1 Domesday data on values and resources

The economic data available in 1086 for manors in Essex and Wiltshire, which have been mapped by Darby (1952, 209–63; 1967, 1–66), include: the annual value, and occasionally the rent; the number of plough-teams both on the demesne and 'belonging to the men'; the numbers of freemen, sokemen, villeins, bordars (or cottars and coscets), and slaves; the amount of woodland, pasture, and meadow; and finally, the number of mills, fisheries, and vineyards. In addition, there are a number of variables recorded for only one or other of the two counties. For Essex there are data on: extra plough-teams that could have been employed; numbers of livestock, including cows, sheep, swine, goats, and horses; salt pans; and beehives. And for Wiltshire, the ambiguous ploughlands variable has been recorded. In contrast to the abundant data available for 1086, that for 1066 is somewhat limited. The 1066 data is restricted to Essex, and includes only plough-teams, freemen, sokemen, villeins, bordars, and slaves.

To reduce the number of explanatory variables to a manageable level, some—labour and livestock—have been combined to produce the following ten resource variables for each holding: plough-teams (Pl), livestock (Li), horses (H), labour (N), slaves (S), woodland (W), meadow (Me), pasture (P), mills (M), and beehives (B). First, labour (N) is a combination of freemen, sokemen, villeins, and bordars (or cottars and coscets), weighted equally on the grounds that they performed a similar economic function, despite the different proportion of their time distributed between working their own land and that of their lords. Further, according to Maitland (1897, 43–5), the wergild, or payment that had to be made to their families by anyone causing their death, was the same for each of these categories, and, probably most importantly, there was considerable mobility between these groups between 1066 and 1086. Slaves were included separately because their economic function differed from that of the peasants, and, as they seem to be associated with demesne plough-teams, there could be some correlation between these two variables. Secondly, with the exception of horses, all livestock were combined into one variable using market values as the weighting system.[12] Horses have been excluded because, as suggested in the literature (Postan 1972, 80), during the Anglo-Norman period they were used largely for non-productive purposes such as war and leisure. It was not until the thirteenth and fourteenth centuries that ploughing with horses became common.[13] To the extent that horses were used for non-productive purposes, horses and value will not be significantly related; and further, if keeping horses also involved substantial costs, horses and value will be inversely related.

Thirdly, beehives have been included because of the importance of honey in the Domesday economy, both as an essential item of consumption (as the only sweetener, as the main ingredient in mead, and as a raw material for candles) and as one of the methods used by peasants to pay their obligations to their lord.[14] As there is a suggestion that data on beehives were not comprehensively collected (Darby 1977, 279), this may not be a significant variable. Fourthly, although mills have been included in our analysis as an important capital variable, there is some uncertainty in the literature as to whether mill renders have been included in the annual values. Darby (1977, 210) assumes that the mill renders have been included in the annual values, whereas Finn (1971, 11) guesses that they have been excluded. Mills should only be treated as an explanatory variable if their renders have been added to the values. Resolution of this uncertainty would be an important outcome of our analysis. Finally, a number of variables, such as saltpans, fisheries, and vineyards, have been omitted from the list of independent variables, both because the available data appeared incomplete or ambiguous, and because they were not considered to be major determinants of income.

5.5.2 An analysis of manorial values in 1086

The major problem with Darby's analysis is that a systematic relationship cannot be properly tested by examining a few observations. Darby's method is only valid under two unlikely conditions: that the data are entirely free of measurement errors, and that the relationship between value and resources is exact. Only under these very special circumstances, which do not apply to the data in Domesday Book, will one failure of the hypothesis cause it to be rejected. The hypothesis that all swans are white, for example, can be rejected by the sighting of one black (Australian) swan only if the sighting is completely accurate.

   The statistical procedure employed here allows for some measurement error and a non-exact (or stochastic) relationship between value and resources. Also, instead of examining just a few observations, or even a random sample of observations, we have used all the data: for Essex, this involves 682 lay and 179 ecclesiastical manors, and for Wiltshire, 425 lay and 107 ecclesiastical manors. As in Chapter 4, we have allowed the data to determine the functional form, because economic theory merely tells us that income increases as more resources are employed; and we have allowed for heteroskedasticity in the regression equation, with the variance depending upon the size of the manor (as measured by the plough-teams variable). Discussion of these procedures can be found in 8.10 and 8.11.

5.5.2.1 Lay manors in Essex

The regression results for Essex lay manors, which were generated by the Box–Cox model, are presented in Table 5.1.[15] They provide information on four important hypotheses about the annual values: whether there is a relationship between all economic resources and value (regression 1); whether omitting mills makes any difference (regression 2); whether we were correct in initially assuming that horses were not an economic resource (regression 3); and

Table 5.1. The annual value–resources relationship for Essex and Wiltshire lay manors, 1086

		Const.	Pl	Li	N	S	W	Me	P	B	M	H	$\bar{R}^2$
I Essex													
regression 1	β	4.52	1.35	0.042	0.307	0.311	0.034	0.113	0.055	0.007	−0.111		0.865
	t	26.2	17.9	6.4	6.7	6.7	2.8	4.2	4.1	0.1	−1.2		
	E		0.55	0.07	0.17	0.11	0.03	0.06	0.04	0.00	−0.02		
regression 2	β	4.67	1.34	0.041	0.303	0.308	0.033	0.106	0.055	0.005			0.865
	t	39.4	17.8	6.3	6.7	6.7	2.7	4.1	4.1	0.09			
	E		0.55	0.07	0.17	0.11	0.03	0.06	0.04	0.00			
regression 3	β	4.48	1.35	0.044	0.307	0.312	0.034	0.112	0.055	0.007	−0.104	−0.039	0.865
	t	24.4	17.8	5.5	6.7	6.7	2.7	4.2	4.1	0.1	−1.1	−0.6	
	E		0.55	0.07	0.17	0.11	0.03	0.06	0.04	0.00	−0.02	−0.01	
regression 4	β	4.86	1.43		0.343	0.350	0.037	0.101	0.065				0.856
	t	53.5	18.7		7.4	7.4	2.9	3.8	4.7				
	E		0.58		0.19	0.12	0.04	0.06	0.05				
II Wiltshire													
regression 1	β	5.10	0.868		0.406	0.260	−0.014	0.101	0.120		0.048		0.803
	t	30.8	9.5		6.8	4.2	−1.0	3.2	8.3		0.5		
	E		0.36		0.22	0.10	−0.01	0.06	0.12		0.01		
regression 2	β	5.04	0.870		0.411	0.260	−0.013	0.103	0.120				0.804
	t	46.5	9.6		7.0	4.2	−0.9	3.3	8.4				
	E		0.36		0.23	0.10	−0.01	0.06	0.12				
regression 3	β	5.52	0.858		0.435	0.264	−0.017	0.101	0.123		0.285		0.814
	t	31.8	9.0		7.0	4.1	−1.2	3.1	8.3		2.7		
	E		0.34		0.23	0.10	−0.02	0.06	0.12		0.07		

Notes: The dependent variable in all regressions is the annual value, except in Wiltshire regression 3, where it is the sum of annual value and mill render. All relationships are Box–Cox extended transformations (for the Essex regressions, which were based on 682 observations, $\lambda = 0.280$, for Wiltshire regressions 1 and 2, based on 425 observations, $\lambda = 0.260$, and for Wiltshire regression 3, based on 415 observations, $\lambda = 0.27$).

The first row (labelled β) gives the Box–Cox extended parameter estimates of the intercept or constant and the following explanatory variables: plough-teams (Pl), livestock (Li), peasants (N), slaves (S), woodland (W), meadow (Me), pasture (P), bees (B), and mills (M). (H refers to horses.) The second row (labelled t) gives the conventional t-ratios, and the third row gives the partial resource–annual value elasticities, evaluated at the sample mean of annual value and the resource.

For all regressions, the hetero (a) and hetero (b) tests did not reveal significant heteroskedasticity in the disturbances. Details of the estimation procedure and tests are given in Chapter 8.

whether there is anything in Sawyer's suggestion that livestock are critical to the value–resources relationship (regression 4).

In Essex regression 1, all coefficient estimates (line β), apart from mills, are positive, and, with the exception of the variables for mills and beehives, highly significant (line t). In addition, this estimated functional form is able to 'explain' a remarkably high proportion (86.5 per cent) of the variation in annual values, as indicated by a $\bar{R}^2$ of 0.865. While coefficients of determination of this size are common for time-series data, they are very rare for cross-sectional data. In other words, our results show, in contrast to the interpretation of Darby, that there is a very strong and positive relationship between value and resources: that an increase in one or more resources leads to an increase in value. The impact of the resource variables on annual value is reflected in the partial elasticities (line E): for example, a 1 per cent increase in plough-teams will result in approximately a 0.55 per cent increase in value, whereas a 1 per cent increase in labour inputs will produce only a 0.17 per cent increase in value. As the sum of the partial elasticities is almost unity, it implies that, on average, a small percentage change in all resources will lead to the same percentage change in values.

Of considerable interest is the finding in regression 1 that the coefficient estimate for mills is not significantly different from zero. In other words, the mills variable does not appear to be a determinant of annual value. To test this further, the mills variable was omitted from the regression equation. The results, which are presented in Essex regression 2, show that, when the mills variable is omitted, the other coefficient estimates (line β) and the test statistics (line t) are largely unchanged. It would appear, therefore, that the mill renders were not included in the annual values. This helps to clear up the ambiguity in the literature about this issue. The most likely explanation of the exclusion of mill renders from annual values is that William was interested in agricultural rather than manufacturing activities, because land was considered to be the only true source of income and wealth, and because land was the foundation of the feudal structure. Certainly there is, as discussed in 2.1.2.2, a surprising dearth of information in Domesday Book on towns and secondary industries.

To test our assumption that horses were not an economic resource in Anglo-Norman England, they were subsequently included in the first regression. The results, which are presented in Essex regression 3, show that the estimated coefficient on the horses variable is insignificant from zero at all conventional significance levels. This result supports the suggestion in the literature, and confirms our assumption in regression 1, that horses were not an economic resource. Clearly they were mainly used for war, leisure, and public display.

As livestock numbers are not available for most Domesday counties (only for those in Little Domesday and Exeter Domesday), it is important to examine the effect of omitting them from our regression equation. The importance of this test is highlighted by the argument between Darby and Sawyer about whether livestock is critical in the value–resources relationship.

Essex regression 4 indicates that there is some slight fall in the coefficient of determination ($\bar{R}^2$) and a slight increase in the values of most resource variables and t-ratios; but overall the changes are not very marked. It appears that it is possible even without livestock data to obtain good approximations to the relationship between value and resources. The explanation is that the importance of animal husbandry is reflected in the shares of non-arable land— pasture, meadow,and woodland—as well as in the numbers of livestock, and that direct information on livestock has little effect upon the estimates. This is not to say that livestock are unimportant, only that their statistical influence upon annual value is largely captured by the non-arable land variables. This result is very important for two reasons: it suggests that the method developed here can be applied to counties (like Wiltshire) for which livestock numbers are unavailable; and it indicates that Sawyer's argument, *contra* Darby, that livestock numbers are essential to any relationship between value and resources, is not correct.

5.5.2.2 Lay manors in Wiltshire

The statistical results for Wiltshire lay manors are also presented in Table 5.1. Because livestock numbers are not recorded for Wiltshire (nor for any other county in Great Domesday), there are fewer equations for this county. It is valid, however, to compare the Wiltshire results with those of Essex, because it was shown in 5.5.2.1 that omission of livestock makes no significant difference. From Wiltshire regression 1 it can be seen that, with the exception of mills and woodland, all coefficients are positive and highly significant. Even the coefficient of determination ($\bar{R}^2 = 0.803$) is very similar to that for Essex. Once again, there is close relationship between manorial value and resources, which further confounds the interpretation imbedded in the literature.

Once again, the results show that the mills coefficient is not significantly different from zero, and hence not a determinant of annual value. Even when the mills variable is omitted from our regression equation, as in Wiltshire regression 2, the results are virtually identical in every respect. This provides additional support for our hypothesis, based upon the data for Essex, that mill renders are not included in the annual values. But we can go one step further for Wiltshire. As data on both values and mill renders (in shillings) are contained within the Wiltshire folios, it is possible to make a fairly conclusive test of our hypothesis. If the coefficient for mills is not significantly different from zero in Wiltshire regression 1, and if our hypothesis is true, then by adding mill renders to annual values, and rerunning regression 1, the coefficient for mills should be positive and significant. The results are presented in Wiltshire regression 3 in Table 5.1. As the mills variable is both positive and significant, and as the regression equation passes the diagnostic tests, it can be concluded quite confidently that the mill renders have not been included in the annual values for Wiltshire, nor (as the results in regression 1 for both Wiltshire and Essex are very similar) in those for Essex.[16] Notice also that the fit for regression 3 ($\bar{R}^2 = 0.814$) is better than for regression 1 ($\bar{R}^2 = 0.804$). This is a very important result that could not have been determined other than by the type of statistical method employed here.

There are, however, a number of differences between the results for lay manors in Wiltshire and Essex. The first concerns woodland. For Essex the woodland coefficient is positive and significant, but for Wiltshire it is insignificant. It is tempting to explain this in terms of the more complicated way in which Wiltshire woodland has been recorded—with linear dimensions as well as acres—except that pasture and meadow are measured in the same way, and their estimated coefficients are both positive and significant. A possible alternative explanation is that woodland in Essex was fully exploited economically, but in Wiltshire it was not, perhaps because woodland was used largely for leisure activities such as hunting in this Wessex county.

A second difference between the results for Essex and Wiltshire lay manors concerns the relative importance of resources in determining the annual values, which is reflected in the partial elasticities. For Wiltshire, on average, plough-teams are considerably less important and pasture is much more important than in Essex. In other words, arable activities were relatively more important for Essex than for Wiltshire. This conclusion, which will be analysed in Chapter 6, is particularly interesting because it has been arrived at even though the Wiltshire folios do not record livestock numbers. This is one of the strengths of the statistical method we have employed.

5.5.2.3 *Ecclesiastical manors in Essex*

The broad features of ecclesiastical manors, as presented in Essex regression 1 in Table 5.2, are similar to those for lay estates: there is a strong and positive relationship between annual values and the main manorial resources of plough-teams, peasant labour, and pasture. Even the relative importance of these resources in determining the annual values is similar, except for the slightly greater influence of ecclesiastical plough-teams. The only difference between ecclesiastical and lay manors is that the coefficients for livestock, meadow, woodland, and slaves are not quite significant at the 5 per cent level. However, if the pastoral variables—livestock, meadow, and pasture—are grouped together, on the grounds that they are inputs for the same activity, their coefficients are jointly significant. Once again the coefficient of determination ($\bar{R}^2 = 0.895$) is remarkably high—even higher than that for lay manors ($\bar{R}^2 = 0.865$), which probably reflects either a lower degree of measurement error (possibly due to better records held by ecclesiastical manors) or a higher degree of aggregation. Whatever the reason, something like 90 per cent of the variation in annual value can be accounted for by the variation in manorial resources.

The mills coefficient is, once more, insignificant (regression 1), and when omitted from the initial regression equation (as in Essex regression 2), the coefficient estimates and t-ratios of the remaining variables are not much

Table 5.2. *The annual value–resources relationship for Essex and Wiltshire ecclesiastical manors, 1086*

		Const.	Pl	Li	N	S	W	Me	P	B	M	H	R̄²
I Essex													
regression 1	β	4.70	1.26	0.023	0.283	0.142	0.013	0.065	0.058	−0.063	0.259		0.895
	t	15.8	9.6	1.9	3.2	1.8	0.7	1.6	3.0	−0.6	1.9		
	E		0.60	0.03	0.17	0.05	0.01	0.03	0.05	−0.02	0.07		
regression 2	β	4.37	1.29	0.023	0.297	0.146	0.010	0.084	0.060	−0.044			0.893
	t	17.9	9.7	1.8	3.3	1.9	0.5	2.2	3.1	−0.4			
	E		0.61	0.03	0.18	0.06	0.01	0.04	0.05	−0.01			
regression 3	β	4.69	1.26	0.024	0.283	0.143	0.013	0.065	0.058	−0.063	0.260	−0.009	0.894
	t	14.8	9.5	1.6	3.2	1.8	0.7	1.6	2.9	−0.6	1.9	−0.01	
	E		0.60	0.03	0.17	0.05	0.01	0.03	0.05	0.02	0.00	−0.00	
regression 4	β	4.55	1.34		0.291	0.174	0.014	0.085	0.064				0.893
	t	27.2	10.3		3.3	2.3	0.7	2.2	3.3				
	E		0.63		0.18	0.07	0.02	0.04	0.05				
II Wiltshire													
regression 1	β	4.63	1.15		0.285	0.114	0.002	0.046	0.111		0.212		0.919
	t(w)	12.0	6.6		1.8	1.4	0.1	0.9	5.7		1.9		
	E		0.57		0.17	0.05	0.00	0.03	0.12		0.07		
regression 2	β	4.30	1.20		0.307	0.104	0.001	0.066	0.116				0.916
	t(w)	12.4	6.8		1.8	1.2	0.05	1.4	5.5				
	E		0.60		0.19	0.04	0.00	0.04	0.12				
regression 3	β	6.98	1.64		0.256	0.228	0.002	0.061	0.127		0.715		0.901
	t(w)	8.0	6.9		1.2	1.3	0.1	0.7	5.4		3.2		
	E		0.54		0.12	0.05	0.00	0.03	0.14		0.12		

Notes: The dependent variable in all regressions is the annual value, except in Wiltshire regression 3, where it is the sum of annual value and mill render. All the relationships are Box–Cox extended transformations (for the Essex regressions, which were based on 179 observations, $\lambda = 0.240$, and for the Wiltshire regressions, based on 107 observations, $\lambda = 0.210$ in regressions 1 and 2 and $\lambda = 0.330$ in regression 3).

The first row (labelled β) gives the Box–Cox extended parameter estimates of the intercept or constant and the following explanatory variables: plough-teams (Pl), livestock (Li), peasants (N), slaves (S), woodland (W), meadow (Me), pasture (P), bees (B), and mills (M). (H refers to horses.) The second row (labelled t) gives the conventional t-ratios, and the third row gives the partial resource–annual value elasticities evaluated at the sample mean of annual value and the resource.

For all Essex regressions, the hetero (a) and hetero (b) tests did not reveal significant heteroskedasticity in the disturbances. For the Wiltshire regressions, the hetero (b) (but not the hetero (a)) tests indicated heteroskedasticity at the 5 per cent significance level, so White's t-ratios (which allow for heteroskedasticity) are given for these regressions. Details of the estimation procedure and tests are given in Chapter 8.

changed. The only exception is that the meadow coefficient is now significantly different from zero. Finally, regressions 3 and 4 confirm our earlier conclusions that horses are not an economic resource, and that the omission of livestock makes only a marginal difference to the results. The main change is that the coefficient for slaves now becomes significant. Indeed, with the omission of mills and livestock, all the major resource coefficients, with the exception of woodland, are significant determinants of annual value.

5.5.2.4 Ecclesiastical manors in Wiltshire

Wiltshire regression in Table 5.2 indicates a very strong relationship between annual value and two important resource variables, plough-teams and pasture. We have become accustomed to very high coefficients of determination ($\bar{R}^2$), but in this case they have achieved the truly remarkable level of 0.919, a tribute to the methods used in the collection of this data. That peasant labour is not a significant variable is, at first glance, a surprising feature of these results; but this is due to the fact that peasant numbers were not recorded for a number of large manors. When the regression was rerun to eliminate these manors (no manor could be operated without labour), the t-ratio for peasant labour increased to 2.1, which made it significant, and the t-ratio for mills fell even lower, to 1.6. Further, it was found that when the pastoral variables were grouped together, they were jointly significant. The coefficients for slaves, woodland, and mills, however, remain insignificant—a similar result to that for Essex's ecclesiastical manors. It is possible that slaves were required to fulfil a non-economic, perhaps religious role; woodland, it will be recalled, was insignificant for Wiltshire lay manors; and mills has been insignificant in all regressions.

The mills variable is of special interest. When mill renders were added to annual values, as was done in Wiltshire regression 3, the mills coefficient became significant. This confirms the result achieved for Wiltshire lay manors, and provides further confidence in the important conclusion that mill renders were not included in the annual values.

5.5.3 An analysis of manorial values in 1066

Very little information is available for 1066 in Domesday Book. The only data recorded in Great Domesday involve values and tax assessments. Little Domesday Book, being a more detailed circuit return, provides additional data on plough-teams, peasant labour, and slaves. Consequently it is only possible to analyse the value–resources relationship for Essex. Table 5.3 presents the Essex results for both 1066 and 1086 using the same sample size.

The relationship between value and the main manorial resources in 1066 (see regression 1), like that in 1086, is strong and positive for lay manors. All the available resource variables are significant, and the coefficient of determination ($\bar{R}^2 = 0.794$) is, as we have come to expect of Domesday data, unusually high. The 1066 results are similar to those for 1086 (regression 1)

Table 5.3. The annual value–resources relationship for Essex lay and ecclesiastical manors, 1066 and 1086, restricted sample

		Const.	Pl	N	S	$\bar{R}^2$
1066						
regression 1	β	3.95	1.22	0.100	0.217	0.794
lay manors	t	52.5	17.5	2.2	6.1	
	E		0.74	0.07	0.13	
regression 2	β	3.87	1.34	0.053	−0.006	0.854
ecclesiastical	t	30.4	13.1	0.7	−0.1	
manors	E		0.87	0.04	−0.00	
1086						
regression 1	β	4.80	1.46	0.318	0.227	0.830
lay manors	t	45.9	17.3	6.1	5.3	
	E		0.67	0.19	0.09	
regression 2	β	4.63	1.25	0.393	0.134	0.855
ecclesiastical	t	21.0	8.2	3.6	1.5	
manors	E		0.61	0.25	0.05	

Notes: All relationships are Box–Cox extended transformations. (For 1066 regression 1, which was based on 464 observations, $\lambda = 0.170$, and for regression 2, based on 125 observations, $\lambda = 0.150$; for 1086, using the same number of observations, for regression 1, $\lambda = 0.240$, and for regression 2, $\lambda = 0.230$.)

The first row (labelled β) gives the Box–Cox extended parameter estimates for the intercept or constant and the following explanatory variables: plough-teams (Pl), peasants (N), and slaves (S). The second row (labelled t) gives the conventional t-ratios, and the third row gives the partial resource–annual value elasticities evaluated at the sample mean of annual value and the resource.

For all regressions the hetero (a) and hetero (b) tests did not reveal significant heteroskedasticity in the disturbances. Details of the estimation procedure and tests are given in Chapter 8.

when the same observations are employed for both years, with the exception that the relative importance of peasant labour and slaves (as reflected in the partial elasticities in line E) is reversed. This probably arises from the greater number of missing labour variables for 1066.

Ecclesiastical manors in 1066 present a greater problem, once again because of missing labour variables. While the coefficient of determination ($\bar{R}^2 = 0.854$) is remarkably high, only the plough-team coefficient is significant. The estimated relationship, therefore, is between value and plough-teams, which, alone of all resources, were regularly recorded for 1066. The reason could be that records for ploughbeasts in 1066 were probably still available at the time of the Survey. As Church land was usually leased out complete with livestock, including ploughbeasts (Raftis 1957), which had to be accounted for at the end of the lease, detailed records would have been essential. A comparison with the restricted sample for 1086 (regression 2) indicates that the coefficient for peasant labour was significant but that for slaves was not.

5.6 CONCLUSIONS AND IMPLICATIONS

Contrary to the conventional wisdom, which extends back to Round and Maitland, the statistical results described in this chapter demonstrate a very strong and positive relationship between the values (or income) and resources of lay and ecclesiastical manors in Essex and Wiltshire in 1066 and 1086. This is particularly interesting in view of the marked differences in the size distribution of annual values for the various manorial groups. The implications of this finding for the study of both the economic and the political history of the eleventh century are wide-ranging. In the first place, there is every reason to believe that a close study of the production process in Domesday England will be a profitable exercise. A beginning has been made in Chapter 6, where the broad outlines of the nature of manorial production have been sketched. Had Darby been correct, there would have been no point in proceeding further with a study of the Domesday economy, because it would have been necessary to dismiss the data as meaningless. Secondly, the implications of our results are important for political studies. Quite clearly, the best indicator of income and wealth is annual value. Such an indicator can be employed confidently in studies of the relationship between economic wealth and political power. There is no need to hedge around this issue, as appeared necessary when it was obscured by the long shadow of doubt cast by Round, Maitland, Galbraith, and Darby.

Our results also help to clarify debates in the literature concerning the nature and importance of economic variables in Domesday Book. In the first place, it has been shown that the omission of livestock from the function makes little difference to the estimated results. This is important because it suggests both that our model can be applied to the large number of counties contained in Great Domesday Book for which livestock are not recorded, and that the potentially important debate between Darby and Sawyer has no substance. Secondly, our results make it possible to clarify the uncertainty about whether the important mill renders were included in the annual values. While Darby assumes they were included, the results presented here (particularly for Wiltshire) show quite clearly that mill renders were not included in the annual values. Thirdly, our results support the suggestion in the literature that, in the main, horses were not an economic resource in Domesday England.

Finally, a number of wider implications can be drawn from our analysis. Any lingering doubts concerning the reliability of Domesday Book data must be dispelled once and for all by the results in this chapter. The remarkably close fits ($\bar{R}^2$) between our estimated functions and the data—fits rarely found using modern cross-sectional data—are a measure of the unusual accuracy of this source. William's thorough and costly survey methods are surely vindicated by the very high quality of the data collected. This is a very important conclusion, because it suggests that it is possible to penetrate the apparently bewildering detail of Domesday Book to the reality from which it emerged.

Our statistical results also suggest that there was a high degree of consistency in the way estates were managed in the Anglo-Norman period. Such remarkable consistency is most likely to have arisen from the pursuit of the desire to maximize material returns (as opposed to the application of conventional rules), but further work is required to demonstrate this conclusively. We return to this issue in Chapters 6 and 7.

Notes

1. For example, Hollister (1965) and Stenton (1932).
2. Some manors, particularly those belonging to the king, also received income from the territorial courts.
3. Rents in Domesday Book are not as straightforward as might be assumed. In the first place, the payment of rents was widespread and consisted of a mixture of money renders and renders in kind. Secondly, some of these leases may have concerned not only land, but both land and stock: at least, there is some evidence to this effect in the records of ecclesiastical estates in the twelfth century. Thirdly, there is some evidence that rents were not fixed indefinitely, but varied quite regularly. Domesday Book makes regular reference to rents that a short time before had been set at a level considerably higher than the recognized value of the manor (Lennard 1959, ch. 7).
4. The most convincing explanation of this divergence is that, when the hundred juries considered rents on leased properties to be excessive, they recorded both the excessive *reddit* as well as the more usual *valet*. When the rent was not considered unduly high, or when the lord worked the manor himself, only the *valet* was recorded. (As there were only six cases of excessive rents in Essex, this was not an important problem here.) For a discussion of excessive rents, see Darby (1977, 211–14); Lennard (1959, 116–23); Round (1903, 361, 363–5).
5. A precursor was Baring (1898); also see Lemmon (1966).
6. For example, Darby (1952, 220) and Darby (1977, 10).
7. For example, Darby and Maxwell (1962, 43, 125, 199, 302–3, 352, etc.). There is, of course, a degree of internal inconsistency in the first of these statements.
8. It should be recalled that at this time in history the margin between life and death was slim, and could disappear entirely during adverse climatic periods. This would be incentive enough to husband one's resources as effectively as possible.
9. Harvey (1980, 131) provides an example of how contemporaries used the results in Domesday Book.
10. Darby's third measure of values per plough-team is not particularly useful, as it contains elements of both different yields and the different economic structure between arable and pastoral activities.
11. Essex had suffered numerous Viking raids from 894 to 1049 (Fleming 1983, 1001); but these do not appear to have been particularly devastating, since the county had completely recovered in terms of yields and labour productivity by the time of the Survey (see 5.4).
12. The system of weights was: cows, 30; swine, 8; sheep, 5; and goats, 4. See Maitland (1897, 44); Ballard (1906, 27); Round (1903, 367); Raftis (1957, 62).
13. Horses cost more to keep than oxen, because of the cost of shoeing and the need to feed them oats in winter, whereas oxen could survive on hedge clippings. A recent

discussion of the relative costs of using horses and oxen can be found in Langdon
(1982, 31–40). Also see Hallam (1981, 54).

14. Darby (1977, 277–8); Lennard (1959, 368–76).

15. It is important to realize that the linear and log-linear functional forms were found
    to be inappropriate when a series of diagnostic tests were undertaken. In both cases
    the estimated equations were mis-specified, and there was a high degree of
    heteroskedasticity in the disturbance terms. A detailed discussion can be found in
    8.13.

16. As mill renders were not available for ten of these manors, Wiltshire regression 3 in
    Table 5.1 was estimated using 415 observations, rather than 425, as in Wiltshire
    regression 1. For comparative purposes, Wiltshire regression 1 was rerun using the
    smaller sample; the results were very similar to those presented.

6

The system of manorial production

6.1 INTRODUCTION

Domesday England's basic economic institution was the manor, which produced a range of agricultural commodities, mainly for internal consumption, but also for trade. Although the existing literature describes the main features of the manorial system (see 2.1.2), it is possible to go further and analyse the production process by employing economic and statistical methods. It is possible to provide answers to the following questions that economists usually ask about any system of production. How does output change when there is a given increase in manorial resources? What are the key resources, and what are their relative contributions to manorial output? To what degree is it possible to substitute one resource, say villeins, for another, say plough-teams, and still maintain a given output? Are there economies of scale, so that a doubling of all resources leads to more than a doubling of output? Answers to these questions can be given by estimating production functions, provided the data employed are sufficiently detailed and of the appropriate quality.

In the light of the analysis in previous chapters, it is reasonable to conclude that Domesday Book data are appropriate for this purpose. It was shown in Chapter 5 that a strong relationship exists between annual values and resources, and that the data are both detailed and remarkably free from measurement error, particularly in comparison with modern sources. Also, the relatively simple nature of the Domesday economy means that we do not have to contend with a number of serious problems that normally bedevil production functions estimated for modern economies.[1] Accordingly, it should be possible to estimate appropriate production functions, which, in providing information about the technical relationship between the quantities of various resources (or inputs) and the quantity (or value) of output produced, will suggest answers to the questions posed about the manorial economy. As this work has implications for all those interested in Domesday England, these matters will be outlined in a non-technical way and with a minimum of jargon. A more technical account can be found in Chapter 10 (particularly sections 10.7 and 10.8).

6.2 A MODEL OF MANORIAL PRODUCTION

To interpret the Domesday production function estimates, it is necessary to develop a model of the manorial system as it existed in mid-eleventh-century England. The model of the Domesday manor presented here has been based upon the descriptive detail given in 2.1.2 (where our main assumptions can be verified), but does not pretend to encompass all aspects of that historical reality. An economic model is not a precise description of reality, but rather an abstract characterization of the way in which an economic system works: a characterization that, it is hoped, captures the essence of the economic system. Basically, our model assumes that the landholder maximizes manorial income, subject to feudal institutional constraints that have the effect of fixing input levels in the short run. This model provides a more satisfactory basis for interpreting our Domesday production results than that usually employed by economists, in which a profit-maximizing firm in a perfectly competitive environment is able to vary its input levels in the short run. Briefly, the model of Domesday manorial production is as follows.

First, in our model the land of the manor is divided into two parts, the lord's demesne and the peasants' land, a division which is allowed to vary widely between manors (see 2.1.2.1). While the demesne is used to produce tradable goods to meet the lord's consumption demands, the peasants' land is required to maintain the peasants and their plough-teams, usually at subsistence level. Because of the division of the manor, it is important to distinguish between the gross or total manorial output, which is the sum of production on the demesne and the peasants' land, and the net output, which accrues to the lord from working the manor (or from leasing it to a subtenant).[2] The annual value correponds to the latter and, from the manorial lord's point of view, is the value added by the production process. It can be regarded as the gross value of production less intermediate goods (such as grain seed), and goods produced on the manor (such as fodder and rough shelter for livestock; food, clothing, and shelter for slaves; and the subsistence output of the peasants' land) to maintain the manorial resources. Annual value, in other words, is the return to the lord from owning or controlling the manorial resources, and includes a return for risk, together with economic rents and quasi-rents extracted from factors that are scarce or in fixed supply in the short-run.[3]

Secondly, we postulate that the resources employed on the demesne are in fixed supply in the short-run. The peasants, mainly villeins and bordars, work on the lord's demesne in return for 'protection' (an arrangement in which they have little choice) and the use of land to grow their own crops, while the slaves receive only food and shelter (see 2.1.2.1). Not only is the manor worked by a resident rather than an outside work-force, but the standard arrangement between peasants and lord, which involves a given amount of week work and seasonal (or boon) work, is essentially fixed in the short-run (Postan 1966, 552). Similarly, the various types of land and capital are relatively fixed in the short run. Losses in ploughbeasts, for example, can only be made good by the long process of breeding new stock, because a well-developed market for factor inputs does not exist.[4] As a first approximation, therefore, the Domesday manor can be portrayed as a unit of production with a fixed set of resources, and with fixed payments being made to a dependent labour force.

Thirdly, all goods produced on the manorial demesne can be regarded as tradable, although not all are traded. In the main, these goods include cereals, vegetables, cheese, meat, wool, honey, fish, and salt. These commodities enter into both local and international trade (see 2.1.2.3 and 2.1.2.4), in return for commodities that cannot be produced upon the manor, including agricultural tools and military hardware, building materials (particularly glass and lead), finely crafted furnishings, textiles, and fine clothing. Therefore, while the peasants and slaves consume goods produced only upon the manor, the lord consumes many outside goods and services. In addition, it is necessary for a manor to sell a sufficient proportion of its output to pay the geld. In 1086 the geld was a heavy burden upon the manor, representing about 16 per cent of its annual value, which had to be met either in coin (which is the usual interpretation) or in goods. Whatever the method of payment, trading—either explicit or implicit—was required.

In the absence of trade, all the goods produced on the manor will be consumed on the manor. Such a situation makes it difficult to interpret the results of our production function estimates, because it becomes difficult to draw a distinction between the manor as a unit of production and as a unit of consumption: manorial production behaviour will be inextricably combined with the lord's consumption preferences (or utility function). The underlying reason is that the implicit prices of output reflect both the production and the consumption behaviour of the manor, rather than just the costs of manorial production. Because trade did occur in Domesday England, at prices that did not vary too greatly between one manor and another in a given region (see 2.1.2.3 and 2.1.2.4), it is reasonable to conclude that our production function results largely reflect the technical conditions of production, rather than the consumption behaviour of manors.

Fourthly, it is assumed that the same rural technology is available to all manors within a single county. This assumption is necessary if the results are to be interpreted as reflecting the nature of the commonly experienced technology. It is not necessary, however, that all manors apply this basic technology in the same way. There is good evidence for the assumption. In 2.1.2.1 it was shown that manorial arable land was organized on the basis of large open fields with a two-field rotation. These large fields were in turn divided into long narrow strips, which were ploughed using large plough-teams (of up to eight oxen) and a heavy iron plough. Naturally, within this general technical framework there was some local variation in details such as the balance between arable and pasture, the crop mix, and certain 'rules and institutions' by which this technology was applied. But basically there was uniformity of agricultural technique over a large part of Domesday England.

Finally, it is assumed that the lord of the manor attempts to organize production in a technically efficient way, and to choose outputs in order to maximize the net value of goods produced. In view of the results obtained in Chapters 4 and 5, we are persuaded that this is a reasonable assumption. The monarch, for example, was clearly attempting to maximize his tax revenues, and, according to the *Anglo-Saxon Chronicle*, he went to considerable lengths to maximize the rents from his own estates. There is no reason to believe that the king was unique in this respect. Indeed, the statistical results in Chapter 5 suggest that manorial lords were operating their estates in a highly consistent manner, as if they were attempting to obtain the highest return possible. The assumption of maximizing behaviour on the part of the manorial lord, therefore, appears to be a reasonable approximation to reality (see 7.2.3).

A virtue of our model is that it can explain why manors were operated with widely different resource ratios (such as the ratio of peasants to plough-teams) and at very different production levels. The remarkable variation in manorial size and resource combination recorded in Domesday Book can be accounted for by the history and geography of a particular region, natural processes such as fertility and disease, and the requirements of a feudal society. A lord being granted a manor by the Conqueror received a set of endowments, which included a precisely defined amount of land together with a given number of peasants, slaves, plough-teams, livestock, and other assets of various types. In the short term there was little the new lord could do to change either the maximum scale of production or the combination of resources, because, although there was a market for output, there was little trading in capital and labour resources. The resources could be increased only by long-term breeding programmes that could be suddenly and adversely affected by unexpected droughts, floods, disease, and Viking raids. In these circumstances, the only short-term option available to the manorial lord was to take the amount of each resource as given and attempt to organize production in a technically efficient way in order to maximize the net value of the goods produced.

Our manorial model also suggests that any estimated relationship between manorial annual values and resources reflects the agricultural technology employed in the county under study. Accordingly, differences in this estimated relationship for several counties can be interpreted as arising from variations in the technology employed by manors within these counties. Similarly, changes in the estimated relationship over time can be interpreted as changes in agricultural technology.

6.3 THE THEORY OF DOMESDAY PRODUCTION

A system of production can be analysed by estimating an economic production function, which involves a technical relationship between the quantities of various inputs used and the quantity, or value, of the good(s) produced. It can be used to describe the way in which an increase in inputs of labour, capital, and land affects output; the manner in which one input can be substituted for another without reducing output; and whether a given percentage increase in all resources will lead to an equal, greater, or lesser percentage increase in output. To analyse manorial production in this way will considerably enhance our understanding of the Domesday economy. Accordingly, an intuitive introduction to production functions, illustrated by a hypothetical Domesday manor, is given in this section. A more formal discussion can be found in Chapter 9.

Explanation of the production process can be simplified by focusing upon a hypothetical Domesday manor in which two resources, say villeins and plough-teams, can be varied by the lord, while all other resources remain constant. Of course, in practice the manorial lord was unable to vary any of the resources in the short run, as explained in 6.2, but this conceptual experiment makes it easier to understand the nature of the estimated production function. At the end of this section an attempt will be made to translate the theoretical concepts from a temporal to a spatial basis.

We will focus upon a hypothetical and simplified Domesday manor held by, say, Roger 'God Save the Ladies', which produces wheat with its given set of resources, of which only villeins and plough-teams can be varied.[5] The first question to be asked is: what is the (maximum) output of wheat in quarters that can be produced using various combinations of villeins and plough-teams? Our answer will depend upon the state of technology existing in Essex in 1086. In 2.1.2.1 it was shown that Domesday technology involved the use of a communal form of agriculture, based upon scattered strips in large open fields with a two-field system of crop rotation. This form of agricultural technology restricted the number of quarters of wheat that could be produced. By the eighteenth century the open fields were being enclosed, and new techniques were being applied, so that the same input of ploughs and labourers produced a larger number of quarters of wheat. Between the eleventh and eighteenth centuries, the production function moved outwards because the state of technology changed.

If we go back to our hypothetical Domesday manor, and assume a given technology, it will be discovered that, were Roger 'God Save the Ladies' able to change the combinations of plough-teams and villeins, the output in terms of quarters of wheat would vary. By holding the number of plough-teams constant and gradually increasing the number of villeins, Roger would find that the output of wheat increased. This increase in quarters of wheat resulting from the addition of a further villein can be called the marginal product of peasant labour. Let us suppose that Roger noted carefully how many additional quarters of wheat were produced when each additional villein was put to work, and that, when graphed, these observations traced out a curve, like the total product curve in Figure 6.1, which becomes flatter as the number of villeins increases. In other words, the additional or marginal product of

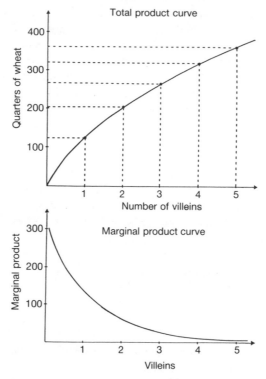

Figure 6.1. Total and marginal product on a hypothetical Domesday manor (held by Roger 'God Save the Ladies')

peasant labour declines progressively as additional villeins are employed, as can be seen reflected in the marginal product curve (which is derived from the total product curve) in Figure 6.1. This is known as the law of diminishing returns. Similarly, had Roger been able to hold the number of villeins constant, and progressively increased the number of plough-teams, possibly by one ox at a time, it is likely he would have noticed that the marginal product of plough-teams also declined.

Economic theory can also provide a number of useful insights into the way in which one resource can be substituted for another in the production process. Had he been inclined to do so, Roger could have discovered, by a series of experiments, that it is possible to produce the same number of quarters of wheat by using a variety of combinations of plough-teams and villeins. By plotting these observations on a graph similar to Figure 6.2, a number of interesting features of production can be highlighted. With OP_1 plough-teams and OV_1 villeins, Roger could have produced, say, five quarters of wheat. By reducing the number of plough-teams to OP_2, and increasing the number of villeins to OV_2, he would have been able to produce the same quantity of

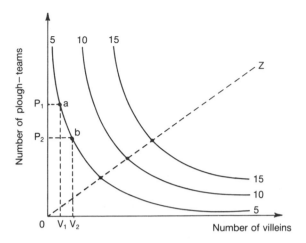

Figure 6.2. Manorial equal-product curves of a hypothetical Domesday manor (held by Roger 'God Save the Ladies')

wheat. Indeed, Roger could have confirmed this by further experiments with different combinations of these two resources. The curve joining these various observations can be called the five-quarter equal-product curve (or isoquant), because all points on it involve different but equally efficient combinations of plough-teams and villeins which produce five quarters of wheat (or an equal level of output). Similarly, an equal-product curve can be drawn by observing the results of doubling the quantity of plough-teams and villeins. In the case of Roger's manor the output of wheat is doubled, to ten quarters. Figure 6.2 illustrates two important properties of equal-product curves: that those further from the origin correspond to higher levels of output, and that, for reasons explained in Chapter 9, they cannot intersect.

Figure 6.2 can be used to examine the theory of factor substitution. A matter of some interest in this study is the rate at which villeins can be substituted for plough-teams in order to maintain a given output of, say, five quarters of wheat. If production on Roger's manor initially corresponded to *a* on the five-quarter equal-product curve, and he wished to move to a position equivalent to *b* by using one more villein and fractionally fewer plough-teams, he would discover that the marginal rate of substitution was equal to the ratio of the (absolute) change in numbers of plough-teams to the change in numbers of villeins, or, in terms of Figure 6.2, $(P_1 - P_2)/(V_2 - V_1)$. In this instance the marginal rate of substitution measures the change in plough-teams required for a unit change in villeins, in order to maintain the same output of wheat. The marginal rate of substitution depends upon the absolute value of the slope of the equal-product curve: the greater the absolute value of the slope, the greater the marginal rate of substitution, and the greater the scope for the substitution

of inputs. Another, often more useful, measure of input-substitution
.possibilities is a dimensionless measure called the elasticity of substitution,
which measures the curvature rather than the slope of the equal-product curve
(see 9.4).

Finally, we wish to know how the output of wheat will be affected by a large
increase, say a doubling, of the numbers of plough-teams and villeins.
Obviously such a large increase in the scale of the manor could only be
achieved by Roger in the long run. There are three possibilities. A doubling of
all manorial resources may lead to more than a doubling of the output of
wheat on Roger's manor. In this case his manor would be experiencing
increasing returns to scale. It may also lead to less than a doubling, or exactly a
doubling, of wheat output, which are known respectively as decreasing and
constant returns to scale. The way in which manorial output responds will
determine the spacing of the equal-product curves in Figure 6.2: with constant
returns to scale, the curves will be equally spaced (as in this case), with
increasing returns, they will be progressively closer together; and with
decreasing returns, they will be progressively further apart, as we move out
from the origin on a straight line *OZ*.

In the case of our hypothetical Domesday manor, increasing returns to scale
may result from the fact that a larger manor will enable more efficient use of the
large plough-teams, whereas decreasing returns may result from the increasing
difficulty of supervising and co-ordinating large teams of bonded peasants. It
is often the case in the modern world that increasing returns are experienced by
firms at low output levels, and constant or decreasing returns are experienced
at higher output levels. It will be interesting to discover if this is true for manors
in Domesday England.

Aspects of the theory of production have been developed here in terms of
developments within a single hypothetical manor over time, largely because
this is the usual and the most straightforward method of analytical exposition.
In this form, however, the theory is not directly relevant to the Domesday
economy, because all manorial inputs were fixed in the short run, and
Domesday Book contains cross-sectional rather than time-series data.
Nevertheless, it is possible to translate these theoretical concepts from a
temporal to a spatial basis. Indeed, a considerable proportion of the work
done on estimation of production functions has been based upon cross-
sectional data. The Domesday Book data are particularly appropriate for this
work, as they contain manors that vary greatly in size: as shown in 5.4, the size
of manors as measured by annual values, ranged from 2.5 shillings (in both
cases) to 1,800 shillings for Essex and 2,120 shillings for Wiltshire. When
evaluating the results in this chapter, it is necessary to remember that the
observations are for numerous manors with different input and output levels
at a point in time, rather than for different input and output levels for an
individual manor over time. For example, in the theoretical discussion we
examined the consequences of a manor substituting villeins for plough-teams;

in the context of Domesday Book, this should be thought of as a comparison between manors with different combinations of villeins and plough-teams. In other words, the points on the equal-product curve represent different manors, with different resource combinations, producing the same output at a point in time.

6.4 A DOMESDAY PRODUCTION FUNCTION

A variety of production functions has been applied to data for modern firms. Often the function that is chosen is not the one that is most appropriate, but rather the one that is easiest to estimate. Ease of estimation, however, does not necessarily make for accuracy of interpretation. Unfortunately, the simple production functions make strong assumptions about the nature of the production process, which, in most cases, forces the data into a very restricted form, and limits what they can tell us about the production system.

A simple and widely employed production function, known as the Cobb–Douglas production function (see section 9.6), makes a number of very strong assumptions. To enable ease of estimation, this model imposes a predetermined functional form (which is linear in its logarithms) upon the data, rather than allowing the data to select the appropriate form. In turn, this imposes strong assumptions on the substitution of factors, such that villeins can only be substituted for plough-teams in a particular manner or, to put it another way, that the equal-product curve has a predetermined shape (see Figure 6.3*b*). The reason is that the elasticity of substitution for the Cobb–Douglas function is forced to be equal to one. It is far preferable, however, to allow the data to inform us about the nature of substitution than to impose a set of restrictive assumptions. While this can be done by employing more flexible production functions, such functions do become increasingly difficult to estimate.

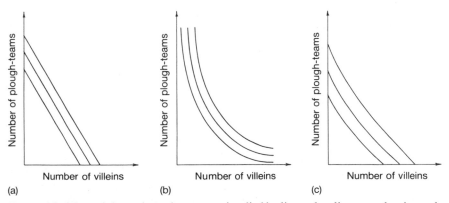

Figure 6.3. Manorial equal-product curves implied by linear, log-linear, and estimated (BCE) production functions: (*a*) linear function (elasticity of substitution equal to ∞); (*b*) log-linear function (elasticity of substitution equal to 1); (c) estimated function (BCE) (elasticity of substitution equal to 1.39)

A function more flexible than the Cobb–Douglas has already been employed in Chapter 5, where the relationship between annual values and resources was investigated. Although no attempt was made to examine production relationships there, the statistical framework employed (the Box–Cox extended model), can be interpreted as the constant elasticity of substitution (or more commonly, the CES) production function (see 10.7). This model allows the elasticity of substitution to assume any value, which can be estimated from the data. The Cobb–Douglas function is a special case of the CES production model (with an elasticity of substitution equal to 1). It will be recalled that the Box–Cox extended model allowed us to use the data to estimate the most appropriate functional form which lay between the linear and log-linear functions (see Figure 8.20, p. 168). The estimated function can be interpreted as a CES production function, with factor substitution properties similar to those represented by Figure 6.3(c): an elasticity of substitution equal to 1.39, and the combined output elasticities equal to 1 implying constant returns to scale. The log-linear function in the Box–Cox extended model corresponds to the Cobb–Douglas production function. Consequently, our estimated function in Chapter 5 has different properties concerning the substitution of villeins for plough-teams from the Cobb–Douglas production function. This means that the equal-product curves differ as between the two functions: for the Domesday production function the curves cut the axes, while for the Cobb–Douglas function they approach but never touch the axes (see Figure 6.3a and b). The implication is that, on our hypothetical manor (see Figure 6.2), a given level of output, say five quarters of wheat, can be produced without the assistance of one of the inputs (say plough-teams).

Yet the CES function, while allowing different substitution properties, assumes that they are constant for all combinations of plough-teams and villeins (or at all points on the equal-product curve). Also when more than two inputs are taken into account, the substitution behaviour between all pairs of resources (say, villeins and plough-teams, plough-teams and livestock, villeins and slaves) is assumed to be the same.

Ideally, we wish to employ a production function that allows the data to be used to estimate all properties of both substitution and return to scale. This is possible with a very flexible model called the generalized quadratic function (see 9.12), but the computing difficulties are formidable because, in our case, it is necessary to estimate over fifty parameters. As a compromise, we have employed more flexible forms of the CES function, including the Sato two-level form. In the Sato function, the inputs (which are more disaggregated than in Chapter 5) are grouped into the three 'higher'-level categories of land (pasture, meadow, and woodland), labour (freemen-sokemen, villeins, bordars, and slaves) and capital (demesne plough-teams, peasant plough-teams, and livestock). Pairs of resources have the same substitution behaviour if they come from the same 'higher'-level category, but the substitution behaviour can differ if they come from different 'higher'-level categories. The Domesday data are used to estimate the appropriate substitution behaviour at each level.[6]

6.5 THE SYSTEM OF DOMESDAY PRODUCTION, ESSEX, 1086

6.5.1 Disaggregation of labour and capital data

Comprehensive statistical analysis of the system of manorial production is possible only for Essex. Of all the counties, only Essex has detailed and unambiguous data for all the resources employed upon Domesday manors, and this only for 1086.[7] The statistical results in Chapter 5 suggest that the Essex data for 1086 are sufficiently straightforward and reliable to enable them to be employed at a more disaggregated level than was attempted when analysing the manorial income–resources relationship. Intead of grouping all peasant labour categories together, as in Chapter 5, this resource has been subdivided into the three groups of freemen-sokemen, villeins, and bordars. Also, plough-teams have been subdivided into those 'on the demesne' and those 'belonging to the men'.

A subdivision of the labour and capital variables is necessary for a detailed analysis of manorial production, because of the substantially different contribution they can be expected to make to net production.[8] In the case of plough-teams, those belonging to the lord were used only on the demesne and were maintained at his expense. The peasants' teams, however, were put to work on both the demesne and the land allocated to the peasants, and they were maintained by the peasants. Although the direct costs of maintaining the peasants' teams were borne by the men, the ultimate cost was shouldered by the lord in terms of the forgone output on the land he allocated to his men. As the input of plough-teams is not standardized in terms of hours worked per week, it can be expected that the lord's teams will make a greater contribution to annual value than will the peasants' teams. Also, it is likely that the lord's teams will be in better condition than the peasants' teams, as they probably had the advantage of the best pasture and meadow. But the major reason for any difference in the contribution to net production of these two categories of plough-teams will be due to the difference in hours worked on the demesne.

For similar reasons, the contribution of the various types of labour to net production will differ. Manorial labour consisted mainly of villeins, bordars, and slaves, but those freemen and sokemen who are recorded as being associated with a particular manor appear to have made a contribution (even if only through the payment of customary dues). One scholar (Ballard 1906, 152–5) has suggested that villeins worked on the demesne for approximately two to three days a week, in return for fifteen to thirty acres of land, while bordars worked one day a week for the lord in return for five to fifteen acres of land. Although there must have been considerable variation in these exchanges of labour for land from region to region, it does suggest that, as the labour input was not standardized for hours worked per week, we can expect that the contribution made by villeins to net production was greater than that of bordars. A significant difference in the physical quality of various types of labour is unlikely. Possibly the motivation of villeins and bordars differed, but it is difficult to say what the effect may have been: perhaps the villein, who had more land to farm, would have been keener to complete his work for the lord in a shorter time than the bordar, which, as their work was supervised, would have resulted in a higher level of productivity for villeins. But this is merely speculation.

It is difficult a priori to say how the contribution of slaves should relate to that of the peasants. Much will depend upon the way in which their services were distributed between agricultural and household activities. The general view (Darby and Finn 1967, 27) is that they were associated with the demesne plough-teams, but there is no hard evidence for this. It is highly likely that some slaves were required to work entirely in the lord's household, or that they worked some of the time in the fields and some in the household (possibly on a seasonal basis). We will not be able to resolve this issue until the production function results are examined: if the contribution is no greater than that of the villeins (who worked about one-third to one-half of the week for the lord), then it will be necessary to revise the orthodox view about slaves being closely associated with the plough. Of course, some allowance will need to be made for the lower motivation of slaves compared with that of the peasants.

6.5.2 The reality of Domesday production

The main results presented in this section (Table 6.1) are generated by a CES production function for which the conditions of substitution and returns to scale are estimated using disaggregated data. As this function assumes that all pairs of inputs experience the same resource substitution conditions, further results are given from the estimation of a more flexible (the Sato two-level) production function that allows variation in this matter. The technical details are given in 10.8.

In Table 6.1 all coefficients, with the exception of beehives, are positive and significant, and the coefficient of determination ($\bar{R}^2$) is a remarkably high 0.969. The CES production function, therefore, provides a very good fit for the Domesday data on net production and economic resources, and it shows that an increase in inputs (with the exception of beehives) will lead to an increase in output (which means that marginal products are positive).

6.5.2.1 The relative importance of manorial resources

Of particular interest is the relative importance of the main resources, which can be seen reflected in the partial output elasticities (line *E*, Table 6.1). The capital resources of ploughs and livestock are of overwhelming importance, as

Table 6.1. CES production function estimates for Essex lay manors, 1086

	Constant	Demesne ploughs	Peasant ploughs	Livestock	Freemen-sokemen	Villeins	Bordars	Slaves	Woodland	Meadow	Pasture	Bees	$\bar{R}^2$
β	0.79	0.895	0.333	0.018	0.087	0.244	0.134	0.177	0.014	0.059	0.032	−0.042	0.969
t	5.1	6.2	4.0	4.8	2.1	4.6	4.2	3.9	2.4	3.4	4.0	−1.2	
E		0.41	0.16	0.09	0.03	0.15	0.11	0.08	0.03	0.06	0.04	−0.01	Σ = 1.15

Note: For greater detail see 10.8 (and particularly Table 10.2).

they accounted for 57.4 per cent of the combined elasticities. Labour resources, of freemen, villeins, bordars, and slaves (32.2 per cent), and non-arable land resources of pasture, meadow, and woodland (11.3 per cent) are of lesser importance. Possibly part of the reason for the dominance of plough-teams is the absence of a variable for arable land. Because of this, plough-teams should probably be regarded as an indicator of the contribution of all arable inputs. By comparing the elasticity of plough-teams with those of all non-arable inputs, we can gain an approximate idea of the relative importance of these two activities. Such a comparison suggests that arable activities were 2.59 times as important as pastoral activities. In 1086, therefore, the manorial economy was dominated by the production of grain and other crops.

The relative importance of individual resources can be examined within these broad groupings, thereby providing a number of important insights into the manorial system of production. For example, the contribution of demesne plough-teams to net production (measured by the ratio of partial output elasticities) was 2.56 times greater than that of peasants' plough-teams. This difference is largely a measure of the relative hours worked per week on the manorial demesne by these two categories of teams (see 6.5.1).

Of the labour variables, villeins made the greatest contribution to net production, followed by bordars, slaves, and freemen. There are a number of interesting issues here. First, as indicated in 6.5.1, it was expected that villeins would add more to net production than would bordars, because it is known that they worked more hours per week on the demesne. Our results suggest that, on average, villeins worked 36.4 per cent more hours per week on the demesne than bordars, which is probably less than is usually thought. Secondly, the contribution of slaves to net production was about one-half of that made by villeins, who probably worked about one-third to one-half of the week on the lord's demesne. This suggests that slaves worked, on average, no more than one-and-a-half days per week on the demesne. In turn, this suggests that slaves were employed on household duties to a much greater degree than was previously thought to be the case. The fact that they appear to be associated with plough-teams in Domesday Book has led to an overrating of their economic importance. It appears instead that a large proportion were personal slaves. Finally, our results suggest that freemen and sokemen attached to large manors played a small but not insignificant role in the manorial economy. Their contribution to the lord's net production was about one-fifth of that of a villein.

Of the non-arable land variables, meadow was the most important. The contribution of pasture was two-thirds that of meadow, and woodland was one-half. Probably the difference between meadow and pasture largely reflects the higher quality of land that was regularly inundated by rivers depositing rich and deep layers of silt. This natural land renewal was particularly important to an economy that had only limited ways of enriching the soil apart from leaving it fallow (see 2.1.2.1). And, because of its fertility, meadowland was vital to the manorial economy. The role of meadow is even more important than suggested by these results, because much of its contribution to output was indirectly transmitted through the ploughbeasts which it maintained. Of course, it also served a non-economic purpose in maintaining England's warhorses. Finally, the lesser contribution of woodland probably reflects its poorer grazing qualities, and its economic underutilization.

6.5.2.2 The conditions of manorial resource substitution

The CES production function provides valuable information about the different ways in which manorial resources were combined in Domesday England. Our estimates suggest that the equal-product curves for Domesday manors are similar to those drawn in Figure 6.1(c) (which are based upon our value–resources function in Chapter 5), except that the elasticity of substitution (i.e. a measure of the rate at which inputs are substituted for each other) is slightly higher (1.76 rather than 1.39). The equal-product curves, therefore, are convex to the point of origin, which means that attempts to substitute, say, villeins for plough-teams could only be achieved by giving up increasing numbers of villeins for a given number of plough-teams. In other words, Domesday manors experienced diminishing marginal rates of substitution.

These results are based upon the assumption that the conditions of substitution are the same for all pairs of resources. Further information about substitution can be obtained from the estimation of a less restrictive two-level (Sato) CES production function, which allows for different substitution behaviour between pairs of resources from different 'higher'-level categories of land, labour, and capital.[9] The results, which are discussed more formally in 10.8, suggest that substitution between pairs of resources from different 'higher'-level resource categories (land, labour, and capital) is somewhat less than perfect, but that within these categories individual resources are very highly substitutable. The substitution behaviour between these 'higher'-level categories can be represented graphically by Figure 6.3(c), where the equal-product curves are convex; and substitution within these categories can be represented by Figure 6.3(a), where the equal-product curves are straight lines. Hence, in the first case labour can be substituted for capital in order to maintain a given output only by adding an increasing number of peasants for a given unit of capital (diminishing marginal rates of substitution), whereas in the second case, bordars can be substituted for villeins, or peasants' plough-teams substituted for demesne plough-teams, at a constant rate. This conclusion is a close approximation to reality, and provides greater confidence in the overall results achieved by applying production functions of this type to the Domesday data. Also, it confirms an earlier conclusion about the different types of both plough-teams and labour: the main difference in contribution to output was in terms of hours worked on the demesne.

6.5.2.3 Manorial returns to scale

What can be said about returns to scale in the Domesday economy? The CES production function results in Table 6.1 show that the combined partial output elasticities amount to 1.15. Accordingly, if all manorial inputs are increased by 100 per cent, manorial net production will increase by approximately 115 per cent. The implication is that, on average, Domesday manors experienced modest increasing returns to scale. While this result is not greatly different from constant returns, there appears to have been a minor economic incentive to increase the size of manors in 1086. Clearly, the costs of supervising production on large manors were not proportionately greater than on small manors, or, at least, they were offset by economies in the use of plough-teams (or other resources). But, as was suggested earlier, the ability to increase manorial size was severely restricted by the nature of the feudal system in Domesday England, and by the lack of well-developed markets for the scarce resources of capital and labour. Finally, as production costs did not increase more rapidly than manorial size, it would appear that Fenoaltea (1975) has, in his debate with North and Thomas (1971), overrated the importance of supervision costs.

6.6   AN EXTENSION OF THE ESSEX 1086 RESULTS

While it is possible to apply sophisticated production functions only to Essex lay manors in 1086, these results can be extrapolated in an approximate way to other regions, to ecclesiastical manors, and to 1066. This can be done by using the simple production function framework employed in Chapter 5, which was applied to the more limited data for Wiltshire, and for 1066. A justification for this approach is that, generally speaking, the inferences drawn from both the simple CES and the Sato functions, when estimated for Essex lay data in 1086, are similar. We wish to emphasize, however, that our interest is not in the precise values of our results for these other regions, institutions, and period, but in their relation to Essex lay manors in 1086. Our concern, therefore, is with regional, institutional, and intertemporal differences in relation to the benchmark of Essex lay manors in 1086.

6.6.1 Regional differences

An approximate picture of regional differences in production methods can be obtained from Table 5.1 (p. 87). A comparison of Essex regression 4 and Wiltshire regression 2 reveals a number of important similarities, as well as some minor differences. The main characteristic these two regions have in common is that an increase in resources will lead to an increase in manorial output (in other words, marginal products of manorial resources are positive). There are differences, however, in the relative importance of the main resources. First, the relative contribution of plough-teams is considerably greater in Essex (55.8 per cent of the combined output elasticities) than in Wiltshire (41.9 per cent), which appears to be compensated for by the much greater role played by the non-arable resources of meadow and pasture in Wiltshire (20.9 per cent) than in Essex (10.6 per cent). The interesting implication, as foreshadowed in Chapter 5, is that pastoral activities were more important in Wiltshire than in Essex. Secondly, the contribution of peasant labour was somewhat higher in Wiltshire (26.7 per cent) than in Essex (18.3 per cent), which implies that, on average, manors in Wiltshire were more labour-intensive than those in Essex.

Further information about the substitution of resources in Wiltshire can be obtained by estimating the elasticity of substitution for manors in that county and comparing it with that for Essex manors. The elasticity of substitution for Wiltshire regression 2 in Table 5.1 is 1.35, which compares very closely with the figure of 1.39 for Essex regression 4. This suggests that, on average, the conditions of factor substitution on manors were very similar between the two counties: in particular, the shapes of the equal product curves are similar (and can be represented as (c) in Figure 6.3), exhibiting diminishing marginal rates of substitution.

Something can also be said about the returns to scale in Wiltshire by comparing the combined output elasticities for both counties. In Essex regression 4, the sum of output elasticities is 1.04, and that for Wiltshire regression 2 is 0.86. This is an interesting difference. When the more general CES production function in 6.5.2 was estimated for Essex, the combined output elasticity was 1.15, which suggested modest increasing returns to scale. If the Wiltshire result is adjusted by the same factor, a rough estimate of 0.95 is obtained for Wiltshire, which is very close to constant returns to scale. Therefore, if Essex can be said to have experienced modest increasing returns to scale, Wiltshire can be deemed to have operated under constant returns to scale. In other words, there was no economic incentive to increase the size of manors in Wiltshire, even if there had been any scope to do so.

6.6.2 Institutional differences

It is reasonable to expect differences in production methods as between lay and ecclesiastical manors, because of differences in both organization and size (see 5.4). To test for this, it is possible to compare lay and ecclesiastical manors in Essex by reference to Essex regression 4 in both Tables 5.1, and 5.2 (pp. 87 and 91). It can be seen that marginal products are positive in both cases, and that the relative contribution of resources to net production is similar, although for ecclesiastical manors the role of plough-teams (63.6 per cent) is slightly greater than that for lay manors (55.8 per cent). Also, it is interesting that the economic role of slaves on ecclesiastical manors (7.1 per cent) is less than that on lay manors (11.5 per cent) in Essex, which implies that Church slaves were employed to a greater extent in household (or religious) activities. In view of the differences in organization and size between lay and ecclesiastical manors, the overall similarity of these results is remarkable, and suggests a common form of technology.

Similar also are the combined output elasticities, 0.99 for ecclesiastical and 1.04 for lay manors, which suggests that returns to scale were almost identical. If these are adjusted in accordance with the more sophisticated results, it can be concluded that both lay and ecclesiastical manors experienced modest increasing returns to scale. Even the conditions of resource substitution were, on average, very similar, with an elasticity of substitution of 1.32 for ecclesiastical and 1.39 for lay manors.

6.6.3 Intertemporal differences

The best comparison that can be made between 1066 and 1086 is that for Essex lay manors. Even so, as there are only three main resources for 1066, this comparison is somewhat limited. Yet it is important to gain some impression of changes in production methods that may have taken place between the Anglo-Saxon and Anglo-Norman regimes. From Table 5.3 it can be seen that, overall, the results are basically similar, but that there are some differences concerning the relative contribution of the main resources. Plough-teams are more important for 1066 (78.7 per cent) than for 1086 (70.5 per cent), which is balanced by peasant labour being less important and slave labour more important in 1066 than 1086. Yet, as there is no pastoral variable, this result is not easy to interpret. It appears to mean that there was an increase in the relative importance of pastoral activities over these twenty years, and that the balance between slaves and peasants declined. Certainly, it is known from other sources that the latter was true. Overall, these results suggest that the English economy was becoming more diversified and more sophisticated.

Finally, the combined output elasticities in Table 5.3 indicate that the returns to scale were virtually identical in 1066 (0.94) and 1086 (0.95). When adjusted by our results in 6.5.2, this suggests that modest increasing returns to scale were experienced in both periods. Thus the economic incentive to increase the scale of production had not changed. In addition, conditions of resource substitution appear to have been only slightly different between 1066 (when the elasticity of substitution was 1.20) and 1086 (when it was 1.32). This suggests that the scope for substitution between resources was slightly greater at the time of the Survey than it had been at the time of the Conquest, due to a slight change in the system of production.

6.7   CONCLUSIONS

An attempt has been made in this chapter to analyse the results of applying reasonably sophisticated production functions to the Domesday data for Essex lay manors in 1086. These results have been extended to other regions, periods, and institutions by employing the more restricted results in Chapter 5. It has been possible to interpret these results by developing a simple economic model of manorial production in Domesday England. The model can be characterized in terms of a manorial lord producing tradable goods by the use of a common technology and a set of resources that are fixed in the short run. The manorial lord is unable to vary input levels in the short run, and therefore attempts to organize production in a technically efficient way so as to maximize the net value of production. In this manner the annual value–resource observations trace out (or define) the common agricultural technology. An important prediction of the manorial model, in contrast to that embodying perfect competition with variable inputs, is that manors will be operated with different combinations of resources and at different levels of production. This model is broadly consistent with the usual picture of the Domesday manor that is sketched from historical records.

The application of this model to our production function results has for the first time provided significant insights into the process of production in the Domesday economy. Previous scholarship has described the nature of economic institutions in this period, but has been unable to show exactly how the production process worked. Our analysis provides results of varying degrees of sophistication. Owing to the detailed data, we have been able to provide a well-focused image of the production process for Essex lay manors in 1086. Although less clearly focused, the images for Wiltshire, for ecclesiastical manors, and for 1066 add to our overall perception of the Anglo-Norman economy.

In the case of Essex lay manors, it was discovered that manorial production increased as resources or inputs increased, a conclusion denied by Darby (1977); that the increments to production diminished as one input, say villeins, was substituted for another, say plough-teams (diminishing marginal rates of substitution); that a given manorial output could be achieved with a wide range of resource combinations (a high degree of substitutability of resources); and that a doubling of all inputs resulted in slightly more than a doubling of output (modest increasing returns to scale). These results also confirm the dominance of arable farming, suggest that demesne plough-teams made a greater contribution to production than peasants' plough-teams, and suggest that the role of villeins was greater than that of bordars, which in turn was greater than that of slaves. Indeed, slaves appear to have worked to a greater degree in the lord's household than has hitherto been suspected.

While the main features of the production process for Essex lay manors have also been confirmed for Wiltshire, ecclesiastical estates, and 1066, a number of interesting differences have emerged. First, the main regional differences are that pastoral activity was relatively more important (but still subordinate to arable production) in Wiltshire than in Essex, and that Essex experienced modest increasing returns to scale while those for Wiltshire were constant. Secondly, the system of production in both lay and ecclesiastical manors was remarkably similar, given their differences in size and organization. The only marked difference is that slaves on ecclesiastical manors appear to have been less important as an economic resource, probably because their main duties were in the manorial households. Finally, the main intertemporal differences in the nature of manorial production appear to have been a growth in the role of pastoral activities and a decline in the role of slaves between 1066 and 1086.

The analysis in this chapter, therefore, has made it possible for the first time to show how the Domesday manorial economy functioned. What has been discovered could not have come to light without the application of economic and statistical techniques. Yet this is only the beginning of what can be achieved with techniques of this nature, as will be suggested in the following chapter.

Notes

1. In the first place, as the manorial lord was unable to vary inputs in the short run (that is, inputs were exogeneously determined), there are none of the usual problems of sorting out the causal connection between output and inputs that are determined together (simultaneity). Secondly, the serious problems, both conceptual and practical, associated with the measurement of capital inputs, do not apply, because the basic item of capital in the Domesday economy was the number of plough-teams.

2. Gross output subsumes all forms of manorial income including rents, customary dues and fines. These are, of course, all related to agricultural production on the manor.

3. Economic rents are defined as the return to those owning scarce resources, generally land. In Domesday England, however, land was abundant, and labour could be thought of as the scarce resource. Quasi-rents are defined as the return to owners of those resources the supply of which is inelastic, or fixed, in the short run. In Domesday England all resources were fixed in the short run.

4. As shown in 2.2.4, it was difficult, even for periods as long as seventeen years, to replace major losses in plough-teams.

5. The real Roger 'God Save the Ladies' (*Deus Salvet Dominas*), was a tenant-in-chief of the king in Essex, holding three manors at Rivenhall, Felsted, and Great Baddow, worth a modest total of 100 shillings.

6. For a more detailed and more technical discussion of the Sato function, see 9.10.

7. A similar range of resources is available for Norfolk and Suffolk (and, in more fragmented form, for the counties in Exon. Domesday), but the complexities, due to the influence of Danish settlement, make it very difficult to apply production functions.

8. This was not considered desirable in the case of the value–resources analysis in Chapter 5. First, direct comparisons between 1066 and 1086 would have been complicated by the very large relocation of labour between these detailed categories. Secondly, the labour categories differ between regions.

9. Because of their complexity the results have not been recorded here, but they can be found in 10.8.

7

Towards an economics of
Domesday England

7.1 INTRODUCTION

Our re-examination of Domesday Book, using contemporary economic and statistical techniques, has provided many new insights into the Anglo-Norman economy. By adopting a new approach to this period, it has been possible not only to demonstrate that the traditional economic interpretation is incorrect, but also to cast new light upon a number of central economic and political issues, and, most importantly, to reconstruct the system of manorial production in Domesday England. Yet this is only the beginning: it is, in the words of Maitland (1897, 407), 'intended to be no more than a distant approach towards the truth'. A fully comprehensive account of the Domesday economy will require further work of this nature in a number of new directions. It remains now to review what has been achieved, and to look ahead to what needs to be done: to look, that is, towards a definitive economics of Domesday England.[1]

7.2 A CONTRIBUTION TO DOMESDAY STUDIES

The contribution made to Domesday studies in this book can be reviewed under five headings: the reinterpretation of economic relationships; pitfalls in the application of the new approach to Domesday Book; new economic insights; wider political implications; and textual interpretation.

7.2.1 Reinterpretation of economic relationships

The traditional interpretation of economic relationships in Domesday England was based upon an inadequate analysis of the remarkable wealth of data contained in the document. In turn, this resulted from a failure to employ satisfactory statistical techniques. Indeed, the conclusions of the traditional scholars were based largely upon an impressionistic evaluation of the data, usually buttressed by a more formal, but still subjective, scrutiny of a handful of non-random observations. Only Maitland attempted to analyse a representative selection of Domesday entries. Unfortunately, he did not advance his claims, particularly in relation to Round's work, with sufficient vigour and clarity. As a result, Maitland's pioneering statistical work was overlooked, and was not taken further by other Domesday scholars, even after the development of scientific sampling and regression techniques in the 1910s and 1920s. The neglect of Maitland's work has until now resulted in the persistence of untenable economic interpretations.

The traditional interpretation concerns both the revenue-raising procedures of the Anglo-Saxon and Anglo-Norman states, and the operation of the Domesday economy at the manorial level. Traditionally it has been argued, on the first issue, that tax assessments for geld were imposed arbitrarily upon landholders and, on the second issue, that there is no systematic relationship between manorial annual values and resources. Neither interpretation makes any economic sense. Our initial reaction was that either the traditional interpretation was incorrect on both counts, or the data in Domesday Book were without meaning. The former appeared most likely, because of the great pains to which William went to obtain accurate data. By employing, in Chapters 4 and 5, regression analysis to examine all the lay and ecclesiastical data for Essex and Wiltshire in both 1066 and 1086, the traditional interpretation was found to be incorrect: there was an unusually strong and positive relationship both between tax assessments and capacity of manors to pay and between manorial annual values and resources. Further, the unusually good fit for each of our functions suggests that the Domesday data are highly reliable. These results, together with existing information about the procedures of William's Survey, suggest that the Domesday data contain considerably less measurement error than modern economic survey or census data.

7.2.2 Pitfalls in the new approach

Our statistical analysis, however, has highlighted a number of problems with the data in Domesday Book, for which appropriate allowance must be made. First, it was discovered that the conventional functional forms—the linear and log-linear—are generally not appropriate for estimating economic relationships from Domesday data. The linear form was not appropriate on any occasion, and the log-linear form was only a reasonable approximation for one relationship, that between assessments and values. It is important, therefore, to employ a statistical model (such as the Box–Cox extended model) which utilizes the data to estimate the most appropriate functional form, otherwise the relationship cannot be determined with precision. Secondly, it is essential to test the assumptions underlying regression analysis, particularly regarding homoskedasticity. If this is not done, inferences cannot be made with confidence, and unsound conclusions may be drawn.

7.2.3 New economic insights

In addition to clarifying the basic nature of economic relationships in the Domesday data, our analyses in Chapters 4 and 5 have brought to light interesting information about other economic issues. Probably the most interesting additional discovery concerns the highly consistent nature of the economic responses of manorial lords, which is reflected mainly by the strength of the relationship between manorial income and resources. The most convincing explanation of such high goodness-of-fit values (with $\bar{R}^2$ as high as 0.92) is that the manorial lords were attempting to maximize their incomes. Any other hypothesis, such as manorial lords (or their agents) responding to 'conventional rules', appears unsatisfactory. If the concept of 'conventional rules' is to have any meaning, these rules should be resistant to changing economic circumstances across regions and across time—for otherwise they would be little more than an illusion, masking the attempt by manorial lords to respond to changing conditions. But, if the rules were inflexible over the longer term in the face of regional economic changes, and if they were closely followed by all manorial lords, then it is highly unlikely that the goodness-of-fit coefficients would be as high as those in Tables 5.1 to 5.3 (pp. 87–93). Our results suggest that the 'production rule' adopted was highly responsive to economic conditions, which is the outcome one would expect if manorial lords displayed income-maximizing behaviour.

Secondly, our results in Chapters 4 and 5 provide new information about taxes and manorial income. It was discovered, for example, that the geld was not a land tax, as some have claimed, but either an income tax or a total resources tax. It was also found that the geld was a regressive tax, in that the marginal rate declined as income increased. There is even some evidence to suggest that tax deductions were granted on meadowland, in order to encourage lords to invest in programmes designed to extend this critical resource. Finally, it was shown that horses were not a determinant of manorial income, but were kept for the purposes of war and leisure.

7.2.4 Wider political implications

A number of political implications have emerged from the analysis of tax assessments in Chapter 4. First, as the assessments for geld were closely related to the capacity of manors to pay the impost, it is clear that William was not imposing his authority arbitrarily, but was acting in a way that would generate the least opposition and thereby return the greatest amount of taxes. In other words, William was acting in an economically rational way, which is consistent with the picture of him painted by the Anglo-Saxon Chronicler. This conclusion begs a further question. If William did not impose his authority arbitrarily in respect of taxes, it is possible that he did not do so in other spheres, such as the feudal demands he made upon his tenants-in-chief, particularly concerning knight service. This question will be investigated further, because the results presented in Chapter 4 provide strong grounds for thinking that William's rule, and possibly that of other medieval monarchs, was less arbitrary than has been thought previously.

Secondly, the ability of Anglo-Saxon and Anglo-Norman monarchs not only to adopt the concept of capacity to pay as the basis of their taxation programmes, but also to measure it so accurately, is direct evidence that state administrations in medieval England were highly sophisticated and efficient. These administrations were able to measure effectively the wealth of manorial lords despite the changing structure and growing complexity of the manorial economy in the eleventh century. Neither Round nor even Maitland appear to have appreciated the degree of administrative sophistication that had been reached by 1086, which accounts for their diverting preoccupation with attempts to discover simple administrative rules of thumb (such as the 'five-hide unit' and 'one pound, one hide'). The Anglo-Norman world was far too complex to be viewed so simply. While the attitude to this issue has changed considerably since the 1890s (see Harvey 1971; Campbell 1975), the evidence employed is of an indirect institutional nature. In contrast, we have been able directly to employ the data gathered by the Norman bureaucracy, in order to test the state's administrative effectiveness.

Thirdly, the results presented in Chapter 4 suggest that a review of the operation of territorial administration in Anglo-Norman England is required. Because Round's artificiality hypothesis must be rejected, it is also necessary to question the resulting emphasis that has been placed upon the role of the vill in relation to the manor (Loyn 1963). As the manor rather than the vill appears to have been the basis for tax assessment, the former should become the focus of greater attention than in the past. We are not, however, disputing the administrative role of the hundred.

Finally, the results in Chapter 5 demonstrate, contrary to the conventional wisdom, that the annual values can be used confidently as an index of wealth in studies of the relationship between economic and political power. Had Darby been correct, the annual values could not have been used to test this relationship. Other manorial variables, such as plough-teams, could also be employed for this purpose, but they are only partial indices, and will be misleading when variations in manorial economic structure (that is, the arable/pastoral relationship) are significant.[2] There are also problems involved in employing tax assessments as an index of economic power, because they do not reflect manorial endowments as strongly as do the annual values, and because some manors were assessed more leniently than others.

7.2.5 Textual interpretation

The results in earlier chapters have assisted in the interpretation of entries in Domesday Book. In the first place, as has been argued elsewhere, the statistical estimates in Chapters 4, 5, and 6 provide a sound basis for considerable confidence in the accuracy of Domesday data. These results provide independent confirmation of existing arguments about data accuracy, which have been based upon evidence concerning the administrative procedures employed in conducting the Survey (Harvey 1980). The problem with institutional evidence is that it impinges only indirectly upon the issue in question. It is possible, for example, for survey administrative procedures to be comprehensive, but for the recorded data to be riddled with major errors. By contrast, our results provide a direct test for the accuracy of the data in Domesday Book.

Secondly, it has been possible to resolve the important question of whether mill renders were included in the annual values. This issue is important because it has implications for the way in which the annual values are interpreted, and for the type of accounting procedure adopted: should the separate sums for annual values and mill renders be left as they are, added together, or subtracted one from the other? As we have been able to demonstrate in Chapter 5 that mill renders were not included in the annual values, the latter must be interpreted as the financial return to the rural activities, and the former to the industrial activities, on Domesday manors. The separate sums can now be dealt with sensibly, according to the purpose of the research in hand.

Finally, the estimates in Chapter 4 provide some ground for questioning whether the Wiltshire assessments were, as they appear from the text of Domesday Book, made prior to 1066. It may be the case that our results merely reflect less accurate data for 1066 than 1086, but further investigation of the issue appears warranted.

7.3 AN ECONOMICS OF DOMESDAY ENGLAND

7.3.1 What has been achieved?

It is possible to learn more about the economy of Domesday England than of any other until the twentieth century. The reasons are that the data in Domesday Book are remarkably detailed, uniquely comprehensive, and contain an unusually small proportion of measurement errors. Hence we are able to apply sophisticated economic and statistical techniques to this data. In fact, in some respects Domesday Book is more suitable for this purpose than modern sources, not only for data reasons, but also because the input–output relationship is considerably less complicated.

The results of estimating production functions, which have been discussed in Chapter 6, are very encouraging. With these estimates, we have been able to provide a detailed picture of the system of manorial production in Domesday England. While more sophisticated production functions, such as the Sato two-level CES, could only be applied Essex lay manors in 1086, the similarity of the inferences to those derived from simpler CES functions enabled an extrapolation of the detailed Essex results to other regions, periods, and institutional groupings. Interpretation of the production function results was considerably enhanced by characterizing or modelling the manorial system. In our model, the landholder attempts to maximize his income through the production of tradable goods, by utilizing a common technology and a set of resources that are fixed in the short run.

What do the estimates tell us about the manorial system in Domesday England? In the first place, the nature of the manorial economy was found to be remarkably similar between regions, over time, and across institutional divisions. Secondly, it was possible to quantify the structure of the manorial economy in Domesday England. For example, arable activities were more than twice as important as pastoral activities in 1086, and even more important in 1066. And, not surprisingly, there was some regional variation in economic structure. Thirdly, considerable definition was given to our picture of the process of manorial production. Contrary to the traditional interpretation, we found that manorial output was a positive function of inputs, and that a given level of output was produced with a wide range of resource combinations. It was also possible to quantify the relative contribution to manorial production of these resources—of demesne plough-teams, peasants' plough-teams, villeins, bordars, slaves, pasture, and meadow—for lay and ecclesiastical manors. And, finally it was shown that Domesday manors operated under either constant or modestly increasing returns to scale.

7.3.2 What further work is required?

Although substantial progress has been made in the above chapters, considerable further work will be required to write a definitive account of the Domesday economy. Yet the foundations have been laid, and we have a clearer idea concerning the form of the finished structure. It suggests that we will need to extend the macro-economic work in this volume to include additional counties that did not experience normal economic conditions in 1086, and also to undertake an analysis of micro-economic relationships (including that of manorial income distribution).

7.3.2.1 *Macro-economic relationships*

The macro-economic work in this book has been concerned only with the normal operation of the Domesday economy. Work at this aggregated level can be extended by analysing a sample of counties experiencing various types of economic problems, and by attempting a nationwide study. The first of these studies will involve an examination of the Domesday economy in crisis. Many English counties in 1086 were suffering from various forms and degrees of hardship. The southern counties, for example, were seriously affected in 1066 when the Conqueror's military forces moved in a great arc from Hastings to London. William's army consisted of more than 6,000 men (Stenton 1943, 593), together with large numbers of horses, all of which needed to live off the land as they went. In the two to three months that the Normans took to march to London, the numbers of livestock and reserves of food must have been severely depleted throughout the surrounding countryside. In addition, the rebellions of 1068, 1069–70, and 1075 had a devastating impact. William's savage policy of 'harrying the north' after the 1069–70 rebellion was so severe that substantial areas of Yorkshire were still waste in 1086. Finally, counties in border areas and along vulnerable coastlines suffered regularly from Viking and Celtic raids, as well as the defensive scorched-earth policies of English and Norman administrations.

A manor unfortunate enough to suffer heavy losses of ploughbeasts, livestock, and peasants could only recover slowly, because of insufficiently developed factor markets. A good illustration of this problem is provided (in 2.2.4) by a manor in Essex that lost half its peasants and plough-teams. In that example, the path to recovery was through diversification into sheep production, probably because sheep were more prolific breeders than oxen. It will be important, therefore, to analyse a sample of counties that were attempting to recover from similar economic problems.

A second extension of our work in the macro-economic field will involve analysing data at the national level. As mentioned earlier, by adopting this approach it will be necessary to negotiate considerable problems of both a technical and an interpretative nature. The technical problems, at least, can be tackled in the knowledge that the effort will be worthwhile, as it is now known that the data are sufficiently accurate. Also, the project will be less hazardous in the interpretative sense, because it will build upon knowledge gained from a number of regional studies. It will be easier to interpret the national results in the light of the earlier studies.

7.3.2.2 Micro-economic relationships

So far, only average economic relationships, at either the county or national levels, have been considered. Estimation of production functions at these levels of aggregation, however, can obscure a number of interesting features of the production process. For example, this approach lumps together large and small manors, arable and pastoral activity, manors close to towns and those isolated in the countryside, and manors held by lords with varying degrees of entrepreneurial talent. Differences in the Domesday economy may emerge if manors are arranged and analysed on the basis of size, specialization, nearness to towns, and ownership. By taking subsamples of the county data in this way, greater refinement of our production function estimates will be achieved. Work of this nature is feasible because of the large number of observations within each county. In a similar way, the issue of income distribution could be considered.

A few brief examples will illustrate the possibilities inherent in the micro-economic approach. In the first place, an assumption made in our production function work, that output prices are similar, is more likely to be met for small local areas in which manors are grouped around market towns. Working with subsamples of this nature will make it possible to obtain more refined production function estimates. It will also demonstrate the effect upon the structure and system of manorial production of proximity to markets. Secondly, it will be of considerable interest to discover how manorial production differs between the estates of different tenants-in-chief. To this end, we wish to isolate the estates of a sample of large landholders with manors scattered throughout England. In this way it should be possible to analyse the role played by the entrepreneur in the Domesday economy. Further, it will highlight the economic problems associated with the supervision of widely scattered estates. Thirdly, it will be important to consider the nature of income distribution arising from the Domesday system of manorial production. A promising framework for such an investigation has been provided by a recent speculative extension of game theory to encompass medieval institutions (David 1982).

There are many questions still to be answered, but, when the answers are forthcoming, a great deal will be known about the Domesday economy.

Notes

1. It is anticipated that this volume will be the first in a series of studies on the economics of Domesday England.
2. If a strong relationship between the annual values and manorial resources had not been found, considerable doubt would have been cast upon the reliability of other Domesday variables such as plough-teams.

PART II
ECONOMIC AND STATISTICAL METHODS

8

Statistical methods

8.1 INTRODUCTION

In most sciences, the principal method used to assess whether numerical evidence supports or contradicts a theory is statistical method. Often a theory can be represented in terms of a relationship between variables, an example being the relationship between manorial tax assessments and annual values. Given a set of data on manorial assessments and values, statistical analysis can be applied to determine whether or not a relationship exists and, if so, to quantify that relationship.

In this chapter we have attempted to convey some of the flavour of statistical method and to explain the statistical procedures employed in Part I. The chapter is not a general introduction to cliometrics or econometrics; rather, our aim has been to provide an intuitive understanding of the statistical methods, and to document clearly where proofs and further information are available in the literature. As the statistical results have been derived many times in the literature, few proofs are given. We have also attempted to reduce the notation to a minimum. There are many excellent introductory texts on econometrics, including Intriligator (1978); Kmenta (1971); Pindyck and Rubinfeld (1981); and Thomas (1973). More advanced books are Judge *et al.* (1980); Schmidt (1976); and Theil (1971).

The plan of the chapter is as follows. In 8.2 we explain how a scatter of observations on two variables can be summarized by the least squares method. An alternative justification for the least squares method in terms of sampling properties is given in 8.3; and the key concepts of a model, an estimator, and the sampling distribution of an estimator are illustrated in 8.4. The properties of the least squares method, given that the data are generated by the normal regression model, are then summarized in 8.5. Section 8.6 is concerned with using a computer to undertake the least squares calculations, and 8.7 with the properties of the least squares estimators when the sample size is large. An alternative estimation procedure, maximum likelihood estimation, is introduced in 8.8. Section 8.9 generalizes the methods to allow for several explanatory variables. In 8.10 and 8.11, the problems of establishing the functional form of a relationship using the Box–Cox method, and variation in the variance of the regression disturbances, or heteroskedasticity, are discussed. Some tests for functional form and heteroskedasticity are described in 8.12. In 8.13 we apply the Box–Cox extended maximum likelihood method, allowing for heteroskedastic disturbances, to the Essex lay annual value–resources 1086 data; and, finally, in 8.14, we describe some simpler estimation procedures that can be carried out with less sophisticated computer software.

8.2 SUMMARIZING A SCATTER OF OBSERVATIONS BY THE LEAST SQUARES METHOD

In Table 8.1 we have listed data on tax assessments and annual values relating to a sample of ten manors. The data are the (natural) logarithms of the assessments (expressed in fiscal acres) and annual values (expressed in shillings) of the ten manors. The reason for taking logarithms will be explained in sections 8.10 and 8.14. In Part I, we postulated that tax assessments depend on the manorial annual values; consequently we will call the logarithm of assessment the *dependent variable* and the logarithm of annual value an *explanatory variable*.

Table 8.1. The logarithm of the tax assessments (y_t) and annual values (x_t) of ten manors

Manor number	Logarithm of tax assessment y_t	Logarithm of annual value x_t
1	3.8	2.0
2	5.0	2.3
3	6.8	6.0
4	5.2	3.4
5	6.0	3.8
6	7.6	5.2
7	6.4	4.2
8	5.4	4.0
9	4.2	1.6
10	4.2	2.2

The data can be exhibited on a scatter diagram (see Figure 8.1). On this diagram the dependent variable, the logarithm of tax assessment, is measured on the vertical axis, and the explanatory variable, the logarithm of annual value, along the horizontal axis. We will denote the logarithm of tax assessment for the first manor, y_1 and the logarithm of annual value for this manor, x_1. The joint observation, (x_1, y_1), relating to the first manor is represented by the scatter point in the bottom left-hand corner of the scatter diagram, which is located a distance representing 3.8 upwards and 2.0 rightwards from the origin. The other nine joint observations can be similarly represented by scatter points on the diagram. In total, then, there are ten joint

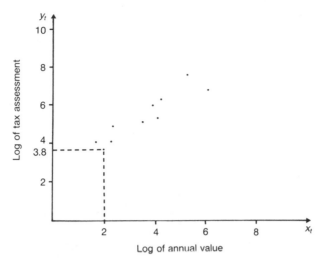

Figure 8.1. Scatter diagram of logarithm of tax assessment against logarithm of annual value for ten manors.

observations on tax assessments and annual value which give rise to ten scatter points on the diagram. The typical joint observation can be denoted (x_t, y_t) where t takes the value 1 for the first manor, 2 for the second manor and 10 for the last. The ten observations can be denoted (x_t, y_t), $t = 1, 2, \ldots 10$.

The scatter points approximately trace out a line. This suggests that we can *summarize the information in the scatter diagram* by a straight line fitted through the scatter points. One possibility is to fit a line by eye. A problem with this approach is that, since ideas on the line that best fits the scatter will differ, different people will fit different lines to the scatter. A more objective fitting procedure is to fit a line so that the sum of squared deviations of the fitted line from the scatter of points is as small as possible. We will measure the deviations in the vertical direction. The criterion for fitting the line, then, is to *fit the line that minimizes the sum of squared deviations measured in the vertical direction.*

To see more clearly what this means, consider Figure 8.2, in which three joint observations (x_1, y_1), (x_2, y_2) and (x_3, y_3) are plotted. Superimposed on the diagram is a (any) line. $\hat{e}_1$ is the vertical deviation of the first scatter point (x_1, y_1) from the line. $\hat{e}_2$ is the vertical deviation of (x_2, y_2) from the line and $\hat{e}_3$ is the vertical deviation of the third scatter point (x_3, y_3) from the line. The criterion for fitting the line which best summarizes the average relationship exhibited by the scatter is to fit the line so that the sum of squared vertical deviations is as small as possible, that is, fit the line for which $\hat{e}_1^2 + \hat{e}_2^2 + \hat{e}_3^2$ is minimized. If there were n joint observations on the dependent and explanatory variables, then the criterion would be to fit the line such that $\hat{e}_1^2 +$

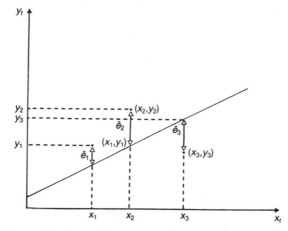

Figure 8.2. Measuring vertical deviations from a line

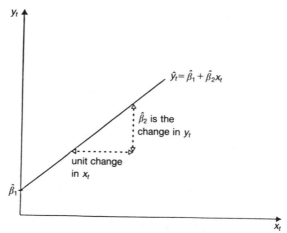

Figure 8.3. The equation for a straight line

$\hat{e}_2^2 + \ldots + \hat{e}_n^2$ is minimized. A shorthand way of writing $\hat{e}_1^2 + \hat{e}_2^2 + \ldots + \hat{e}_n^2$ is $\sum_{t=1}^{n} \hat{e}_t^2$, which says, sum the $\hat{e}_t^2$ from $t = 1$ to $t = n$.

We can now write the criterion in another way. The equation for a straight line with slope $\hat{\beta}_2$ and vertical intercept $\hat{\beta}_1$ is

$$\hat{y}_t = \hat{\beta}_1 + \hat{\beta}_2 x_t$$

In Figure 8.3 we see that $\hat{\beta}_1$, the vertical intercept, is the value on the y_t-axis where the line cuts this axis, and the slope $\hat{\beta}_2$ is equal to the change in y_t (when we move along the line) resulting from a unit change in x_t. As an example,

$$\hat{y}_t = 3 + 2x_t$$

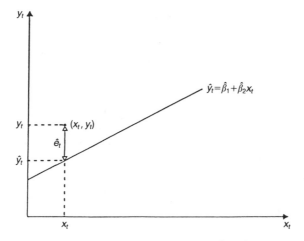

Figure 8.4. Showing that $\hat{e}_t = y_t - \hat{\beta}_1 - \hat{\beta}_2 x_t$

represents the line that cuts the y_t-axis at $y_t = 3$ and has a slope of 2, that is, a unit change in x_t results in a 2-unit change in y_t. In Figure 8.4, the line $\hat{y}_t = \hat{\beta}_1 + \hat{\beta}_2 x_t$ and a joint observation (x_t, y_t) are shown. The vertical deviation of the scatter point from the line is $\hat{e}_t$, which is equal to $y_t - \hat{y}_t$,

that is, $$\hat{e}_t = y_t - \hat{y}_t$$

But, $$\hat{y}_t = \hat{\beta}_1 + \hat{\beta}_2 x_t$$

so, $$\hat{e}_t = y_t - \hat{\beta}_1 - \hat{\beta}_2 x_t$$

The criterion for fitting the line is to fit the line so that $\sum_{t=1}^{n} \hat{e}_t^2$ is minimized, or, equivalently, $\sum_{t=1}^{n} (y_t - \hat{\beta}_1 - \hat{\beta}_2 x_t)^2$ is minimized.

This criterion for fitting a straight line to a scatter diagram is called the *least squares* (**LS**) criterion. The values $\hat{\beta}_1$ and $\hat{\beta}_2$, which minimize the sum of squared deviations measured in the vertical direction, are called the least squares (**LS**) estimates. We will denote them by b_1 and b_2.

If the mean value of the observations on the explanatory variable, x_t, is denoted $\bar{x}$ (that is, $\bar{x} = (x_1 + x_2 + \ldots + x_n)/n$) and the mean value of the observations on the dependent variable by $\bar{y}$ (that is, $\bar{y} = (y_1 + y_2 + \ldots + y_n)/n$), then it can be shown that

$$b_2 = \frac{\sum_{t=1}^{n} (y_t - \bar{y})(x_t - \bar{x})}{\sum_{t=1}^{n} (x_t - \bar{x})^2}$$

and $$b_1 = \bar{y} - b_2 \bar{x}.^1$$

For a given value of the explanatory variable, x_t, the LS estimate of y_t will be denoted $\tilde{y}_t$, so $\tilde{y}_t = b_1 + b_2 x_t$.

We will denote the LS vertical deviation or residual associated with the t-th joint observation (x_t, y_t) by e_t, so $e_t = y_t - \tilde{y}_t$. Also, since $\tilde{y}_t = b_1 + b_2 x_t$, $e_t = y_t - b_1 - b_2 x_t$. (It should be noted that $\hat{\beta}_1, \hat{\beta}_2, \hat{y}_t$ and $\hat{e}_t$ relate to *any* arbitrarily chosen line, and $b_1, b_2, \tilde{y}_t$ and e_t relate to the LS fitted line.)

To illustrate these ideas we will use the data on the logarithm of tax assessments and annual values for the ten manors listed in Table 8.1, to calculate the LS estimates b_1 and b_2. We will then superimpose the LS fitted line on the scatter diagram, Figure 8.1. Finally, we will calculate the LS estimates of the dependent variable, y_t, corresponding to the explanatory variable observations for the ten manors and calculate the LS residuals. (In order to simplify calculations, we will work to one decimal place only; in practice, however, more figures should be calculated to ensure accuracy.)

Illustration

$y_1 = 3.8$	$x_1 = 2.0$
$y_2 = 5.0$	$x_2 = 2.3$
$y_3 = 6.8$	$x_3 = 6.0$
$y_4 = 5.2$	$x_4 = 3.4$
$y_5 = 6.0$	$x_5 = 3.8$
$y_6 = 7.6$	$x_6 = 5.2$
$y_7 = 6.4$	$x_7 = 4.2$
$y_8 = 5.4$	$x_8 = 4.0$
$y_9 = 4.2$	$x_9 = 1.6$
$y_{10} = 4.2$	$x_{10} = 2.2$

$$\sum_{t=1}^{10} y_t = 54.6 \qquad \sum_{t=1}^{10} x_t = 34.7$$

$\bar{y} = 5.46$ or 5.5 to one decimal place $\bar{x} = 3.47$ or 3.5 to one decimal place

$y_1 - \bar{y} = -1.7$	$x_1 - \bar{x} = -1.5$	$(y_1 - \bar{y})(x_1 - \bar{x}) = 2.6$	$(x_1 - \bar{x})^2 = 2.3$
$y_2 - \bar{y} = -0.5$	$x_2 - \bar{x} = -1.2$	$(y_2 - \bar{y})(x_2 - \bar{x}) = 0.6$	$(x_2 - \bar{x})^2 = 1.4$
$y_3 - \bar{y} = 1.3$	$x_3 - \bar{x} = 2.5$	$(y_3 - \bar{y})(x_3 - \bar{x}) = 3.3$	$(x_3 - \bar{x})^2 = 6.3$
$y_4 - \bar{y} = -0.3$	$x_4 - \bar{x} = -0.1$	$(y_4 - \bar{y})(x_4 - \bar{x}) = 0.0$	$(x_4 - \bar{x})^2 = 0.0$
$y_5 - \bar{y} = 0.5$	$x_5 - \bar{x} = 0.3$	$(y_5 - \bar{y})(x_5 - \bar{x}) = 0.2$	$(x_5 - \bar{x})^2 = 0.1$
$y_6 - \bar{y} = 2.1$	$x_6 - \bar{x} = 1.7$	$(y_6 - \bar{y})(x_6 - \bar{x}) = 3.6$	$(x_6 - \bar{x})^2 = 2.9$
$y_7 - \bar{y} = 0.9$	$x_7 - \bar{x} = 0.7$	$(y_7 - \bar{y})(x_7 - \bar{x}) = 0.6$	$(x_7 - \bar{x})^2 = 0.5$
$y_8 - \bar{y} = -0.1$	$x_8 - \bar{x} = 0.5$	$(y_8 - \bar{y})(x_8 - \bar{x}) = -0.1$	$(x_8 - \bar{x})^2 = 0.3$
$y_9 - \bar{y} = -1.3$	$x_9 - \bar{x} = -1.9$	$(y_9 - \bar{y})(x_9 - \bar{x}) = 2.5$	$(x_9 - \bar{x})^2 = 3.6$
$y_{10} - \bar{y} = -1.3$	$x_{10} - \bar{x} = -1.3$	$(y_{10} - \bar{y})(x_{10} - \bar{x}) = 1.7$	$(x_{10} - \bar{x})^2 = 1.7$

$$\sum_{t=1}^{10} (y_t - \bar{y})(x_t - \bar{x}) = 15.0 \qquad \sum_{t=1}^{10} (x_t - \bar{x})^2 = 19.1$$

$$b_2 = \frac{\sum\limits_{t=1}^{10}(y_t - \bar{y})(x_t - \bar{x})}{\sum\limits_{t=1}^{10}(x_t - \bar{x})^2} = \frac{15.0}{19.1} = 0.8 \text{ (to one decimal place).}$$

$$b_1 = \bar{y} - b_2\bar{x} = 5.5 - 0.8(3.5) = 2.7$$

The LS line (or regression equation) is $\tilde{y}_t = 2.7 + 0.8x_t$. This line cuts the y_t-axis at $y_t = b_1 = 2.7$, so the line goes through the point $x_t = 0$, $y_t = 2.7$, which can be denoted $(0, 2.7)$. Its slope is $b_2 = 0.8$, that is, a unit change in x_t results in a 0.8 increase in y_t. Hence, since the line goes through the point $x_t = 0$, $y_t = 2.7$, it also goes through the point $x_t = 0 + 1$, $y_t = 2.7 + 0.8$ or $(1, 3.5)$. The LS fitted line is the line passing through these two points on the scatter diagram (see Figure 8.5).

The LS estimate of the dependent variable when the explanatory variable is $x_1 = 2.0$ is $\tilde{y}_1 = 2.7 + 0.8(2.0) = 4.3$.

Similarly, $\tilde{y}_2 = 2.7 + 0.8(2.3) = 4.5$.

The LS residual associated with the first manor is

$$e_1 = y_1 - \tilde{y}_1 = 3.8 - 4.3 = -0.5$$

Similarly,

$$e_2 = y_2 - \tilde{y}_2 = 5.0 - 4.5 = 0.5$$

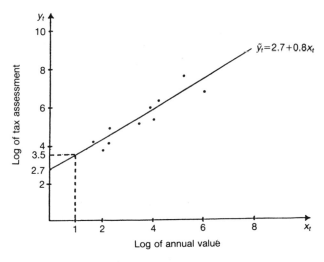

Figure 8.5. Scatter diagram and LS fitted line for logarithm of tax assessment against logarithm of annual value for ten manors

The LS estimates of the dependent variable and the LS residuals for the ten manors are listed below.

Manor	Dependent variable y_t	LS estimate of dependent variable $\tilde{y}_t$	LS residual e_t
1	3.8	4.3	−0.5
2	5.0	4.5	0.5
3	6.8	7.5	−0.7
4	5.2	5.4	−0.2
5	6.0	5.7	0.3
6	7.6	6.9	0.7
7	6.4	6.1	0.3
8	5.4	5.9	−0.5
9	4.2	4.0	0.2
10	4.2	4.5	−0.3

The LS fitted line measures the *average relationship* between the dependent and explanatory variables. Usually the fitted line will not pass through all the points on the scatter diagram. It is useful, then, to have some measure of the *dispersion* of scatter points about the average relationship. A measure of 'goodness of fit' or dispersion of the scatter points about the LS line is the *coefficient of determination*, denoted R^2, and defined

$$R^2 = \frac{\sum_{t=1}^{n} (\tilde{y}_t - \bar{y})^2}{\sum_{t=1}^{n} (y_t - \bar{y})^2}$$

R^2 is the ratio of two sums of squares. The numerator (top) is the sum of squares of the LS estimated dependent variable values about $\bar{y}$. The denominator is the sum of squares of the observed dependent variable values about $\bar{y}$.

R^2 is greater than or equal to zero (written $R^2 \geqslant 0$), because the square of any number other than zero is a positive number, so the sum of squared numbers must be positive or zero, as must the ratio of two sums of squares. horizontal, whatever the value of the explanatory variable, the LS estimated value of the dependent variable is equal to $\bar{y}$, so that the fitted line suggests that

R^2 is also less than or equal to one (written $R^2 \leqslant 1$), as can be shown by the following argument. First, it can be shown that

$$\sum_{t=1}^{n} (\tilde{y}_t - \bar{y})^2 = \sum_{t=1}^{n} (y_t - \bar{y})^2 - \sum_{t=1}^{n} e_t^2$$

that is, the sum of squares of the LS estimated dependent variable values about $\bar{y}$ is equal to the sum of squares of the observed dependent variable values about $\bar{y}$ minus the sum of squares of the LS residuals.[2] Secondly, notice that $\sum_{t=1}^{n} (\tilde{y}_t - \bar{y})^2$, $\sum_{t=1}^{n} (y_t - \bar{y})^2$ and $\sum_{t=1}^{n} e_t^2$ are all sums of squares and hence cannot be negative numbers. It follows that $\sum_{t=1}^{n} (\tilde{y}_t - \bar{y})^2$ cannot be larger than $\sum_{t=1}^{n} (y_t - \bar{y})^2$ and will be smaller if $\sum_{t=1}^{n} e_t^2$ is not zero. Consequently $R^2 \leqslant 1$.

To understand how R^2 measures the dispersion of scatter points about the LS line, it is useful to consider the two polar cases, $R^2 = 1$ and $R^2 = 0$.

Case 1. If the LS fitted line is not a horizontal line and passes through all the scatter points, then all the LS estimated values of the dependent variable will equal the observed values, that is, $\tilde{y}_t = y_t$, all t, hence $\sum_{t=1}^{n} (\tilde{y}_t - \bar{y})^2 = \sum_{t=1}^{n} (y_t - \bar{y})^2$ and $R^2 = 1$. Figure 8.6 illustrates this case. Notice that all the LS residuals are zero, that is, $e_t = 0$, all t, and hence $\sum_{t=1}^{n} e_t^2 = 0$.

Case 2. If, as in Figure 8.7, the LS fitted line is horizontal, so that $b_2 = 0$, then the LS estimated dependent variable values will all equal $\bar{y}$, that is, $\tilde{y}_t = \bar{y}$, all t, hence $\sum_{t=1}^{n} (\tilde{y}_t - \bar{y})^2 = 0$ and $R^2 = 0$. Notice that if the LS fitted line is

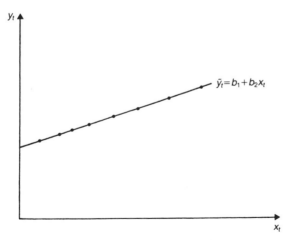

Figure 8.6. The case when $R^2 = 1$

the explanatory variable does not help to explain the behaviour of the dependent variable.

We have shown that R^2 may take the values 0 or 1 or any value between 0 and 1. If, for a given sample, the value of the explanatory variable exactly determines the value of the dependent variable, then $R^2 = 1$. If the explanatory variable does not in fact help to explain the behaviour of the dependent variable, then $R^2 = 0$. Generally speaking, the closer the value of R^2 to unity, the greater the explanatory power of the explanatory variable and the smaller the dispersion of scatter points about the LS fitted line. A value of R^2 close to zero indicates that, for the sample, the explanatory variable does not explain the behaviour well and corresponds to a wide dispersion of scatter points about the fitted LS line.[3]

The value of R^2 for the illustrative example involving ten manors can be calculated as follows. (Again, for simplicity all calculations are made to one decimal place.)

$y_1 - \bar{y} = -1.7$	$(y_1 - \bar{y})^2 = 2.9$	$\tilde{y}_1 - \bar{y} = -1.2$	$(\tilde{y}_1 - \bar{y})^2 = 1.4$
$y_2 - \bar{y} = -0.5$	$(y_2 - \bar{y})^2 = 0.3$	$\tilde{y}_2 - \bar{y} = -1.0$	$(\tilde{y}_2 - \bar{y})^2 = 1.0$
$y_3 - \bar{y} = 1.3$	$(y_3 - \bar{y})^2 = 1.7$	$\tilde{y}_3 - \bar{y} = 2.0$	$(\tilde{y}_3 - \bar{y})^2 = 4.0$
$y_4 - \bar{y} = -0.3$	$(y_4 - \bar{y})^2 = 0.1$	$\tilde{y}_4 - \bar{y} = -0.1$	$(\tilde{y}_4 - \bar{y})^2 = 0.0$
$y_5 - \bar{y} = 0.5$	$(y_5 - \bar{y})^2 = 0.3$	$\tilde{y}_5 - \bar{y} = 0.2$	$(\tilde{y}_5 - \bar{y})^2 = 0.0$
$y_6 - \bar{y} = 2.1$	$(y_6 - \bar{y})^2 = 4.4$	$\tilde{y}_6 - \bar{y} = 1.4$	$(\tilde{y}_6 - \bar{y})^2 = 2.0$
$y_7 - \bar{y} = 0.9$	$(y_7 - \bar{y})^2 = 0.8$	$\tilde{y}_7 - \bar{y} = 0.6$	$(\tilde{y}_7 - \bar{y})^2 = 0.4$
$y_8 - \bar{y} = -0.1$	$(y_8 - \bar{y})^2 = 0.0$	$\tilde{y}_8 - \bar{y} = 0.4$	$(\tilde{y}_8 - \bar{y})^2 = 0.2$
$y_9 - \bar{y} = -1.3$	$(y_9 - \bar{y})^2 = 1.7$	$\tilde{y}_9 - \bar{y} = -1.5$	$(\tilde{y}_9 - \bar{y})^2 = 2.3$
$y_{10} - \bar{y} = -1.3$	$(y_{10} - \bar{y})^2 = 1.7$	$\tilde{y}_{10} - \bar{y} = -1.0$	$(\tilde{y}_{10} - \bar{y})^2 = 1.0$

$$\sum_{t=1}^{10} (y_t - \bar{y})^2 = 13.9 \qquad\qquad \sum_{t=1}^{10} (\tilde{y}_t - \bar{y})^2 = 12.3$$

$$R^2 = \frac{\sum (\tilde{y}_t - \bar{y})^2}{\sum (y_t - \bar{y})^2} = \frac{12.3}{13.9} = 0.9 \text{ (to one decimal place)}$$

The analysis can be summarized as follows. We obtained data on the logarithm of manorial tax assessments and annual values. Economic theory suggests that we regard the logarithm of tax as the *dependent variable* (denoted by y_t) and the logarithm of annual value as an *explanatory variable* (denoted by x_t). We constructed a *scatter diagram* of the logarithm of tax assessment against the logarithm of annual value. The *average relationship* between the logarithm of assessment and annual value can be represented by a straight line. An objective criterion (called the LS criterion) for fitting the line is to minimize the sum of squared deviations measured in the vertical direction. A measure of

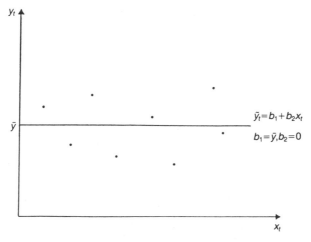

Figure 8.7. The case when $R^2 = 0$

dispersion of the scatter points about the LS line is given by the coefficient of determination, R^2.

8.3 THE LEAST SQUARES METHOD: JUSTIFICATION IN TERMS OF SAMPLING PROPERTIES

The LS method was introduced as an objective criterion for summarizing a scatter diagram. Clearly, other reasonable criteria exist—for example, minimizing the sum of squared deviations in the horizontal direction (see Figure 8.8a), and minimizing the sum of squared deviations measured in the direction at right angles to the fitted line (see Figure 8.8b). The latter method is sometimes called orthogonal regression. If there is little scatter about the fitted line (that is, R^2 is close to 1) then, if we use any of these methods, the fitted lines will be similar. Intuitively, since we are usually interested in estimating the dependent variable for given values of the explanatory variable, it may seem more reasonable to minimize the sum of squared deviations measured in the vertical direction.

The use of the LS method can, however, be justified by an entirely different argument. It can be shown that the LS method of fitting the line often has good sampling properties. In order to clarify the meaning of this statement, it is useful to introduce the ideas of a *random variable*, an *estimator*, and a *model* or mechanism generating the data.

First, let us see how the idea of a *random variable* arises. Consider the simple *random* situation or *experiment* of tossing a coin. There are two possible outcomes: obtaining a head or a tail. If the coin is a regular coin and it is tossed fairly, then the probability of occurrence of either outcome is one-half. The set

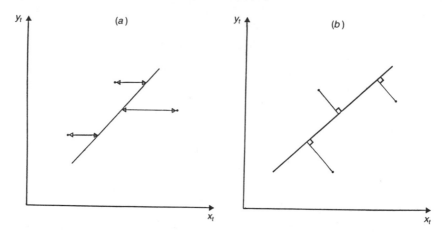

Figure 8.8. Measuring deviations (a) in the horizontal direction and (b) in the direction at right angles to the fitted line

of all possible outcomes together with the associated probabilities of occurrence of the outcomes is called the *sample space* of the experiment. Now, a random variable is a function defined over the sample space. An example of a random variable defined over this sample space is

$$z, \text{ where } z = 1 \text{ if a head occurs}$$
$$z = -1 \text{ if a tail occurs}$$

Notice that the probability that z takes the value 1 is one-half and the probability that z takes the value -1 is also one-half. More generally, a random variable is a variable which can take different numerical values each with a probability of less than one, such that the sum of the probabilities is one. The list of all possible values and the probabilities with which each occur is called the *probability distribution* of the random variable. This information can be presented in a tabular or graphic form (see Figure 8.9). The concepts explored above are summarized in Figure 8.10. Notice that, in the figures, the probability distribution of z is denoted $f(z)$, and, since $z = 1$ with probability one half and $z = -1$ with probability one half, $f(1) = \frac{1}{2}$ and $f(-1) = \frac{1}{2}$.

A slightly more complex random experiment is throwing a die. There are now six possible outcomes, each with probability of occurrence of one sixth. One way we can define a random variable—call it w—on this random experiment is by assigning the number 10 if the die outcome is 1, 20 if the die outcome is 2, 30 if it is 3, and so on. These definitions are summarized in Figure 8.11.

It is often useful to summarize the probability distribution of a random variable by a measure of central tendency and a measure of spread or dispersion of the distribution. A measure of central tendency is the *mean* or *expected value* of the random variable. The mean is simply the weighted

Tabular representation

Value taken by z	Probability that z takes this value, denoted $f(z)$
$z = 1$	$f(1) = \frac{1}{2}$
$z = -1$	$f(-1) = \frac{1}{2}$

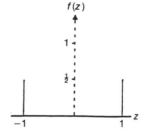

This table can be represented more succinctly as:

z	$f(z)$
1	$\frac{1}{2}$
-1	$\frac{1}{2}$

Figure 8.9. Probability distribution of the random variable z

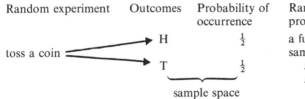

Random experiment	Outcomes	Probability of occurrence	Random variable z with a probability distribution $f(z)$
toss a coin	H	$\frac{1}{2}$	a function defined over the sample space such that
	T	$\frac{1}{2}$	$z = 1$ if H: $f(1) = \frac{1}{2}$ $z = -1$ if T: $f(-1) = \frac{1}{2}$

sample space

Figure 8.10. Summary of concepts relating to the random variable z

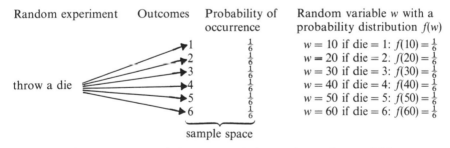

Random experiment	Outcomes	Probability of occurrence	Random variable w with a probability distribution $f(w)$
throw a die	1	$\frac{1}{6}$	$w = 10$ if die $= 1$: $f(10) = \frac{1}{6}$
	2	$\frac{1}{6}$	$w = 20$ if die $= 2$: $f(20) = \frac{1}{6}$
	3	$\frac{1}{6}$	$w = 30$ if die $= 3$: $f(30) = \frac{1}{6}$
	4	$\frac{1}{6}$	$w = 40$ if die $= 4$: $f(40) = \frac{1}{6}$
	5	$\frac{1}{6}$	$w = 50$ if die $= 5$: $f(50) = \frac{1}{6}$
	6	$\frac{1}{6}$	$w = 60$ if die $= 6$: $f(60) = \frac{1}{6}$

sample space

Figure 8.11. Summary of concepts relating to the random variable w

average of the possible values the random variable can take, with the probabilities of the respective values as weights. The mean of z, written $E(z)$, is therefore: one times one-half plus minus one times one-half equals zero, that is,

$$E(z) = 1(\tfrac{1}{2}) + (-1)(\tfrac{1}{2}) = 0$$

The expected value of w is

$$E(w) = 10(\tfrac{1}{6}) + 20(\tfrac{1}{6}) + 30(\tfrac{1}{6}) + 40(\tfrac{1}{6}) + 50(\tfrac{1}{6}) + 60(\tfrac{1}{6}) = 35$$

The *variance* of a random variable is a measure of spread or dispersion about the mean. It is the weighted average of the squares of the deviations from the mean of values the random variable can take, with the probabilities of the respective values as weights. The variance of z, denoted $\mathrm{Var}(z)$, is therefore,

$$\mathrm{Var}(z) = (1-0)^2(\tfrac{1}{2}) + (-1-0)^2(\tfrac{1}{2}) = 1$$

The variance of w is

$$\mathrm{Var}(w) = (10-35)^2(\tfrac{1}{6}) + (20-35)^2(\tfrac{1}{6}) + (30-35)^2(\tfrac{1}{6}) + (40-35)^2(\tfrac{1}{6})$$
$$+ (50-35)^2(\tfrac{1}{6}) + (60-35)^2(\tfrac{1}{6})$$
$$= 625(\tfrac{1}{6}) + 225(\tfrac{1}{6}) + 25(\tfrac{1}{6}) + 25(\tfrac{1}{6}) + 225(\tfrac{1}{6}) + 625(\tfrac{1}{6})$$
$$= 291.7$$

The (positive) square root of the variance is called the *standard deviation* of the random variable. The standard deviation of z, denoted $\mathrm{SD}(z)$, is therefore

$$\mathrm{SD}(z) = \text{square root } (1) = 1$$

and

$$\mathrm{SD}(w) = \text{square root } (291.7) = 17.1$$

The mean, variance and standard deviation are sometimes referred to as *parameters* of the distribution of the random variable.

The two random variables z and w are an example of two *independent* random variables. They are independent because the value that z takes is completely unrelated to the value that w takes. (This is clearly the case, because z and w are generated by entirely unrelated random experiments.) Another example of independent random variables is the following. Suppose now we toss a coin twice. Let the first toss generate a random variable z_1, defined such that $z_1 = 1$ if a head occurs, $z_1 = -1$ if a tail occurs; and the second toss generate z_2 such that $z_2 = 1$ if a head occurs, $z_2 = -1$ if a tail occurs. The two random variables z_1 and z_2 are independent random variables because the outcome of the second toss does not depend on the outcome of the first toss. Let us now define a random variable z^* as being equal to the sum of z_1 and z_2, that is, $z^* = z_1 + z_2$ (so that if, for example, we obtain a head on the first toss and a tail on the second $z^* = 1 + (-1) = 0$). z^* is clearly not independent of either z_1 or z_2.

The random variables we have considered so far are examples of *discrete* random variables, that is, they are random variables that can only take a specific number of (real) values. Sometimes it is useful to define random variables which can take any (real) value. These are called *continuous* random variables. An example is the normal random variable u, the probability distribution of which is graphed in Figure 8.12. The normal distribution has a bell shape, and is symmetrical about its mean (in this case zero). The probability distribution, $f(u)$, can no longer be interpreted as the probability

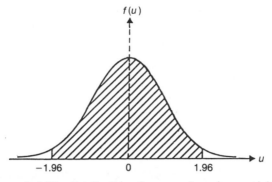

Figure 8.12. The probability distribution of a normal random variable u with mean zero and variance equal to one

that u takes a particular value. However, the area under the curve does have a probability interpretation. For example, for the normal random variable u which has a mean of zero and variance equal to one (that is, $E(u) = 0$ and $\text{Var}(u) = 1$), it can be shown that 95 per cent of the area under the curve (the shaded area) lies between $u = -1.96$ and $u = 1.96$, and the probability that u will take a value between -1.96 and 1.96 is 0.95. Other continuous random variables we will be examining are the 't' and 'F' random variables which follow t and F distributions, respectively.[4]

The random variables z_1 and z_2 have the same probability distribution. It is sometimes useful to regard them as a *sample* of two observations on the same random variable z, defined as $z = 1$ if a head occurs, $z = -1$ if a tail occurs. Now let us suppose that we do not know the probability distribution of z but we do have the two observations z_1 and z_2. We may wish to estimate the mean of the distribution of z. An obvious rule would be to use the *sample mean*, that is, the sum of the two observations divided by two. The sample mean is an example of an *estimator*. An estimator of a parameter (such as the mean of z) is simply a method or rule for determining an estimate of the parameter from the sample observations. The sample mean estimator can be denoted $\bar{z} = \frac{1}{2}(z_1 + z_2)$. Notice that, since z_1 and z_2 are random variables, the estimator $\bar{z}$ is a random variable with a probability distribution which is often called the *sampling distribution* of $\bar{z}$. In fact, it is easy to derive the probability distribution of $\bar{z}$. $\bar{z}$ can take one of three values. If z_1 and z_2 both equal 1, then $\bar{z} = 1$; if z_1 and z_2 both equal -1, then $\bar{z} = -1$; and if either z_1 or z_2 is equal to 1 and the other is equal to -1, then $\bar{z} = 0$. $\bar{z}$ can take the values $1, -1$, or 0, and will do so with probabilities of $\frac{1}{4}, \frac{1}{4}$, and $\frac{1}{2}$, respectively (see Figure 8.13). If the actual values of z_1 and z_2 are 1 and -1, then the *estimate* of the mean of z by using the sample mean rule is 0. For any particular sample, then, the result of applying the rule—that is, the estimate—is not a random variable but a number.

z_1	z_2	$\bar{z}$	$f(\bar{z})$
1	1	1	$\frac{1}{4}$
-1	-1	-1	$\frac{1}{4}$
1	-1	$0 \rbrace$	
-1	1	$0 \rbrace$	$\frac{1}{2}$

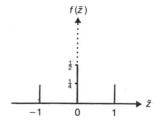

Figure 8.13. The probability distribution of $\bar{z} = \frac{1}{2}(z_1 + z_2)$

If $\bar{z}$ is to be a good estimator of the mean of z we may require that

(*i*) The mean of the sampling distribution of $\bar{z}$ be equal to the mean of z, the parameter we are trying to estimate. (This is in fact the case because the mean of $\bar{z}$, $E(\bar{z})$, $= 1(\frac{1}{4}) + (-1)(\frac{1}{4}) + 0(\frac{1}{2}) = 0$.)

(*ii*) The spread or dispersion of the sampling distribution of $\bar{z}$ about the mean of z be small.

Notice that, in order to determine the sampling properties of $\bar{z}$, we require some general information or *model* of the way in which the sample observations were generated—for instance, that the two sample observations were generated from the experimental situation of tossing a coin described above, and that the successive tosses of the coin were independent of one another. Without this information, or model, we cannot determine the sampling properties of the estimator $\bar{z}$.

We can formalize the two criteria suggested for a good estimator:

(*i*) An estimator is said to be an *unbiased* estimator of a parameter if the mean of the sampling distribution of the estimator is equal to the value of the parameter we are trying to estimate.

(*ii*) An estimator is said to be a *minimum variance* estimator of a parameter if the variance of the estimator is smaller than the variance of any other estimator of the parameter.

On its own, the minimum variance criterion is not very satisfactory. For example, if we used as our estimate of the mean of z the rule of setting our estimate equal to some number, say 3, irrespective of the sample observations, then the variance of the estimator will be zero. Clearly, however, this is not a sensible estimation rule, since it completely ignores the sample information. We must therefore use the minimum variance criterion in conjunction with some other criterion, such as unbiasedness. The following definitions incorporate this idea.

An estimator is the *best unbiased estimator* of a parameter if the estimator is an unbiased estimator of the parameter and if it has the smallest variance of all unbiased estimators of the parameter. An estimator is the *best linear unbiased estimator* of a parameter if the estimator is a linear estimator (that is, a weighted sum of the sample observations), if the estimator is unbiased, and if it has the smallest variance of all linear, unbiased estimators of the parameter.

We will now relate the above discussion about the sampling properties of estimators to the problem of fitting a line to a scatter diagram. A major reason why we adopt the LS criterion for fitting the line is that, if we make some general assumptions about the way that data on the dependent and explanatory variables are generated, the LS estimation method has optimal properties.

Look again at the scatter of observations relating to the logarithm of tax assessments and annual values in Figure 8.1. The observations approximately trace out a line. It is clear, however, that the observations do not all fall exactly on a line. Our general assumptions about the way the data are generated should reflect these characteristics.

If we assumed that the data were generated by the model

$$y_t = \beta_1 + \beta_2 x_t$$

where β_1 and β_2 are fixed numbers called parameters or coefficients, then we would be postulating that the scatter points would all lie on a straight line with slope β_2 and y_t-intercept β_1 (see Figure 8.14). Clearly this model is unsatisfactory because the scatter points lie *about* a line, not all *on* the line. In order to account for this observed characteristic we introduce another element into the model, a *random disturbance* or random variable, which 'explains' why all the observations do not lie exactly on the line. The revised model generating the t-th observation on the dependent variable is

$$y_t = \beta_1 + \beta_2 x_t + \varepsilon_t$$

where ε_t is a random disturbance or random variable with a probability distri-

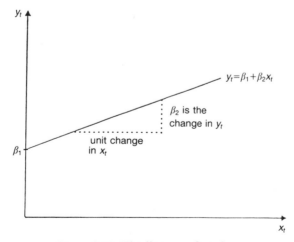

Figure 8.14. The line $y_t = \beta_1 + \beta_2 x_t$

bution. We assume that the mean of the random disturbance is zero (that is, $E(\varepsilon_t) = 0$), so the probability distribution of ε_t will be centred on zero. It could, for example, look like the probability distribution of the random variable z (see Figure 8.9) or the normal random variable u (see Figure 8.12).

The *regression model* we have just described is simply a formal way of saying that the average relationship between the dependent and explanatory variables can be represented by a straight line, and that the actual observations on these variables will not lie *on* the line but randomly *about* the line. Given the model, we can interpret an actual observation on the dependent variable (that is, y_t) to be the sum of the linear effect of the explanatory variable (that is, $\beta_1 + \beta_2 x_t$) and a drawing from a disturbance distribution (that is, ε_t).

The next two statements indicate reasons for preferring the LS estimation method.

(1) If the observations are generated by the regression model described above and we estimate β_1 and β_2 by fitting the line that minimizes the sum of squared deviations measured in the vertical direction (that is, we adopt the LS method), then the estimators of β_1 and β_2 are unbiased.

(2) If, in addition, the random disturbances relating to the dependent variable observations all have the same variance, and if the disturbances are independent of one another, then the LS estimators of β_1 and β_2 are best linear unbiased estimators.[5]

8.4 SUMMARY AND ILLUSTRATION OF THE CONCEPTS INTRODUCED IN 8.3.

In the previous section we gave a justification for using the LS method in terms of the sampling properties of the method. Our argument involved a number of important statistical concepts, which we shall now summarize.

A random variable is a variable which can take different values, each with a probability of less than one, such that the sum of these probabilities is one. A random variable has a probability distribution. The mean and variance are measures of central tendency and spread or dispersion of the probability distribution, and are sometimes referred to as parameters of the distribution. If we have a sample of observations on a random variable, we can estimate the parameters of the probability distribution. An estimator of a parameter is a rule for determining an estimate of the parameter from the sample observations. An estimator is a random variable with a probability or sampling distribution, but the estimate obtained from a particular sample is a number. To determine the sampling distribution of an estimator, we require some general information about, or a model of, the way in which the sample observations were generated. An estimator is said to be unbiased if the mean of the sampling distribution is equal to the parameter we are trying to estimate. A good estimator should have a small dispersion about the parameter value. An estimator is said to be the best linear unbiased estimator of a parameter if the estimator is a linear estimator (that is, a weighted sum of the sample observations), if the estimator is unbiased, and if it has the smallest variance of all linear, unbiased estimators of the parameter.

A reasonable model describing how the sample observations on the logarithm of tax assessments and annual values in Table 8.1 are generated is that the t-th observation on the dependent variable (the logarithm of tax assessment for the t-th manor) is generated by the stochastic, or inexact, relation

$$y_t = \beta_1 + \beta_2 x_t + \varepsilon_t$$

where β_1 and β_2 are fixed numbers or parameters, and ε_t is a random disturbance with a mean of zero. This regression model formalizes the idea that the average relationship between the dependent and explanatory variables can be represented by a straight line, and the actual observations lie randomly about the line.

If the sample observations are generated by the regression model, and we estimate the line (or, equivalently, the intercept, β_1, and slope, β_2) by the LS method, then the estimators of β_1 and β_2 are unbiased.

If, in addition, the random disturbances all have the same variance and are independent of one another, then the LS estimators of β_1 and β_2 are best linear unbiased estimators.

Some of the concepts described above are highly abstract; so it would be useful to illustrate by examples how the data on the dependent variable are conceptually generated, and to show that the estimators of the parameters β_1 and β_2 have sampling distributions.

Illustration 1. To illustrate conceptually how the data are generated, suppose

$$\beta_1 = 2, \beta_2 = 1, \quad \text{so that}$$

$$y_t = 2 + 1x_t + \varepsilon_t$$

Also, let ε_t be a random variable defined on the random experiment of tossing a coin, so that

$$\varepsilon_t = \quad 1 \text{ if a head occurs}$$

$$= -1 \text{ if a tail occurs.}$$

The mean of ε_t is $E(\varepsilon_t) = 1(\tfrac{1}{2}) + (-1)(\tfrac{1}{2}) = 0$, so the data on the dependent variable are indeed generated by a special case of the regression model. Let the observations on the explanatory variable be

$$x_1 = 1, x_2 = 4, x_3 = 5, x_4 = 6$$

We can now generate the observations y_1, y_2, y_3 and y_4.

$$y_1 = 2 + 1(1) + \varepsilon_1 = 3 + \varepsilon_1$$

The value of ε_1 will depend on the outcome of a toss of a coin. If a head occurs, $\varepsilon_1 = 1$, and $y_1 = 3 + 1 = 4$. Let us suppose that when we toss the coin on the second, third, and fourth occasions we obtain a head, a tail, and a head, respectively, thus generating $\varepsilon_2 = 1$, $\varepsilon_3 = -1$, and $\varepsilon_4 = 1$. Consequently,

$$y_2 = 2 + 1(4) + 1 \quad = 7$$

$$y_3 = 2 + 1(5) + (-1) = 6$$

$$y_4 = 2 + 1(6) + 1 \quad = 9$$

Now suppose we have no knowledge of the values of the parameters β_1 and β_2 of the regression model, nor of the disturbance values $\varepsilon_1, \varepsilon_2, \varepsilon_3$, and ε_4. All we observe are the sample observations $(1, 4), (4, 7), (5, 6), (6, 9)$. We can use the LS method to estimate β_1 and β_2. The LS estimator of β_2 is

$$b_2 = \frac{\sum_{t=1}^{4} (x_t - \bar{x})(y_t - \bar{y})}{\sum_{t=1}^{4} (x_t - \bar{x})^2}$$

Now $\bar{x} = 4$ and $\bar{y} = 6.5$, so

$y_1 - \bar{y} = -2.5$	$x_1 - \bar{x} = -3$	$(y_1 - \bar{y})(x_1 - \bar{x}) = 7.5$	$(x_1 - \bar{x})^2 = 9$
$y_2 - \bar{y} = 0.5$	$x_2 - \bar{x} = 0$	$(y_2 - \bar{y})(x_2 - \bar{x}) = 0$	$(x_2 - \bar{x})^2 = 0$
$y_3 - \bar{y} = -0.5$	$x_3 - \bar{x} = 1$	$(y_3 - \bar{y})(x_3 - \bar{x}) = -0.5$	$(x_3 - \bar{x})^2 = 1$
$y_4 - \bar{y} = 2.5$	$x_4 - \bar{x} = 2$	$(y_4 - \bar{y})(x_4 - \bar{x}) = 5$	$(x_4 - \bar{x})^2 = 4$

$$\sum_{t=1}^{4} (y_t - \bar{y})(x_t - \bar{x}) = 12 \qquad \sum_{t=1}^{4} (x_t - \bar{x})^2 = 14$$

The estimate $b_2 = \frac{12}{14} = 0.9$ (to one decimal place).

The LS estimator of β_1 is $b_1 = \bar{y} - b_2\bar{x}$.

The estimate $b_1 = 6.5 - 0.9(4) = 2.9$ (working to one decimal place).

Now let us generate a second sample. Let the observations on the explanatory variable be $x_1 = 1, x_2 = 4, x_3 = 5, x_4 = 6$, as before. Suppose that when we toss the coin we obtain a tail, then a head, a head and then a tail, thus generating $\varepsilon_1 = -1, \varepsilon_2 = 1, \varepsilon_3 = 1, \varepsilon_4 = -1$. Consequently,

$$y_1 = 2 + 1(1) + (-1) = 2$$

$$y_2 = 2 + 1(4) + 1 \quad = 7$$

$$y_3 = 2 + 1(5) + 1 \quad = 8$$

$$y_4 = 2 + 1(6) + (-1) = 7$$

Again suppose we only observe the four observations, which this time are $(1, 2)$, $(4, 7)$, $(5, 8)$, $(6, 7)$, and we use the LS method to estimate β_1 and β_2. $\bar{x} = 4$ and $\bar{y} = 6$, so

$y_1 - \bar{y} = -4$	$x_1 - \bar{x} = -3$	$(y_1 - \bar{y})(x_1 - \bar{x}) = 12$	$(x_1 - \bar{x})^2 = 9$
$y_2 - \bar{y} = 1$	$x_2 - \bar{x} = 0$	$(y_2 - \bar{y})(x_2 - \bar{x}) = 0$	$(x_2 - \bar{x})^2 = 0$
$y_3 - \bar{y} = 2$	$x_3 - \bar{x} = 1$	$(y_3 - \bar{y})(x_3 - \bar{x}) = 2$	$(x_3 - \bar{x})^2 = 1$
$y_4 - \bar{y} = 1$	$x_4 - \bar{x} = 2$	$(y_4 - \bar{y})(x_4 - \bar{x}) = 2$	$(x_4 - \bar{x})^2 = 4$

$$\sum_{t=1}^{4} (y_t - \bar{y})(x_t - \bar{x}) = 16 \qquad \sum_{t=1}^{4} (x_t - \bar{x})^2 = 14$$

The estimate $b_2 = \frac{16}{14} = 1.1$ and the estimate $b_1 = 6 - 1.1(4) = 1.6$ (working to one decimal place).
Note that:

The LS estimates are different in the two samples.
The LS estimators or rules have sampling distributions—that is, the estimators take different values with certain probabilities.
Since the data were generated by the regression model, the estimator b_1 is an unbiased estimator of β_1 and b_2 is an unbiased estimator of β_2.
Finally, in our example, all the random disturbances, ε_1, ε_2, ε_3, ε_4, have the same probability distribution and hence the same variance and the random disturbances are independent of each other. It follows that the estimator b_1 is the best linear unbiased estimator of β_1 and b_2 the best linear unbiased estimator of β_2.

Illustration 2. Now consider an example that relates more directly to the tax assessment–annual value sample in Table 8.1 (p. 128). Suppose the values for the explanatory variable are $x_1 = 2.0$, $x_2 = 2.3$, $x_3 = 6.0$, $x_4 = 3.4$, $x_5 = 3.8$, $x_6 = 5.2$, $x_7 = 4.2$, $x_8 = 4.0$, $x_9 = 1.6$, $x_{10} = 2.2$ —that is, the same as in Table 8.1. In addition, suppose the β-parameter values (usually unknown to the researcher) are $\beta_1 = 2.7$ and $\beta_2 = 0.8$, so

$$y_t = 2.7 + 0.8x_t + \varepsilon_t$$

Finally, let ε_t be a random variable defined over the random experiment of throwing a die, so that

$$\varepsilon_t = -0.7 \quad \text{if die} = 1$$
$$= -0.5 \quad \text{if die} = 2$$
$$= -0.25 \quad \text{if die} = 3$$
$$= 0.25 \quad \text{if die} = 4$$
$$= 0.5 \quad \text{if die} = 5$$
$$= 0.7 \quad \text{if die} = 6$$

Note that

$$E(\varepsilon_t) = (-0.7)(\tfrac{1}{6}) + (-0.5)(\tfrac{1}{6}) + (-0.25)(\tfrac{1}{6}) + 0.25(\tfrac{1}{6}) + 0.5(\tfrac{1}{6}) + 0.7(\tfrac{1}{6}) = 0.$$

We invite you to generate the disturbances $\varepsilon_1, \varepsilon_2, \ldots \varepsilon_{10}$, obtain the observations on the dependent variable, then use the observations on the dependent and explanatory variables to compute the LS estimates of β_1 and β_2, and finally compare your results with Figure 8.5. When we undertook the experiment we obtained the following results. (The estimates are rounded to one decimal place.)

ε_1	ε_2	ε_3	ε_4	ε_5	ε_6	ε_7	ε_8	ε_9	ε_{10}
0.5	0.25	−0.7	−0.5	−0.25	0.7	−0.25	0.5	0.25	−0.25

y_1	y_2	y_3	y_4	y_5	y_6	y_7	y_8	y_9	y_{10}
4.8	4.8	6.8	4.9	5.5	7.6	5.8	6.4	4.2	4.2

$$b_2 = \frac{\sum\limits_{t=1}^{10} (y_t - \bar{y})(x_t - \bar{x})}{\sum\limits_{t=1}^{10} (x_t - \bar{x})^2} = 0.7$$

$$b_1 = \bar{y} - b_2\bar{x} = 3.0.$$

The scatter points and LS line are exhibited in Figure 8.15.

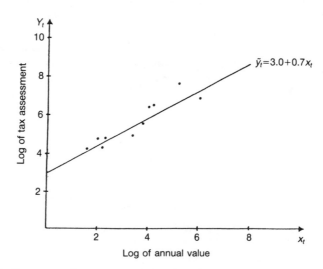

Figure 8.15. The scatter diagram and LS fitted line for the sample used in Illustration 2

8.5 PROPERTIES OF THE LEAST SQUARES METHOD IN THE NORMAL REGRESSION MODEL

Our model describing the experiment of tossing a coin was very simple. The outcome was regarded as random, with a probability of one-half assigned to the occurrence of a head and a probability of one-half assigned to the occurrence of a tail. Alternatively, we could have attempted to develop a deterministic model to describe the experiment. This would be an extremely difficult undertaking involving the laws of physics, measuring the velocity imparted on the coin as it was tossed, the height it was dropped, the bias of the coin, and many other factors. To predict the outcome from this model, a huge amount of information would be required. Even if it were possible to develop a deterministic model, the simple probabilistic model would for many purposes be more useful.

The regression model can likewise be regarded as a useful simplification of the real-world situation. Except when we are trying to explain extremely simple phenomena, our theories must always be less complex than reality and concentrate on the most important aspects of a relationship. To the extent that we ignore some factors which influence the dependent variable, the relationship will be inexact. For example, a manorial tax assessment will depend not only on the annual value of the manor but on many other less important factors, such as the effect of irregular revision of the tax assessment and minor tax concessions to some lords. The effect of these omitted factors or variables on the assessment is summarized in the form of the random disturbance, which also allows for some measurement error in the dependent variable such as rounding errors, collection errors, and clerical errors.[6]

In the illustrations of the previous section, we have characterized the disturbance as a discrete random variable which can only take a few values. Since the disturbance is conceptually the random effect of a multitude of factors, it is more reasonable to characterize it as a continuous random variable, such as the normal random variable, which can take any value. If the normal random variable has a mean of zero, then the probability that it will take very large or small values will be small, and the probability that it will take values close to zero large. The normal distribution is also symmetrical about zero. For these and other reasons, the normal distribution has been regarded as an attractive way of characterizing a disturbance distribution about which we have very little a priori knowledge.

If the data on the dependent variable are generated by the regression model with independent normal random disturbances each with a mean of zero and the same variance (we will call this the *normal regression model*), the LS estimators have very attractive properties. First, the LS estimator of β_1 (that is b_1) is the best unbiased estimator of β_1, which means that it is an unbiased estimator of β_1 and has the smallest variance of all unbiased estimators of β_1.[7] Similarly, the LS estimator of β_2 (that is, b_2) is the best unbiased estimator of

β_2. Secondly, we can estimate the common random disturbance variance. If we denote the common variance of the disturbances by $\text{Var}(\varepsilon_t) = \sigma^2$, an unbiased estimator of the variance is given by the sum of the squares of the LS residuals divided by the number of observations in the sample less 2. (2 is subtracted because two parameters, β_1 and β_2, have been estimated.) In our notation, an unbiased estimator of $\text{Var}(\varepsilon_t) = \sigma^2$ is

$$\tilde{\text{V}}\text{ar}(\varepsilon_t) = \frac{1}{n-2} \sum_{t=1}^{n} e_t^2$$

Thirdly, we can obtain an unbiased estimator of the variance of the sampling distribution of the LS estimator b_1. Let us denote this unbiased estimator by $\tilde{\text{V}}\text{ar}(b_1)$. It can be shown that

$$\tilde{\text{V}}\text{ar}(b_1) = \tilde{\text{V}}\text{ar}(\varepsilon_t) \left(\frac{\sum_{t=1}^{n} x_t^2}{n \sum_{t=1}^{n} (x_t - \bar{x})^2} \right)$$

Also, an unbiased estimator of the variance of b_2, denoted $\tilde{\text{V}}\text{ar}(b_2)$, is

$$\tilde{\text{V}}\text{ar}(b_2) = \frac{\tilde{\text{V}}\text{ar}(\varepsilon_t)}{\sum_{t=1}^{n} (x_t - \bar{x})^2}$$

Finally, it is possible to undertake tests of hypotheses relating to the coefficients β_1 and β_2.

The idea of statistical testing is quite complex. A good introduction is given in Kmenta (1971, 112–53). We will only give a brief description here. To fix ideas, let us assume that the data on the logarithm of tax assessment in Table 8.1 were generated by the normal regression model, and consider the problem of testing that β_1 is equal to some number of interest, say $\beta_1 = 2$. It would seem sensible to base the test on the difference between the LS estimate of β_1 (that is, $b_1 = 2.7$) and the number 2, and to take into consideration the estimated variance of the sampling distribution of b_1 (that is, $\tilde{\text{V}}\text{ar}(b_1)$), which can be calculated using the formula above. For this example $\tilde{\text{V}}\text{ar}(b_1) = 0.2$). A *test statistic* that does this is

$$\frac{b_1 - 2}{\tilde{\text{S}}\text{D}(b_1)}$$

where $\tilde{\text{S}}\text{D}(b_1)$ is the square root of $\tilde{\text{V}}\text{ar}(b_1)$:

$$\frac{b_1 - 2}{\tilde{\text{S}}\text{D}(b_1)} = \frac{2.7 - 2}{0.4} = \frac{0.7}{0.4} = 1.8 \text{ (to one decimal place)}$$

Although for a particular sample the test statistic is a number, in the same way that an estimator has a sampling distribution, so the test statistic rule has a

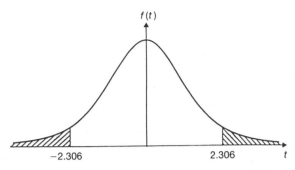

Figure 8.16. The probability distribution of a t random variable with 8 degrees of freedom

sampling distribution. It can be shown that, if $\beta_1 = 2$ is true, then the sampling distribution of the test statistic rule is a t distribution. The probability distribution of a t random variable is exhibited in Figure 8.16. A t random variable (or, equivalently, the test statistic rule when $\beta_1 = 2$) can take any value. It follows that the only decision rule based on the test statistic that will always accept the hypothesis $\beta_1 = 2$, when it is in fact true, is to accept $\beta_1 = 2$ for all observed values of the test statistic. If we impose this rule, however, we will never reject the hypothesis $\beta_1 = 2$. We will therefore always commit an error when $\beta_1 = 2$ is not true. Clearly, we will need to compromise between committing this kind of error and committing the error of rejecting the hypothesis $\beta_1 = 2$ when it is true.

Although the t random variable can take any value, the probability that it takes very high or low values is small. Note that the test statistic will take very high or low values when the estimate b_1 is not close to 2. This suggests that we reject the hypothesis $\beta_1 = 2$ if the test statistic takes a sufficiently high or low value. In Figure 8.16 we have shaded the lower $2\frac{1}{2}$ per cent and upper $2\frac{1}{2}$ per cent of the area under the curve. The cut-off points on the horizontal axis (called the lower and upper *critical values*) are -2.306 and 2.306. A decision rule is to reject $\beta_1 = 2$ if the test statistic value lies outside these critical values and accept $\beta_1 = 2$ if the test statistic value lies on or within them. If $\beta_1 = 2$ is true, then the probability that the test statistic rule will give a value lying outside the critical values is 0.05. The test is said to have a *size* of 5 per cent because we will reject $\beta_1 = 2$ five per cent of the time when $\beta_1 = 2$ is true. $\beta_1 = 2$ is called the *null* hypothesis; β_1 not equal to 2 (that is, $\beta_1 \neq 2$) is called the *alternative* hypothesis.

A minor complication is that the type of t distribution the test statistic rule follows depends on the sample size, n. t distributions are categorized by their *degrees of freedom*. The test statistic rule follows a t distribution with $n - 2$ degrees of freedom. (Two degress of freedom are lost because two parameters are estimated. In the example there are $10 - 2 = 8$ degrees of freedom.) The $2\frac{1}{2}$ per cent critical values for the various t distributions have been tabulated (see, for example, Kmenta 1971, 621). For the t distribution with 8 degrees of freedom they are -2.306 and 2.306. To carry out the test, we calculate the test statistic value and look up the critical values of the appropriate t distribution in the table. Since the test statistic value is 1.8, which lies within the critical values, we accept the null hypothesis $\beta_1 = 2$ at the 5 per cent significance level.

We can also test hypotheses concerning β_2. For example, we may wish to test the null hypothesis that $\beta_2 = 0$, which corresponds to the condition that the logarithm of tax assessment does not depend linearly on the logarithm of manorial value. For this test, the test statistic is

$$\frac{b_2 - 0}{\widetilde{SD}(b_2)} = \frac{0.8 - 0}{0.12} = \frac{0.8}{0.12} = 6.7 \text{ (to one decimal place)}$$

When $\beta_2 = 0$ is true, the sampling distribution of the test statistic rule is again the t distribution with $n - 2 = 8$ degrees of freedom. For a 5 per cent test of $\beta_2 = 0$ against the alternative $\beta_2 \neq 0$, the lower and upper critical values are therefore -2.306 and 2.306. Since the test statistic value is 6.7, we reject the null hypothesis at the 5 per cent significance level.

$\beta_1 = 2$ and $\beta_2 = 0$ are examples of linear hypotheses. It is also possible to test two linear hypotheses simultaneously—that is, to test, for example, the null hypothesis that $\beta_1 = 2$ and $\beta_2 = 0$ against the alternative that either or both hypotheses are not true. It seems sensible to reject the null hypothesis if, when we impose it, the calculated residual sum of squares is considerably greater than when we do not. When the null hypothesis $\beta_1 = 2$, $\beta_2 = 0$ is imposed the first residual will be

$$e_1^* = y_1 - 2 - 0(x_1) = 3.8 - 2 - 0(2.0) = 1.8, \text{ and}$$

$$e_2^* = y_2 - 2 - 0(x_2) = 5.0 - 2 - 0(2.3) = 3.0$$

The other residuals are $e_3^* = 4.8$, $e_4^* = 3.2$, $e_5^* = 4.0$, $e_6^* = 5.6$, $e_7^* = 4.4$, $e_8^* = 3.4$, $e_9^* = 2.2$, $e_{10}^* = 2.2$

The residual sum of squares, called the *restricted residual sum of squares* (RRSS), is $\sum_{t=1}^{n} e_t^{*2} = 133.5$ (to one decimal place). When the null hypothesis is not imposed but β_1 and β_2 are estimated by LS, we earlier calculated the (LS) residuals (in 8.2) to be $e_1 = 0.5$, $e_2 = -0.5$, $e_3 = -0.7$, $e_4 = -0.2$, $e_5 = 0.3$, $e_6 = 0.7$, $e_7 = 0.3$, $e_8 = -0.5$, $e_9 = 0.2$, $e_{10} = -0.3$, so the *unrestricted residual sum of squares* (URSS) is $\sum_{t=1}^{n} e_t^2 = 2.1$ (to one decimal place). To test $\beta_1 = 2$ and $\beta_2 = 0$ against the alternative hypothesis, we use the test statistic.

$$\frac{(RRSS - URSS)/2}{URSS/(n-2)} = \frac{(133.5 - 2.1)/2}{2.1/(10-2)} = \frac{131.4/2}{2.1/8} = 250.3$$

It can be shown that when the null hypothesis is true, the sampling distribution of the test statistic rule is an F distribution. F distributions are categorized by upper and lower degrees of freedom. The test statistic has 2 (because 2 parameters are assigned values under the null hypothesis) and $n - 2$ degrees of freedom. The test statistic will take high values if the restricted residual sum of squares is considerably greater than the unrestricted, so we reject the null hypothesis when the test statistic value is sufficiently large. The critical values for 5 per cent tests have been tabulated for the various kinds of F distribution (see Kmenta 1971, 623). For an F distribution with 2 and 8 degrees of freedom, the critical value is 4.46. Since the test statistic value is greater than 4.46, we reject the null hypothesis.

An F test statistic can also be used to test an hypothesis concerning a single parameter, for example $\beta_2 = 0$ against the alternative hypothesis $\beta_2 \neq 0$. If we impose the null hypothesis $\beta_2 = 0$, the regression equation is

$$y_t = \beta_1 + 0x_t + \varepsilon_t$$

or

$$y_t = \beta_1 + \varepsilon_t$$

β_1 is not assigned a value by the null hypothesis but it can be estimated by the LS method. Let us denote the LS estimate of β_1 given that we set $\beta_2 = 0$ by b_1^*. b_1^* can be shown to be equal to the sample mean of the observations y_1, y_2, ... y_{10} on the dependent variable, that is, $b_1^* = \bar{y} = 5.5$ (to one decimal place). We can now calculate the restricted residuals and hence the restricted residual sum of squares. The calculations are displayed below.

$$
\begin{aligned}
e_1^* &= y_1 - b_1^* = -1.7 & e_1^{*2} &= 2.9 \\
e_2^* &= y_2 - b_1^* = -0.5 & e_2^{*2} &= 0.3 \\
e_3^* &= y_3 - b_1^* = 1.3 & e_3^{*2} &= 1.7 \\
e_4^* &= y_4 - b_1^* = -0.3 & e_4^{*2} &= 0.1 \\
e_5^* &= y_5 - b_1^* = 0.5 & e_5^{*2} &= 0.3 \\
e_6^* &= y_6 - b_1^* = 2.1 & e_6^{*2} &= 4.4 \\
e_7^* &= y_7 - b_1^* = 0.9 & e_7^{*2} &= 0.8 \\
e_8^* &= y_8 - b_1^* = -0.1 & e_8^{*2} &= 0.0 \\
e_9^* &= y_9 - b_1^* = -1.3 & e_9^{*2} &= 1.7 \\
e_{10}^* &= y_{10} - b_1^* = -1.3 & e_{10}^{*2} &= 1.7 \\
\end{aligned}
$$

$$\sum_{t=1}^{10} e_t^{*2} = 13.9 = \text{RRSS}$$

For this test, the test statistic is

$$\frac{(\text{RRSS} - \text{URSS})/1}{\text{URSS}/(n-2)} = \frac{13.9 - 2.1}{2.1/(10-2)} = \frac{11.8}{2.1/8} = 45.0$$

(working to one decimal place), where URSS is the residual sum of squares when both β_1 and β_2 are estimated by LS, that is URSS $= \sum_{t=1}^{10} e_t^2 = 2.1$. (Note that the test statistic formula is slightly different from the previous F test. The numerator is divided by one, not two, because only one parameter is assigned a value under the null hypothesis.)

When the null hypothesis is true, the sampling distribution of the test statistic rule is an F distribution with 1 and $n - 2$ degrees of freedom. From tables of critical values of the F distribution (for example, Kmenta 1971, 627), we can see that the 5 per cent critical value for the F distribution with 1 and 8 degrees of freedom is 5.32. Since the test statistic value is greater than this critical value, we reject the null hypothesis. It can be shown that this F test and the t test of $\beta_2 = 0$ described earlier always lead to the same decision result. They are exactly equivalent tests.

8.6   USE OF A COMPUTER

In all the examples presented so far, we have made the calculations by hand to one decimal place. This simplified the calculations and made the examples easier to follow. In practice, calculations should be made to a higher degree of precision. This can be easily achieved on a computer. In Table 8.2 we present computer output for the LS regression of the tax assessment–annual value data in Table 8.1. The output is selected output from the computer package SHAZAM, with which it is possible to undertake most of the statistical analyses described in this chapter.[8]

From Table 8.2 we see that the computer program gives a listing of the ten observations on the dependent and explanatory variables (the logarithm of manorial tax assessment called 'LOGTAX' and annual value called 'LOG-VALUE', respectively). It then calculates the sample mean, standard deviation, and variance, and the smallest and largest value that these variables take. 'LOGTAX' is designated the dependent variable, then we have the LS regression results. The 'ESTIMATED COEFFICIENTS' are $b_2 = 0.78466$ and $b_1 = 2.7372$. The 'STANDARD ERRORS' are the estimates of the standard deviation of the sampling distribution of b_2 and b_1, that is, in our notation $\tilde{S}D(b_2) = 0.11737$ and $\tilde{S}D(b_1) = 0.43819$. The 'T-RATIOS' are simply the ratios of the 'ESTIMATED COEFFICIENTS' to the 'STANDARD ERRORS', that is, the first is

$$\frac{b_2}{\tilde{S}D(b_2)} = \frac{0.78466}{0.11737} = 6.6851$$

This is the test statistic for testing the null hypothesis $\beta_2 = 0$. Underneath, the observed values of the dependent variable, y_t, the LS estimated values, $\tilde{y}_t$, (referred to as 'PREDICTED VALUES') and the LS residuals, e_t, (referred to as 'CALCULATED ERRORS') are displayed. Finally, 'R-SQUARE' is what we have denoted R^2, the coefficient of determination, and 'VARIANCE OF THE ESTIMATE' is what we have denoted $\tilde{V}ar(\varepsilon_t)$, that is, an unbiased estimate of the common variance of the disturbances $Var(\varepsilon_t) = \sigma^2$. Notice that

Table 8.2. Computer output from SHAZAM relating to the manorial tax assessment–annual value data in Table 8.1

```
LISTING OF ALL INCLUDED OBSERVATIONS
          LOGTAX        LOGVALUE
   1      3.8000        2.0000
   2      5.0000        2.3000
   3      6.8000        6.0000
   4      5.2000        3.4000
   5      6.0000        3.8000
   6      7.6000        5.2000
   7      6.4000        4.2000
   8      5.4000        4.0000
   9      4.2000        1.6000
  10      4.2000        2.2000
```

VARIABLE NAME	MEAN	STANDARD DEVIATION	VARIANCE	MINIMUM	MAXIMUM
LOGTAX	5.4600	1.2367	1.5293	3.8000	7.6000
LOGVALUE	3.4700	1.4515	2.1068	1.6000	6.0000

```
DEPENDENT VARIABLE =      LOGTAX
```

VARIABLE NAME	ESTIMATED COEFFICIENT	STANDARD ERROR	T-RATIO 8 DF
LOGVALUE	0.78466	0.11737	6.6851
INTERCEPT	2.7372	0.43819	6.2467

OBSERVATION NO.	OBSERVED VALUE	PREDICTED VALUE	CALCULATED ERROR
1	3.8000	4.3065	-0.50655
2	5.0000	4.5419	0.45806
3	6.8000	7.4452	-0.64520
4	5.2000	5.4051	-0.20507
5	6.0000	5.7189	0.28106
6	7.6000	6.8175	0.78253
7	6.4000	6.0328	0.36720
8	5.4000	5.8759	-0.47587
9	4.2000	3.9927	0.20732
10	4.2000	4.4635	-0.26348

```
R-SQUARE = 0.8482
VARIANCE OF THE ESTIMATE =   0.26122
```

the estimates are a little different from those calculated by hand. This illustrates the importance of making the calculations to several significant figures. Also, notice that the interpretations we have placed on the output statistics rely on assumptions about the way the data were generated, in particular on the assumption that they were generated by the normal regression model.

8.7   LARGE SAMPLE PROPERTIES OF LEAST SQUARES ESTIMATORS IN THE REGRESSION MODEL

If the LS estimates are based on a large sample, it can be shown that the hypothesis tests described in section 8.5 are approximately valid even when the disturbances are not normal random variables.[9] This is a very important statistical result, and a major justification for undertaking the regressions described in Part I of the book. For some situations a sample of about 40 observations is sufficiently large for the approximation to be good. For the Essex and Wiltshire lay 1086 data, the sample sizes are much greater (683 and 425 respectively).

The LS estimators also have attractive properties. b_1 is the best linear unbiased estimator of β_1 (that is, of all linear, unbiased estimators it has the smallest variance) and b_2 is the best linear unbiased estimator of β_2. b_1 and b_2 are also *consistent* estimators of β_1 and β_2, respectively. Roughly speaking, an estimator is consistent if the sampling distribution of the estimator collapses on the true value of the parameter as the sample size becomes very large. This idea is illustrated graphically in Figure 8.17 for the case of b_1. There we see that

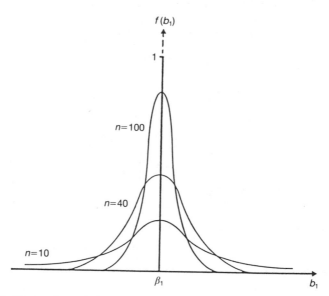

Figure 8.17. Illustration of the property of an estimator, b_1, being a consistent estimator of a parameter, β_1

for a small sample size (say, $n = 10$), the sampling distribution of b_1 is dispersed. For a larger sample size ($n = 40$, say), the distribution is more concentrated about the parameter value β_1. For an even larger sample size (say, $n = 100$) the distribution of b_1 is highly concentrated about β_1. Eventually, as the sample size increases still further, the distribution collapses to a spike at the value β_1, so that the probability that b_1 equals β_1 is one and the probability that b_1 is not equal to β_1 is zero.[10]

8.8 MAXIMUM LIKELIHOOD ESTIMATION

So far we have focused on the LS estimation method. Another procedure is the *maximum likelihood method*, which is based on the idea that different models will generate a particular sample with different probabilities, or, put another way, that a given sample is more likely to have been generated by some models than by others. As an example, suppose we consider the random experiment of tossing a coin which may be biased so that the probability of obtaining a head is not equal to one-half. If we toss the coin 100 times and obtain 50 heads and 50 tails, the most likely model generating the sample would be that the probability of obtaining a head is one-half. If we obtained 10 heads and 90 tails, this model would be most unlikely.

To analyse the maximum likelihood estimation idea more closely, let us denote the probability of obtaining a head by p. It follows that the probability of obtaining a tail is $1 - p$. To simplify matters, let us suppose we toss the coin three times only, obtaining a tail, a head, and a head, so the sample of observations is (T, H, H). The maximum likelihood estimate of p is the value of p that is most likely to have generated this sample. One way of calculating the maximum likelihood estimate is to set p equal to a series of different values, calculate the probability of generating the sample for each value, and hence find the value of p which generates the sample with highest probability.

The smallest value p can take is 0. But if $p = 0$, then a head can never be tossed. Similarly, if $p = 1$, we will never observe a tail. For both $p = 0$ and $p = 1$, then, it is not possible to observe the sample (T, H, H)—that is, the probability of observing the sample is 0. If $p = 0.1$, then the probability of obtaining a tail on the first toss is 0.9, the probability of obtaining a head on the second toss is 0.1, and the probability of obtaining a head on the third toss is 0.1. Since these events are independent, the probability of obtaining our sample (T, H, H) is $(0.9)(0.1)(0.1) = 0.009$. If $p = 0.2$, then the probability of obtaining our sample is $(0.8)(0.2)(0.2) = 0.032$. We can calculate the probability of obtaining the sample for any value of p between 0 and 1 and then graph these probabilities against p. This is done in Figure 8.18. The relationship between the sample probability and the value of p is called the *likelihood function* of p for the sample (T, H, H). The maximum likelihood estimate of p is the value of p that maximizes the likelihood function. From Figure 8.18 we see that the maximum likelihood estimate of p is 0.667 or $\frac{2}{3}$.

The example just considered relates directly to a random experiment of tossing a coin. We could, however, have defined a discrete random variable on the experiment, say z, such that,

$$z = \quad 1 \text{ if a head occurs}$$

$$= -1 \text{ if a tail occurs}$$

We would then have observed the sample $(-1, 1, 1)$, p would be the

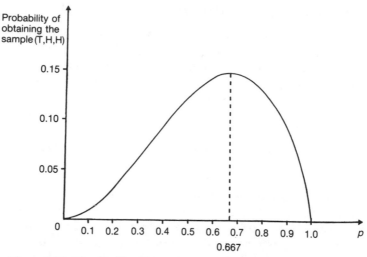

Figure 8.18. The likelihood function of p for the sample (T, H, H)

probability that $z = 1$, and the maximum likelihood estimate of p would be, as before, $\frac{2}{3}$.

For discrete situations or random variables, the value of the likelihood function for a given parameter value (for example, $p = 0.5$) can be interpreted as a probability (for example, the probability of obtaining the sample (T, H, H) when $p = 0.1$). This probability interpretation cannot be made if the sample relates to continuous random variables. Nevertheless, it is still possible to calculate the likelihood function and hence find the maximum likelihood estimate. If the model contains several parameters, then the likelihood function will depend on the values that all of the parameters take, and the maximum likelihood estimates of the parameters are the values for which the likelihood function takes the greatest value (see Kmenta 1971, 174–82 for further information).

If we have a sample of observations from the normal regression model (say, the tax assessment–annual value data in Table 8.1), then it is possible to estimate the unknown parameters of the model (that is β_1, β_2 and $\text{Var}(\varepsilon_t) = \sigma^2$) by the maximum likelihood method. It is interesting that the maximum likelihood estimators of β_1 and β_2 are the LS estimators b_1 and b_2, which we know are best unbiased estimators. The maximum likelihood estimator of σ^2 is equal to the sum of the squared LS (or maximum likelihood) residuals divided by n, that is $1/n \sum_{t=1}^{n} e_t^2$. This is not an unbiased estimator of σ^2 (an unbiased estimator is $1/(n-2) \sum_{t=1}^{n} e_t^2$—see 8.5). This result illustrates the fact that maximum likelihood estimators are not always unbiased estimators. Maximum likelihood estimators do, however, have very attractive properties when based on a large sample of observations. Under general conditions, they are consistent estimators and have the smallest variance of all estimators that are members of a broad class of consistent estimators. (See Schmidt 1976, 16–18 and 254–6, for further details.)

8.9 RELATIONSHIPS INVOLVING SEVERAL EXPLANATORY VARIABLES

In the previous sections we have explained how a relationship between a dependent variable and a single explanatory variable can be estimated. The LS and maximum likelihood estimation methods can also be used to estimate a relationship between a dependent variable and several explanatory variables. As an example, consider the relationship between the annual value and the resources of the Essex lay manors in 1086. In Part I we identified nine different manorial resources; plough-teams, livestock, peasants, slaves, woodland, meadow, pasture, bees, and mills. If we denote the annual value for the t-th manor by V_t and the nine resources of this manor by $R_{t2}, R_{t3}, R_{t4}, \ldots R_{t10}$, then the linear relationship between value and the resources can be written

$$V_t = \beta_1 + \beta_2 R_{t2} + \beta_3 R_{t3} + \beta_4 R_{t4} + \ldots + \beta_{10} R_{t10} + \varepsilon_t$$

(Notice that the notation is slightly different from the previous sections in that the dependent variable is V_t and the explanatory variables $R_{t2}, R_{t3}, R_{t4}, \ldots R_{t10}$.)

The unknown parameters $\beta_1, \beta_2, \beta_3, \ldots \beta_{10}$ can be estimated by the LS or maximum likelihood methods. If the data on the dependent variable, V_t, are generated by the normal regression model, then, as in the single explanatory variable case, the LS and maximum likelihood estimators of the β will be equal and the estimators will be best unbiased estimators of the β. They will also be minimum-variance, consistent estimators. Also, t and F tests similar to those described in 8.5 can be made of hypotheses relating to the values of the β. Moreover, if the sample size is large, these tests will be approximately valid even if the disturbances are not normal random variables (see Kmenta 1971, ch. 10, and Schmidt 1976, ch. 1 for further details).

Table 8.3 gives part of the SHAZAM computer output relating to the LS estimation of the linear relationship between value and the resources of 683 Essex lay manors for 1086. We see that the first five and the last observations on all variables are listed. The mean, standard deviation, variance, minimum and maximum values of the variables are then given. The dependent variable is the variable 'VALUE'. The estimated β-coefficients for the nine explanatory variables and the intercept, β_1, are then given. The LS estimate of β_2, the parameter relating to the resource R_{t2}, 'PLOUGHS' is $b_2 = 12.337$. The LS estimate of the resource R_{t3}, 'LIVESTOC', is $b_3 = 0.19307E - 01 = 0.019307$ (0.19307E − 01 means divide 0.19307 by 10) and the estimate of the intercept is $b_1 = -4.9703$. The column headed 'STANDARD ERROR' gives the estimated standard deviation of the sampling distribution of the LS estimators, so $\tilde{S}D(b_2) = 0.94596$, $\tilde{S}D(b_3) = 0.35065E - 02 = 0.0035065$ and

Table 8.3. Computer output from SHAZAM relating to the LS estimates of the linear relationship between value and resources for 683 Essex lay manors 1086

FIRST FIVE INCLUDED AND LAST OBSERVATION

	VALUE	PLOUGHS	LIVEST	PEASANTS	SLAVES	WOODLAND	MEADOW	PASTURE	BEES	MILLS
1	720.00	21.000	3816.0	45.000	9.0000	750.00	10.000	1100.0	0.00000	0.00000
2	50.000	2.0000	678.00	12.000	3.0000	0.00000	12.000	60.000	0.00000	0.00000
3	60.000	2.5000	268.00	6.0000	0.00000	40.000	0.00000	0.00000	0.00000	0.00000
4	20.000	2.0000	0.00000	0.00000	0.00000	0.00000	0.00000	0.00000	0.00000	0.00000
5	20.000	1.0000	0.00000	2.0000	0.00000	0.00000	0.00000	0.00000	0.00000	0.00000
683	10.000	1.0000	0.00000	1.0000	0.00000	0.00000	15.000	0.00000	0.00000	0.00000

VARIABLE NAME	MEAN	STANDARD DEVIATION	VARIANCE	MINIMUM	MAXIMUM
VALUE	94.623	125.99	15874.	0.00000	1200.0
PLOUGHS	3.6414	4.6787	21.890	0.00000	42.500
LIVESTOC	461.99	633.71	0.40158E+06	0.00000	3816.0
PEASANTS	10.984	15.160	229.83	0.00000	127.00
SLAVES	1.8624	2.6867	7.2186	0.00000	127.00
WOODLAND	90.919	177.92	31655.	0.00000	1500.0
MEADOW	10.600	15.444	238.51	0.00000	120.00
PASTURE	25.164	83.067	6900.2	0.00000	1100.0
BEES	0.81698	2.5343	6.4225	0.00000	30.000
MILLS	0.21376	0.54352	0.29541	0.00000	8.0000

DEPENDENT VARIABLE = VALUE

VARIABLE NAME	ESTIMATED COEFFICIENT	STANDARD ERROR	T-RATIO 673 DF	PARTIAL CORR.	BETA COEFFICIENT	ELASTICITY AT MEANS
PLOUGHS	12.337	0.94596	13.041	0.4492	0.45811	0.47476
LIVESTOC	0.19307E-01	0.35065E-02	5.5059	0.2076	0.97106E-01	0.94264E-01
PEASANTS	1.8978	0.27547	6.8895	0.2567	0.22836	0.22030
SLAVES	7.4711	0.90716	8.2357	0.3026	0.15932	0.14705
WOODLAND	0.24993E-01	0.12440E-01	2.0092	0.0772	0.35294E-01	0.24015E-01
MEADOW	0.62706	0.14867	4.2179	0.1605	0.76863E-01	0.70243E-01
PASTURE	0.10305	0.22851E-01	4.5096	0.1713	0.67940E-01	0.27405E-01
BEES	1.9718	0.79620	2.4766	0.0950	0.39662E-01	0.17025E-01
MILLS	-9.9754	3.7214	-2.6806	-0.1028	-0.43032E-01	-0.22535E-01
INTERCEPT	-4.9703	2.3382	-2.1257			

OBSERVATION NO.	OBSERVED VALUE	PREDICTED VALUE	CALCULATED ERROR
1	720.00	618.79	101.21
2	50.000	91.688	-41.688
3	60.000	43.432	16.568
4	20.000	19.703	0.29694
5	20.000	11.162	8.8380

R-SQUARE = 0.8748   R-SQUARE ADJUSTED = 0.8731
VARIANCE OF THE ESTIMATE = 2013.9

	SS	DF	MS	F
EXPLAINED	0.94710E+07	9.	0.10523E+07	522.547
UNEXPLAINED	0.13553E+07	673.	2013.9	
TOTAL	0.10826E+08	682.	15874	

$\tilde{S}D(b_1) = 2.3382$. The 'T-RATIOS' are the 'ESTIMATED COEFFICIENTS' divided by the 'STANDARD ERRORS', for example, $13.041 = b_2/\tilde{S}D(b_2)$. As before, given that the data are generated by the normal regression model, this 'T-RATIO' is the test statistic for the test of the hypothesis $\beta_2 = 0$. Now, however, the test statistic rule has a t distribution with $n - 10$ degrees of freedom when $\beta_2 = 0$ is true. (10 corresponds to the number of estimated β-coefficients.) Since the test statistic is 13.041, which is greater than the upper $2\frac{1}{2}$ per cent critical value of a t distribution with 673 degrees of freedom (from the t table critical values in Kmenta (1971, 621), we see that this lies between 1.960 and 2.045), we would reject the null hypothesis $\beta_2 = 0$ against the alternative $\beta_2 \neq 0$ at the 5 per cent significance level.

The computer output also lists the actual observations or 'OBSERVED VALUES' on the dependent variable, V_t, the 'PREDICTED VALUES' or LS estimates, $\tilde{V}_t$, and the 'CALCULATED ERRORS' or LS residuals, e_t, relating to the first five observations (all can be listed if required). 'R-SQUARE' is R^2, the coefficient of determination, and the 'VARIANCE OF THE ESTIMATE' is, as before, an unbiased estimate of the variance of the disturbances, $\text{Var}(\varepsilon_t) = \sigma^2$.

Additional output are 'R-SQUARE ADJUSTED', 'EXPLAINED', 'UN-EXPLAINED' and 'TOTAL SS', 'DF', and 'F'. A problem with R^2, the coefficient of determination, as a measure of the goodness of fit of the fitted relation to the scatter of observations is that it takes no account of the number of explanatory variables in the fitted relationship. It can be shown that if we add an explanatory variable to a regression equation, the value of R^2 will usually increase and cannot fall. This is not true for the *adjusted* R^2, which we will denote $\bar{R}^2$. $\bar{R}^2$ does allow for the number of explanatory variables in the regression and may fall if an explanatory variable is added. For this reason it is often a more useful measure of goodness of fit when we are comparing estimated relationships involving a different number of explanatory variables.[11]

'F' is the test statistic for testing the null hypothesis that $\beta_2 = \beta_3 = \beta_4 = \ldots = \beta_{10} = 0$ (that is, that manorial annual values do not depend linearly on the resources) against the alternative that one or more of the β is not zero. The test statistic is equal to

$$\frac{(\text{RRSS} - \text{URSS})/9}{\text{URSS}/(n - 9)} = 522.547$$

where RRSS is the restricted residual sum of squares, that is, the residual sum of squares when the null hypothesis is imposed, (when the null hypothesis is imposed, the LS estimate of the intercept, β_1, is the sample mean of V_t, $\bar{V}$) and URSS is the residual sum of squares when the null hypothesis is not imposed. These residual sums of squares are given by the 'TOTAL SS' (which in our notation is $\sum_{t=1}^{n}(V_t - \bar{V})^2$) and the 'UNEXPLAINED SS' (in our notation

$\sum_{t=1}^{n} e_t^2$), that is $0.10826E + 08 = 10826000$ and $0.13553E + 07 = 1355300$, respectively. ($0.10826E + 08$ means multiply 0.10826 by $100{,}000{,}000$.) The numerator (top) is divided by 9 because 9 restrictions are imposed under the null hypothesis. When the null hypothesis is true, the sampling distribution of the test statistic rule is an F distribution with 9 and 673 degrees of freedom (the first two numbers under 'DF'). The table of critical values for the F distribution in Kmenta 1971, 623 indicates that the 5 per cent critical value of the F distribution with 9 and 673 degrees of freedom lies between 1.88 and 1.96, so we would reject the null hypothesis at the 5 per cent significance level.

Of course, the validity of the tests and the interpretation of the computer output depend critically on assumptions about the way the data were generated, that is, that they were generated by the normal regression model. If the dependent variable is not related linearly to the explanatory variables but is related non-linearly, then this will usually not be an appropriate model. We investigate the question of whether a relationship is linear in the next section.

8.10   DETERMINING THE FUNCTIONAL FORM OF THE RELATIONSHIP: THE BOX–COX METHOD

A major problem in establishing the relationship between manorial annual values and resources is the difficulty of determining the functional form of the relationship. If a relationship exists, a priori we might expect the annual value to be an increasing function of resources, so that greater manorial resources are, on average, associated with a higher annual value. Theoretical reasoning does not, however, indicate the precise functional form of the relationship; whether the relationship is, for example, linear (as we assumed in the previous section) or log-linear (as in the tax assessment–annual value regressions examined in 8.2 and 8.6). This difficulty usually arises when regression methods are used to measure relationships. One way of overcoming the problem is to assume from the outset that the relationship has a particular form, for example linear, and to estimate the parameters of the relationship given that assumption. This strategy will work well if the linear form is a good approximation to the actual functional form, but not otherwise. To guard against the latter possibility, the alternative approach of assuming that the actual functional form can be adequately approximated by a member of a broad class of functional forms can be adopted. The data can then be used to select the functional form from this broad class.

The class of functional forms we will consider is the class defined by the *Box–Cox extended* (*BCE*) *model*, which includes the conventional linear and log-linear functional forms as special cases, together with those forms that are linear in a power transformation of the dependent and explanatory variables. Transforming the variables by taking powers or logarithms often 'straightens out' or linearizes a relationship which is non-linear in the original variables. To see this, let us suppose for simplicity that the annual value, V_t, depends on a

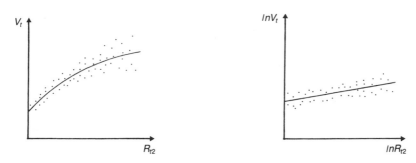

Figure 8.19. Illustration of how transforming the data may induce linearity and homoskedasticity

single resource variable, R_{t2}, only. If the average relationship between annual value and this resource variable is log-linear, the scatter of observations when graphed will trace out a curve rather than a line (see Figure 8.19). Clearly, the average relationship between annual value and the resource variable will not be linear. If, however, the observations on annual value and the resource variable are transformed by taking logarithms, and the logarithm of annual value is graphed against the logarithm of the resource variable, the scatter of observations will trace out a line. In other words, the logarithm of annual value is linearly related to the logarithm of the resource variable, that is

$$\ln V_t = \beta_1 + \beta_2 \ln R_{t2} + \varepsilon_t$$

where β_1 and β_2 are parameters and ε_t is a random disturbance. This log-linear functional form is the member of the BCE class of functions which has a transformation parameter (which we will denote by λ) equal to zero. For some other data set, another transformation may 'straighten out' the curve. For instance, it may be necessary to transform the variables by taking square roots. The functional form that is linear in the square roots of the variables corresponds to the BCE functional form with $\lambda = \frac{1}{2}$. If the data are linear in the original variables, the BCE transformation parameter λ is equal to one, and hence no transformation is required. Box and Cox (1964) explain how λ together with the β-parameters can be jointly estimated by a maximum likelihood method.[12]

8.11 THE PROBLEM OF VARIATION IN THE VARIANCE OF THE REGRESSION DISTURBANCE: HETEROSKEDASTICITY

The data on manorial annual values and resources are *cross-sectional data*, that is, data relating to several units at a point in time. A common problem with regression equations based on cross-sectional data is that the variance of the regression disturbance is not constant over the sample (that is, $\text{Var}(\varepsilon_t) \neq \sigma^2$, for all t) but is related to the size of the unit of measurement—in this case, the size of the manor. When this occurs, the disturbances are said to be *heteroskedastic*, and when the disturbance variance is constant over the sample, homoskedastic. If the regression disturbances are heteroskedastic, then parameter estimates obtained from estimation methods that ignore the heteroskedasticity do not have minimum variance properties and the estimates of the standard deviations of the sampling distribution of estimators and the tests of significance described earlier are invalid.[13]

Transforming the original variables will often make heteroskedastic disturbances more homoskedastic. For example, referring again to Figure 8.19, if in the original variables there is greater variation in annual values at high values of the resource variable, when annual value and the resource variable are transformed by taking logarithms, the variation in the transformed annual value variable at high resource levels will be moderated. It is often the case that there exists a transformation of the original variables that both 'straightens out' the curve and induces homoskedasticity; but it is perhaps optimistic to assume that this is the case for any given data set. Consequently, the method we have used to estimate the relations described in Part I allows for the disturbances in the regression equation, which is linear in the transformed variables, to be heteroskedastic, with the variance of the disturbance depending upon the size of the manor. The plough-teams variable is a measure of the size of the arable land of the manor and, because on most manors arable farming is the major activity, the plough-teams variable was employed as the indicator of manorial size.[14]

8.12 TESTING FOR FUNCTIONAL FORM AND HETEROSKEDASTICITY

The estimation procedure described in the previous section—that is, the BCE method allowing for heteroskedasticity in the disturbances—is complex, requires sophisticated computer software, and is computationally expensive. For some data sets it is not necessary to use the procedure, because a simple linear or log-linear relationship with homoskedastic disturbances adequately characterizes the relationship. Of course, we will need to be able to identify these data sets. Consequently, we require tests for functional form and heteroskedasticity to see if the simpler relationships are appropriate.

Godfrey and Wickens (1981) have developed simple tests of the null hypotheses that a relationship is linear or log-linear, which are designed to have high *power* (that is, to have small error of accepting the null hypothesis when it is false) against the alternative hypothesis that the model is another member of the BCE family of functional forms.

To explain the test of the linear null hypothesis, we will use the LS estimates of the linear relationship between annual values and the resources of the 683

Essex lay manors in 1086 presented in 8.9 and Table 8.3. The first stage is to estimate the linear relationship by LS and generate the variable

$$q_t = (\tilde{V}_t \ln \tilde{V}_t - \tilde{V}_t + 1) - b_2(R_{t2} \ln R_{t2} - R_{t2} + 1) - \ldots$$
$$- b_{10}(R_{t10} \ln R_{t10} - R_{t10} + 1)$$

where $\tilde{V}_t$ is the LS estimated value of V_t and $b_2 \ldots b_{10}$ are the LS estimates of the β. The second stage is to add q_t to the set of explanatory variables, estimate the augmented relationship by LS and calculate the usual t-ratio for q_t. This is the test statistic. Under the assumption that the random disturbances are independent random variables, all with the same probability distribution which has a mean of zero and a variance that is a finite number, in large samples, the test statistic rule is approximately distributed as a t distribution with $n - 11$ degrees of freedom, when the null hypothesis is true. The test statistic value is listed under 'F-FORM' and alongside 'regression 1' in Table 8.4. The value is 3.28, which is greater than 1.96 the upper $2\frac{1}{2}$ per cent critical value of a t distribution with 672 degrees of freedom, so we reject the null hypothesis of a linear relationship at the 5 per cent significance level.

The test of the log-linear hypothesis can be illustrated by considering the LS estimates of the log-linear relationship between the annual values and resources of the Essex lay estates in 1086 (see regression 2, Table 8.4).[15] The test is carried out in a similar way, except that q_t is defined as

$$q_t = 1/2[(\widetilde{\ln} V_t)^2 - b_2(\ln R_{t2})^2 - \ldots - b_{10}(\ln R_{t10})^2]$$

where $\widetilde{\ln} V_t$ is the LS estimated value of $\ln V_t$ and $b_2 \ldots b_{10}$ are the LS estimates of the β in the log-linear regression, that is, regression 2. The t-ratio of q_t in the augmented LS regression was $- 12.53$, which is less than $- 1.96$, the lower $2\frac{1}{2}$ per cent critical value of the t distribution with $n - 11$ degrees of freedom, so we reject the null hypothesis of a log-linear relationship at the 5 per cent significance level. Neither the simple linear nor the log-linear forms seems appropriate on these tests.

Pagan and Hall (1983) describe two tests for heteroskedasticity which we will refer to as hetero (a) and hetero (b). For the hetero (a) test, the null hypothesis is that the random disturbances are homoskedastic (that is, $\text{Var}(\varepsilon_t) = \sigma^2$, all t). The test is designed to have high power against the alternative hypothesis that the disturbance variance is linearly related to the mean value of the dependent variable. The test involves running an LS regression of the squared LS residuals of the relationship being tested on the LS estimates of the dependent variable values (allowing for an intercept in the regression), and then testing that the β-parameter relating to the LS estimated dependent variable values is zero, using the usual t test. For the hetero (b) test, the null hypothesis is that the random disturbances are homoskedastic, and the test is designed to have high power against the alternative hypothesis that the disturbance variance is linearly related to the mean of the expected value of

Table 8.4. The annual value–resources relationship for Essex lay manors, 1086

		Const.	Pl	Li	N	S	W	Me	P	B	M	H	λ	$\bar{R}^2$	F	F-Form	Hetero (a)	Hetero (b)
regression 1 linear form $n=683$	β	−4.97	12.3	0.0193	1.90	7.47	0.0250	0.627	0.103	1.97	−9.98		1	0.873	522.5	3.28	18.6	189.99
	t	2.1	13.0	5.5	6.9	8.2	2.0	4.2	4.5	2.5	−2.7				$F_{(9,673)}$	$t_{(672)}$	$t_{(671)}$	$F_{(2,670)}$
	$t(w)$	1.6	4.8	3.2	3.0	4.0	1.4	2.2	2.8	1.1	−1.9				1.90	±1.96	±1.96	3.01
	E		0.50	0.09	0.22	0.16	0.02	0.07	0.03	0.02	−0.04							
regression 2 log-linear form $n=682$	β	3.11	0.545	0.0370	0.132	0.115	0.0337	0.0464	0.0389	0.0062	−0.0011		0	0.822	350.4	−12.53	−8.4	46.47
	t	47.5	18.2	5.9	6.3	6.7	3.7	3.5	4.2	0.3	−0.0				$F_{(9,672)}$	$t_{(671)}$	$t_{(670)}$	$F_{(2,669)}$
	$t(w)$	40.9	10.9	6.2	4.9	6.4	3.7	3.3	3.9	0.3	−0.0				1.90	±1.96	±1.96	3.01
	E		0.55	0.04	0.13	0.12	0.03	0.05	0.04	0.01	−0.00							
regression 3 BCE transformation $n=682$	β	4.52	1.35	0.0416	0.307	0.311	0.0342	0.113	0.055	0.007	−0.111		0.280	0.865	484.4		0.7	2.52
	t	26.2	17.9	6.4	6.7	6.7	2.8	4.2	4.1	0.1	−1.2				$F_{(9,672)}$		$t_{(670)}$	$F_{(2,669)}$
	E		0.55	0.07	0.17	0.11	0.03	0.06	0.04	0.00	−0.02				1.90		±1.96	3.01
regression 4 BCE transformation $n=682$	β	4.67	1.34	0.0413	0.303	0.308	0.0334	0.106	0.055	0.005			0.280	0.865	544.4		0.8	2.42
	t	39.4	17.8	6.3	6.7	6.7	2.7	4.1	4.1	0.1					$F_{(8,673)}$		$t_{(671)}$	$F_{(2,670)}$
	E		0.55	0.07	0.17	0.11	0.03	0.06	0.04	0.00					1.96		±1.96	3.01
regression 5 BCE transformation $n=682$	β	4.48	1.35	0.0442	0.307	0.312	0.0340	0.112	0.055	0.007	−0.104	−0.039	0.280	0.865	435.6		0.7	2.60
	t	24.4	17.8	5.5	6.7	6.7	2.7	4.2	4.1	0.1	−1.1	−0.6			$F_{(10,671)}$		$t_{(669)}$	$F_{(2,688)}$
	E		0.55	0.07	0.17	0.11	0.03	0.06	0.04	0.00	−0.02	−0.01			1.85		±1.96	3.01
regression 6 BCE transformation $n=682$	β	4.86	1.43		0.343	0.350	0.0368	0.101	0.065				0.280	0.856	675.5		0.5	2.20
	t	53.5	18.7		7.4	7.4	2.9	3.8	4.7						$F_{(6,675)}$		$t_{(673)}$	$F_{(2,672)}$
	E		0.58		0.19	0.12	0.04	0.06	0.05						2.12		±1.96	3.01

Notes: The first row (labelled β) gives the LS parameter estimates of the intercept or constant and the following explanatory variables: plough-teams (Pl), livestock (Li), peasants (N), slaves (S), woodland (W), meadow (Me), pasture (P), bees (B), and mills (M), when annual value is linearly related to these variables. The second row (labelled t) gives t-ratios; and the third row (labelled $t(w)$) t-ratios calculated according to White's method. The fourth row gives partial resource–annual value elasticities evaluated at the sample means of annual value and the resource.

H refers to the horses variable. λ is the BCE transformation parameter. R^2 is the coefficient of determination adjusted for degrees of freedom, and F is the test statistic for testing that the parameters on all resource variables are zero. The value of the F-test statistic is 522.5; $F_{(9,673)}$ in line 2 indicates that when the null hypothesis is true the test statistic rule has an F distribution with 9 and 673 degrees of *freedom*. Five per cent critical values are given underneath. The entries relating to the functional form (F-Form) and hetero (a) and hetero (b) tests can be interpreted in a similar way.

the dependent variable and the square of this value. The test involves regressing the squared residuals on the LS estimates of the dependent variable values and the square of these values (again allowing for an intercept in the regression), and then testing that the β-parameters relating to the explanatory variables are both zero, using the F test.

Table 8.4 gives the test statistics for the hetero (a) and (b) tests of the linear and log-linear annual value–resources relationships for the Essex lay estates. For the linear form, the hetero (a) test statistic is 18.6, much greater than the upper $2\frac{1}{2}$ per cent critical value of the t distribution with 671 degrees of freedom.[16] The test statistic value for the hetero (b) test is 189.99, which is considerably greater than the 5 per cent critical value of the F distribution with 2 and 670 degrees of freedom. The null hypothesis of homoskedastic disturbances is rejected on both tests and this is also the case for the log-linear relationship, regression 2.

8.13 APPLICATION OF THE BOX–COX EXTENDED MAXIMUM LIKELIHOOD METHOD, ALLOWING FOR HETEROSKEDASTIC DISTURBANCES, TO THE ESSEX LAY ANNUAL VALUE–RESOURCES 1086 DATA

The tests for functional form and heteroskedasticity described in the previous section indicate that the linear and log-linear functional forms are inappropriate descriptions of the relationship between annual value and the resources of the Essex lay holdings for 1086. Consequently, we used the BCE maximum likelihood method, allowing for heteroskedasticity, to estimate the relationship. This estimation procedure can be carried out in two stages. The first stage is to calculate the value of the likelihood for a grid of values of λ (the transformation parameter) and γ (the heteroskedasticity parameter), and to search over the grid to find values of λ and γ that maximize the likelihood. For these values of λ and γ, we can then calculate estimates of the β-parameters. The resulting estimates are the maximum likelihood estimates.[17]

We searched over a grid with λ taking values between zero and one, and γ taking values between zero and three. The search indicated that the likelihood was maximized when (to three decimal places) $\gamma = 0$ and $\lambda = 0.280$. As a further check, we set $\gamma = 0$ and found the maximum likelihood estimate of λ, searching over values of λ in the interval from minus four to plus five. The maximum likelihood estimate of λ was again 0.280. As indicated in note 14, $\gamma = 0$ corresponds to homoskedastic disturbances, so the estimates suggest that when $\lambda = 0.280$, the disturbances are homoskedastic.

One way of illustrating the properties of the BCE functional form with $\lambda = 0.280$ is by graphing the estimated relationship between annual value and the most influential explanatory variable, plough-teams. Figure 8.20 shows the value–plough-teams relationship for the estimated linear and log-linear

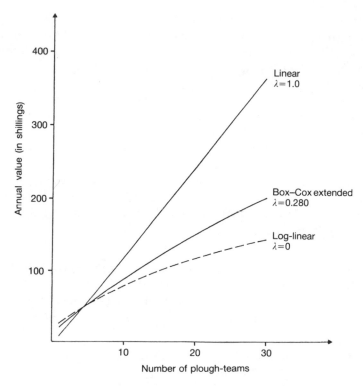

Figure 8.20. The bivariate relationship between annual value and plough-teams for the Essex lay estates, 1086
(All explanatory variables other than ploughs set to zero)

models and the BCE model with $\lambda = 0.280$. The estimated bivariate relationship for the BCE model with $\lambda = 0.280$ is intermediate between those of the estimated linear ($\lambda = 1$) and log-linear ($\lambda = 0$) models, lying somewhat closer to the log-linear curve.

   Regression 3 of Table 8.4 lists the BCE estimates when $\lambda = 0.280$ and $\gamma = 0$. A number of points should be noted. First, the results of a series of diagnostic tests applied to this equation are consistent with the hypothesis that the equation is well-specified. The hetero (a) and hetero (b) tests suggest that the disturbances are homoskedastic. White's t-ratios (see White 1980), which are valid in the presence of heteroskedasticity, were (to one decimal place) equal to the conventional t-ratios (and so are not listed in Table 8.4). This also suggests that the disturbances are homoskedastic. Further, a Chi-squared goodness of fit test for normality suggests that when $\lambda = 0.280$ the disturbances are approximately normally distributed.[18] Secondly, all parameter estimates, other than that for the mills variable, are positive and, with the exception of the mills and bees variables, highly significant.[19] The coefficient of determination adjusted for degrees of freedom, $\bar{R}^2$, has a value of 0.865, which indicates a very good overall fit of the estimated relationship to the data. Although fits of this size are common for aggregated time-series data, they are unusual in the case of individual cross-sectional data of this kind (see Theil 1971, 181). Thirdly, the mills parameter estimate is insignificant from zero at the 5 and indeed 20 per cent level. Further, regression 4 shows that if the mills variable is omitted from the regression, the other parameter estimates and *t*-ratios are only very marginally affected. This evidence is consistent with the hypothesis that mill renders are not included in annual values. Fourthly, regression 5 shows the effect of adding horses to the set of explanatory variables. The estimated parameter on horses is insignificant at all conventional significance levels, which supports the hypothesis that horses were not an income-generating resource.

Regression 6 conveys considerable information on the effect of estimating a value–resource relationship when, as is the case of all but the few counties included in Little Domesday Book and Exeter Domesday Book, livestock data are unavailable. While there is a small fall in the value of the adjusted coefficient of determination and a slight increase in the values of most resource variable parameter estimates and *t*-ratios, the overwhelming impression is that inferences are not much affected. The regression passes the diagnostic tests, and the parameter estimates, *t*-ratios, and elasticities are very similar to those for regressions 3, 4, and 5. These results suggest that good approximations to the value–resource relationship can be obtained even if livestock data are unavailable. (For a possible explanation, see Chapter 5.)

Finally, it should be noted that while it is desirable to indicate the relative importance of the explanatory variables, the estimated regression parameters for the three relationships (the linear, log-linear, and BCE with $\lambda = 0.280$) cannot be compared easily because they apply to differently transformed variables. It is however, meaningful to compare resource–annual value partial elasticities. These elasticities are essentially the percentage changes in annual value with respect to 1 per cent change in the respective resources, evaluated at the sample means of annual value and the resource. They are defined as

$$\frac{\partial V_t}{\partial R_{ti}} \frac{\bar{R}_i}{\bar{V}}$$

where $\bar{R}_i$ and $\bar{V}$ are the sample means of the *i*th resource and annual value, respectively, and

$$\frac{\partial V_t}{\partial R_{ti}}$$

is the partial derivative of annual value with respect to the *i*th resource evaluated at the sample means $\bar{R}_i$ and $\bar{V}$. The lines labelled E in Table 8.4 give these elasticities. In regression 4, which is the preferred equation, the elasticities clearly indicate the importance of the plough-teams variable and, to a lesser extent, peasants and slaves in the value–resources relationship. As expected, the bees variable is much less important. It is interesting that the sum of the elasticities is 1.01 or almost unity, because a sum of unity would imply that if, initially, the manorial value and resource variables are equal to their respective sample means, a small percentage change in all resources will, on average, lead to the same percentage change in value. As the elasticities depend on the initial manorial value and resource values for the BCE model with $\lambda = 0.280$, this characteristic is only approximately true for smaller or larger initial values.

8.14   SIMPLER ESTIMATION PROCEDURES

In all cases, when we have undertaken the BCE maximum likelihood method allowing for heteroskedastic disturbances, we have found that the heteroskedasticity parameter γ estimate is zero. This suggests adopting the simpler procedure of setting $\gamma = 0$, and searching over values of λ for the maximum likelihood estimate of λ, conditional on $\gamma = 0$. The conditional maximum likelihood β-parameters estimates can then be calculated. Finally, we can apply the hetero (a) and hetero (b) tests to these estimates, to test for homoskedastic disturbances. The computer program SHAZAM (White 1978) automatically carries out the required search over values of λ, and then calculates the BCE regression estimates for the value of λ that maximizes the conditional likelihood. The heteroskedasticity tests can then be carried out as indicated in 8.12.

SHAZAM is available for use on many mainframe computer and micro-computer systems; nevertheless, many computer users will not have access to the program. The essential calculations can, however, be performed using a standard LS computer program. For all Domesday relationships examined, we have found that the maximum likelihood λ estimate lies within the zero–one interval. This suggests that the following procedure can be employed. First, estimate the linear and log-linear relationships, and undertake the functional form and heteroskedasticity tests to see if these forms appear appropriate. If one of the forms is appropriate, no further calculations are required. If neither form is appropriate, transform the dependent and explanatory variables data by $(z_t^\lambda - 1)/\lambda$ (where z_t refers to the dependent or explanatory variable), for $\lambda = \frac{1}{4}, \frac{1}{2}$ and $\frac{3}{4}$, and then run linear LS regressions on these data allowing for an intercept in the regressions. Finally, for $\lambda = 0, \frac{1}{4}, \frac{1}{2}, \frac{3}{4}$ and 1, calculate

$$C = -(n/2)\ln(\text{RRS}/n) + (\lambda - 1)\sum_{t=1}^{n} \ln V_t$$

where RSS is the residual sum of squares in the regression involving the transformed data, and V_t is the (untransformed) dependent variable, and select the λ value which gives the largest C value. This should result in the selection of a reasonable value for λ, because the BCE maximum likelihood estimation procedure chooses λ such that C is maximized (see Box and Cox 1964, 215). As discussed earlier, computational problems will occur if some variables take zero values. One way of overcoming these is to adopt a suggestion made by Mosteller and Tukey (1977, 112) of adding a small positive number (e.g. $\frac{1}{6}$) to all observations of such variables before transforming the data.

To illustrate this procedure, we first examine the relationship between tax assessments and manorial annual values for Wiltshire lay estates in 1086. Table 8.5 exhibits the linear and log-linear estimates as regression 1 and regression 2, respectively. On the Godfrey–Wickens functional form test, the linear form is rejected at conventional significance levels (the test statistic is 6.90 and the $2\frac{1}{2}$ per cent critical values ± 1.96), and the hetero (a) and hetero (b) tests indicate significant heteroskedasticity in the disturbances. In contrast, the log-linear form appears appropriate on these tests. The null hypothesis of log-linear form and homoskedastic disturbances is accepted at the 5 per cent significant level on the tests.

Our second illustration is the Essex value–resources relationship for lay holdings in 1086 examined in the previous section. The test statistics in Table 8.4 indicate that the linear form (regression 1) and the log-linear form (regression 2) are inappropriate. Table 8.6 gives the C-function values obtained from the transformed data regressions. $\lambda = \frac{1}{4}$ has the largest C value. The estimates for the BCE model with $\lambda = \frac{1}{4}$ are also exhibited in Table 8.6. The

Table 8.5. The tax assessment–annual value relationship for Wiltshire lay manors, 1086

		Const.	V	λ	$\bar{R}^2$	F	F-Form	Hetero (a)	Hetero (b)
regression 1	β	130.32	4.70	1	0.665	816.0	6.90	11.57	84.51
linear form	t	18.7	29.0				$F(1,423)$	$t(422)$	$t(421)$	$F(2,420)$
$n = 425$	E		0.74				3.86	± 1.96	± 1.96	3.02
regression 2	β	2.66	0.81	0	0.794	1638.4	-1.32	-0.33	0.37
log-linear form	t	33.7	40.5				$F(1,423)$	$t(422)$	$t(421)$	$F(2,420)$
$n = 425$	E		0.81				3.86	± 1.96	± 1.96	3.02

Notes: The first row (labelled β) gives the LS parameter estimates of the intercept or constant when tax assessment is linearly related to annual value. The second row (labelled t) gives t-ratios, and the third row the partial annual value–tax assessment elasticity evaluated at the sample means of tax assessment and annual value.

λ is the BCE transformation parameter; $\bar{R}^2$ is the coefficient of determination adjusted for degrees of freedom; and F is the test statistic for testing that the parameter on annual value is zero. The value of the F-test statistic is 816.0; $F(1,423)$ in line 2 indicates that when the null hypothesis is true the test statistic has an F distribution with 1 and 423 degrees of freedom. Five per cent critical values are given underneath. The entries relating to the functional form (F-Form) and hetero (a) and hetero (b) tests can be interpreted in a similar way.

Table 8.6. C-function and BCE estimates when $\lambda = \frac{1}{4}$ for the Essex annual value–resources relationship, 1086

C-function:

λ	0	$\frac{1}{4}$	$\frac{1}{2}$	$\frac{3}{4}$	1
C	−3177.7	−3094.2	−3141.4	−3305.5	−3557.4

The BCE estimates when $\lambda = \frac{1}{4}$:

	Const.	Pl	Li	N	S	W	Me	P	B	M	$\bar{R}^2$	F	Hetero (a)	Hetero (b)
β	4.34	1.22	0.0416	0.281	0.278	0.0348	0.103	0.054	0.007	−0.087	0.862	472.3	−0.4	2.67
t	28.2	18.0	6.3	6.7	6.7	2.9	4.2	4.1	0.2	−1.1		$F(9,672)$	$t(670)$	$F(2,669)$
E		0.55	0.06	0.17	0.11	0.03	0.06	0.04	0.00	−0.02		1.90	±1.96	3.01

Notes: The first row (labelled β) gives the BCE parameter estimates of the intercept or constant and the following explanatory variables: plough-teams (Pl), livestock (Li), peasants (N), slaves (S), woodland (W), meadow (Me), pasture (P), bees (B), and mills (M). The second row (labelled t) gives t-ratios; and the third row (labelled E) partial resource–annual value elasticities evaluated at the sample means of annual value and the resource. $\bar{R}^2$ is the coefficient of determination adjusted for degrees of freedom, and F is the test statistic for testing that the parameters on all resource variables are zero. The value of the F test statistic is 472.3; $F(9,672)$ in line 2 indicates that when the null hypothesis is true the test statistic rule has an F distribution with 9 and 672 degrees of freedom. Five per cent critical values are given underneath. The entries relating to the hetero (a) and hetero (b) tests can be interpreted in a similar way.

diagnostic tests do not reveal significant heteroskedasticity in the disturbances. The estimates, and in particular the elasticities, are very similar to those of the BCE maximum likelihood estimates listed as regression 3 in Table 8.4. The procedure has indeed produced very good approximations to the maximum likelihood estimates.

Notes

1. See for example Pindyck and Rubinfeld (1981, 8–10, 16–17).
2. For a formal proof, see Schmidt (1976, 3–5).
3. R^2 can also be expressed as

$$R^2 = 1 - \frac{\sum_{t=1}^{n} e_t^2}{\sum_{t=1}^{n} (y_t - \bar{y})^2},$$

that is R^2 is equal to one minus the ratio of the LS residual sum of squares to the sum of squares of the observed dependent variable values about their mean. This can be shown by noting that

$$\sum_{t=1}^{n} (\tilde{y}_t - \bar{y})^2 = \sum_{t=1}^{n} (y_t - \bar{y})^2 - \sum_{t=1}^{n} e_t^2, \text{ so}$$

$$R^2 = \frac{\sum_{t=1}^{n} (\tilde{y}_t - \bar{y})^2}{\sum_{t=1}^{n} (y_t - \bar{y})^2} = \frac{\sum_{t=1}^{n} (y_t - \bar{y})^2 - \sum_{t=1}^{n} e_t^2}{\sum_{t=1}^{n} (y_t - \bar{y})^2} = 1 - \frac{\sum_{t=1}^{n} e_t^2}{\sum (y_t - \bar{y})^2}$$

It can also be shown that the mean of the LS estimated values of the dependent variable is equal to the mean of the observed values of the dependent variable, that is, $(\tilde{y}_1 + \tilde{y}_2 + \ldots + \tilde{y}_n)/n = \bar{y}$. This result can be used to obtain another interpretation of R^2. Because the $1/n$ cancel,

$$R^2 = \frac{\frac{1}{n} \sum_{t=1}^{n} (\tilde{y}_t - \bar{y})^2}{\frac{1}{n} \sum_{t=1}^{n} (y_t - \bar{y})^2}.$$

Now the numerator can be interpreted as the sample variance of the LS estimated dependent variable values or explained sample variance. The denominator is the sample variance of the observed values of the dependent variable. Consequently, we can interpret R^2 as the proportion of the total variance in the dependent variable explained by movements in the explanatory variable. It should be noted that many of the properties of R^2 described above require that there is an intercept in the regression. See Schmidt (1976, 3–6) for further details.

4. In this paragraph we have glossed over a number of difficult mathematical concepts, and the statements are thus somewhat imprecise. The mean and variance of a continuous random variable are defined in a manner slightly different from, but

analogous to, those of a discrete random variable. See Kmenta (1971, 54–66) for further details.

5. This property is true under a weaker condition than independence. The disturbances need only to be uncorrelated (that is, not linearly related): see Schmidt (1976, 1–11) and Kmenta (1971, ch. 7) for proofs of these results.

6. On measurement errors see Schmidt (1976, 105–15). Measurement error in the explanatory variable is less easily accommodated.

7. See Schmidt (1976, ch. 1) and Kmenta (1971, ch. 4) for derivations of this and the other statistical results discussed in this section.

8. SHAZAM was written by, and can be purchased from, K. J. White, Department of Economics, University of British Columbia, Vancouver, BC, Canada V6T 1Y2. A description of the program is given in White (1978).

9. Conditions under which the LS estimators possess the attractive large sample properties are that the data are generated by the regression model such that the random disturbances all have the same distribution which has a mean of zero and a finite variance; that the disturbances are independent of one another; and that the observations on the explanatory variable satisfy some mathematical boundedness and convergence conditions (see lemma 4 of Schmidt 1976, 56). For further information see Schmidt (1976, 55–64) and Kmenta (1971, 162–71).

10. These statements are only intended to convey a rough idea of the concept of a consistent estimator and are not precise. Kmenta (1971, 165) and Schmidt (1976, 249) give more rigorous treatments.

11. From note 3, we see that if the dependent variable is denoted y_t rather than V_t,

$$R^2 = 1 - \frac{\sum\limits_{t=1}^{n} e_t^2}{\sum\limits_{t=1}^{n} (y_t - \bar{y})^2}.$$

$\bar{R}^2$ is defined as

$$1 - \frac{\sum\limits_{t=1}^{n} e_t^2/(n-k)}{\sum\limits_{t=1}^{n} (y_t - \bar{y})^2/(n-1)},$$

where k is the number of estimated β-coefficients (in this case 10). It can be shown that $\bar{R}^2$ is always less than R^2, unless $R^2 = 1$ or $k = 1$, when $R^2 = \bar{R}^2$ (see Theil 1971, 178–9).

12. The BCE model relating to the Essex annual value–resources 1086 data considered in the previous section can be written

$$\frac{V_t^\lambda - 1}{\lambda} = \beta_1 + \beta_2 \left(\frac{R_{t2}^\lambda - 1}{\lambda} \right) + \ldots + \beta_{10} \left(\frac{R_{t10}^\lambda - 1}{\lambda} \right) + \varepsilon_t, \quad \lambda \neq 0$$

$$\ln V_t = \beta_1 + \beta_2 \ln R_{t2} + \ldots + \beta_{10} \ln R_{t10} + \varepsilon_t, \quad \lambda = 0$$

If $\lambda = 1$, the model is

$$V_t - 1 = \beta_1 + \beta_2 (R_{t2} - 1) + \ldots + \beta_{10} (R_{t10} - 1) + \varepsilon_t$$

or

$$V_t = (1 + \beta_1 - \beta_2 - \ldots - \beta_{10}) + \beta_2 R_{t2} + \ldots + \beta_{10} R_{t10} + \varepsilon_t$$

so that V_t is linearly related to the resources $R_{t2} \ldots R_{t10}$ and the intercept is $(1 + \beta_1 - \beta_2 - \ldots - \beta_{10})$.

An implicit assumption underlying the BCE model method is that there exists a value of the transformation parameter, λ, such that the random disturbances, ε_t, and hence $(V_t - 1)/\lambda$ or $\ln V_t$, are normally distributed. However, for λ greater than zero, the latter quantities must be greater than $-1/\lambda$, and for λ less than zero, they must be less than $1/\lambda$; there is a truncation problem, so the quantities can only be approximately normally distributed. If λ equals zero, there is no truncation problem, and if the absolute value of λ is small (which is the case for our estimated models), the truncation is small and the results of Draper and Cox (1969) suggest that inferences are robust with respect to the approximation. For further information on the BCE model, see Box and Cox (1964) and Judge *et al.* (1980, 308–11).

13. For example, the LS estimators $b_1, b_2 \ldots b_k$ (where there are k β-parameters to be estimated) are unbiased, but not best unbiased or best linear unbiased; the estimators $\tilde{V}\text{ar}(b_1), \tilde{V}\text{ar}(b_2) \ldots \tilde{V}\text{ar}(b_k)$ are biased and inconsistent; and the test statistic rules described earlier are not distributed as t or F distributions when the null hypothesis is true (see Schmidt 1976, chs. 1–2). White (1980) describes some tests that are valid in the presence of heteroskedasticity. We refer to these tests in the next section.

14. Formally, it was assumed that the disturbances, ε_t, in the regression equation involving the transformed variables (see note 12 above) are independent normally distributed random variables with a mean of zero and variance $\text{Var}(\varepsilon_t) = \sigma^2 (R_{t2})^\gamma$, where σ^2 is a positive number, R_{t2} is the plough-teams variable for manor t, and γ is a heteroskedasticity parameter, which takes the value zero or a positive number. Notice that if γ equals zero, then $\text{Var}(\varepsilon_t) = \sigma^2$, so the disturbances are homoskedastic and the model reduces to the BCE model. If γ equals two, the variance of the disturbance is proportional to the square of the size-indicator variable, a plausible and commonly used specification for disturbance heteroskedasticity. This model is very similar to that postulated by Lahiri and Egy (1981).

15. A difficulty in applying the log-linear specification is that for some holdings the variables take on zero values and the logarithm of zero is not defined. Only one holding has a value of zero. This is a holding in the hundred of Lexden listed in Domesday Book under 'Free Men of the King'. The entry indicates that the holding was worth 10 shillings in 1066 and reads: 'and when Robert de Montbegon seized it, it was worth 10 shillings, now nothing'. We decided to omit this unusual holding from the sample, so the estimated log-linear relationship is based on 682 observations. To deal with the problem that the resource variables take on zero values for some holdings, we adopted the procedure of adding a small positive number to all explanatory variable observations before taking logarithms. F. Mosteller and J. W. Tukey (1977, 112) call this procedure 'starting the logs'. We adopted their suggestion of adding one-sixth to the observations before taking logarithms. These adjustments were also made to the data when estimating the BCE models. If the observations relating to the holding with zero value are not

omitted from the sample but instead one-sixth is added to the values of all holdings before taking logarithms, then almost identical results to those given in Table 8.4 are obtained.

16. Although there are 683 residuals and hence 683 observations in the second regression, because ten β-parameters were estimated to obtain the residuals, only 673 degrees of freedom remain. Two further β-parameters are estimated in the second regression.

17. For given values of λ and γ, the values of the β and σ^2 that maximize the likelihood function can be calculated. These values, when substituted into the likelihood function, give us the concentrated likelihood function (concentrated on λ and γ). The maximum likelihood estimates of λ and γ are obtained by searching over a grid of values of λ and γ for the values that maximize the value of the concentrated likelihood function. The values of the β and σ^2 that maximize the likelihood function for these values of λ and γ are the maximum likelihood estimates of the β and σ^2. See Lahiri and Egy (1981) for details of this maximum likelihood procedure applied to a similar model.

18. The Chi-squared test was based on 44 subgroups of the residuals from regression 3, and the null hypothesis of normality was not rejected at the 10 per cent level. See Huang and Bolch (1974, 330–5) for details and discussions of the test. Note that our sample size is far greater than the sample sizes employed in the Monte Carlo simulations described in that paper, so the test's performance should be considerably enhanced. The Shapiro–Wilk W-test was not performed because the a_i coefficients and the critical values of the W distribution have not been tabulated for sample sizes greater than 50.

19. The t-ratios exhibited in Table 8.4 are conditional on the maximum likelihood value of λ (that is, $\lambda = 0.280$). Unconditional t-ratios can be computed from a non-linear LS estimation. This is because the BCE maximum likelihood estimation problem can be converted to a non-linear LS problem by dividing all the variables by $\dot{V}^{\lambda-1}$, where $\dot{V}$ is the geometric mean of V_t, thereby reducing the Jacobian of the transformation to unity (see Box and Cox 1964, 216). When the regression equations are estimated by this method, the t-ratios on all explanatory variables are smaller, but nevertheless indicate that the estimates are highly significant. For example, the unconditional t-ratios for the explanatory variables in regression 4 of Table 8.4 are Pl, 8.9, Li, 6.3, N, 5.8, S, 5.2, W, 2.7, Me, 3.9, P, 4.0, B, 0.1. The estimated standard deviation of the sampling distribution of λ is 0.031, so λ is significantly different from both 0 and 1 at the 5 per cent significance level.

9

Economic production functions

9.1 INTRODUCTION

This chapter is an introduction to economic production functions. The treatment of the subject focuses on the analysis of manorial production functions in Chapter 6. In 9.2 some basic characteristics of production functions are introduced. The ideas of the marginal product of a resource and the law of diminishing returns are discussed and illustrated. In 9.3 the concepts of an isoquant, the marginal rate of substitution between two resources, and the convexity of isoquants are reviewed and some properties of isoquants developed. The elasticity of substitution between two resources is defined in 9.4. 9.5 deals with questions relating to returns to scale, homogeneity, and homotheticity. The Cobb–Douglas production function is introduced in 9.6. The main properties of the Constant Elasticity of Substitution production function are derived in 9.7. 9.8 is concerned with generalizing the Constant Elasticity of Substitution production function to allow for more than two resources; the concepts of a partial elasticity of substitution and separability are considered and applied to the basic Constant Elasticity of Substitution production function in three resources. The production function proposed by Mukerji is discussed in 9.9, and the Sato Two-Level Constant Elasticity of Substitution function is considered in 9.10. The idea of flexible functional forms and the Generalized Linear production function are the subject of 9.11. The Generalized Quadratic production function is analysed in the final section.

Amongst the topics not covered are questions of distribution; modelling technical change; analysis when profit maximization, perfect competition, and variable input levels are assumed; and indirect and dual representations of the production function. More general introductory expositions on the subject of production functions are given by Heathfield (1971) and Baumol (1977). A more advanced treatment is Fuss and McFadden (1978), and in particular Fuss *et al.* (1978). Other useful surveys are Bridge (1971, ch. 6) and Intriligator (1978, ch. 8). The mathematical concepts used in this chapter are reviewed in Henderson and Quandt (1980) and Chiang (1974).

9.2   SOME CHARACTERISTICS OF PRODUCTION FUNCTIONS

The manorial annual value is the income accruing to the landholder. If the manor was worked by the landholder or his bailiff this income was the value of output, that is, the value added by the production process. If the manor was leased out, the income was the rent received. It is reasonable to suppose that these rents reflected the value of output that could be generated from the holding. A production function relates the output of a production unit, such as a manor, to the inputs. The annual value–resources relationship can therefore be interpreted as a production function, in which output is measured in money or value terms and the inputs or resource levels are measured in physical terms. The production function is usually regarded as a technical relationship between the quantities of inputs and the maximum amount or value of output which can be produced at prescribed input levels. If there are just two inputs or resources, the production function can be represented as

$$V = f(R_1, R_2) \tag{1}$$

where V is the maximum value of output that can be produced when R_1 units of the first resource and R_2 units of the second resource are used, and f represents the functional form of the relationship. f will vary depending on the particular production function with which we are concerned. Examples of particular production functions are

$$V = 3R_1 + 3R_2 \tag{2}$$

$$V = 3R_1 + 3R_2 + 2(R_1^{\frac{1}{2}} R_2^{\frac{1}{2}}) \tag{3}$$

where $R_1^{\frac{1}{2}}$ denotes the square root of R_1.

Notice that for these production functions the value of V is uniquely determined once the values of R_1 and R_2 are prescribed. For example, for (2), if $R_1 = R_2 = 1$, then $V = 6$. 6 is the maximum value of output that can be produced with 2 units of resource 1 and with 2 units of resource 2. To simplify the analysis that follows, we will assume that the resource levels can be varied continuously, and that the production functions possess first and second derivatives.

For most technologies, if more inputs are used, then output can be increased. This is true for the production functions (2) and (3). For example, for (3), if $R_1 = R_2 = 1$, then $V = 8$ and if $R_1 = R_2 = 2$, $V = 16$. This idea can also be illustrated in Figure 9.1 where, for the production function (3), we have graphed the relationship between V and R_1, when R_2 is fixed at $R_2 = 1$. Notice that, as R_1 increases, V increases. V is said to be a *monotonically increasing function* of R_1 when $R_2 = 1$. This property is also true for (3) when R_2 is fixed at any other value, so we can say that V is a monotonically increasing function of R_1. V is also a monotonically increasing function of R_2, so we can say that V is a monotonically increasing function of both resources.

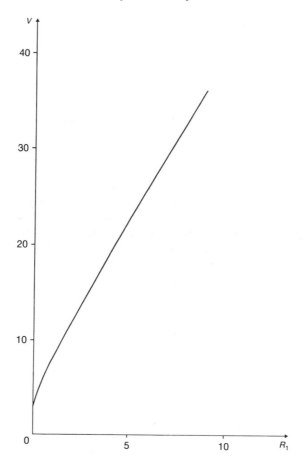

Figure 9.1. The production function $V = 3R_1 + 3R_2 + 2(R_1^{\frac{1}{2}} R_2^{\frac{1}{2}})$
The graph of V against R_1, with $R_2 = 1$

The change in output resulting from a (small) unit change in the level of use of a resource, when the other resources are held constant, is called the *marginal product* of that resource. From Figure 9.1, the marginal product of resource 1, denoted MP_1, is positive for all values of R_1, when $R_2 = 1$. If the marginal product of resource 1 is also positive for all values of R_1 when R_2 is set at any other value, we say that the marginal product of resource 1 is (everywhere) positive, that is, (everywhere) $MP_1 > 0$. A more rigorous definition of the marginal product of resource 1 is in terms of the *partial derivative* of V with respect to $R_1, \partial V/\partial R_1$, which we will denote V_1. We define $MP_1 = V_1$ and note that as with MP_1, V_1 can be evaluated at different values of R_1 and R_2.

If a production function is a monotonically increasing function of both resources, then $V_1 > 0$, and $V_2 > 0$ at all values of R_1 and R_2, and hence $MP_1 > 0$ and $MP_2 > 0$ at all values of R_1 and R_2.

An often observed empirical law is the *law of diminishing returns*, which states that, as more of some resource, say resource 1, is used, all other resource levels held constant, eventually, additional quantities of resource 1 will yield diminishing marginal contributions to output. The law implies that, when resource uses are varied in this way, the marginal product of resource 1 will eventually decrease. Since the marginal product of resource 1 is the first derivative of output with respect to R_1, this means that the second derivative with respect to R_1 will eventually be negative. If we denote $\partial^2 V/\partial R_1^2$ by V_{11}, then eventually $V_{11} < 0$.

For production function (2), $MP_1 = V_1 = 3 > 0$ for all R_1, R_2 values and $MP_2 = 3 > 0$ for all R_1, R_2 values. This production function has the unusual feature that the marginal products do not vary with the level of use of either of the resources. As a consequence, $V_{11} = 0$ for all R_1, R_2 values, $V_{22} = 0$ for all R_1, R_2 values and the function does not admit diminishing returns to either resource. For production function (3), $MP_1 = 3 + R_2^{-\frac{1}{2}}R_2^{\frac{1}{2}}$, where $R_1^{-\frac{1}{2}}$ is the reciprocal of the square root of R_1, and $MP_2 = 3 + R_1^{\frac{1}{2}}R_2^{-\frac{1}{2}}$, so the marginal products are positive at all values of the resources. Also $V_{11} = -\frac{1}{2}R_1^{-\frac{3}{2}}R_2^{\frac{1}{2}}$ and $V_{22} = -\frac{1}{2}R_1^{\frac{1}{2}}R_2^{-\frac{3}{2}}$, which are negative for all positive values of R_1 and R_2, so (3) does admit diminishing returns to both factors. $\partial^2 V/\partial R_1\,\partial R_2 = V_{12} = \frac{1}{2}R_1^{-\frac{1}{2}}R_2^{-\frac{1}{2}} > 0$ for all positive values of R_1 and R_2. This indicates that MP_1 increases when R_2 increases and MP_2 increases when R_1 increases. Notice that $V_{12} = V_{21}$.

9.3 ISOQUANTS AND THEIR PROPERTIES

One way of describing a production function is by graphing some of its isoquants. An *isoquant* is a locus of resource level combinations, all of which are capable of producing the same output. Figure 9.2 is a graph of two isoquants for production function (2). From (2) we can see that $V = 3$ when $R_1 = 1$ and $R_2 = 0$ (i.e. at point A in Figure 9.2), when $R_1 = 0$ and $R_2 = 1$ (at point B) and when $R_1 = \frac{1}{2}$ and $R_2 = \frac{1}{2}$ (point C). The $V = 3$ isoquant must therefore be the combinations of resource levels R_1 and R_2 which lie along the line that travels through these three points. Notice that (2) indicates that positive output ($V > 0$) is possible if only one resource is used, and this corresponds to a $V > 0$ isoquant touching the axes.

The $V = 3$ isoquant in Figure 9.2 has a negative slope. If a production function is a monotonically increasing function of both resources (and hence the marginal products are positive for both resources), then this must be the case. To see this, consider point C in Figure 9.2. If increased resource use leads to greater output, any isoquant through C cannot lie on or to the NE of the dotted horizontal and vertical lines, because this would imply that the same output is produced with more of one or both resources. Similarly, any isoquant through C cannot lie on or to the SW of the dashed horizontal and vertical lines, because this would imply that the same output is produced with

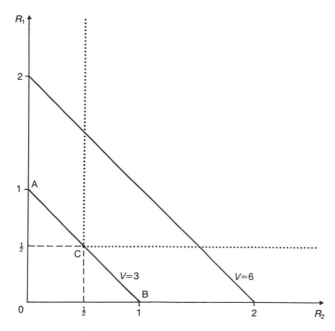

Figure 9.2. The production function $V = 3R_1 + 3R_2$
The $V = 3$ and $V = 6$ isoquants

less of one or both resources. Consequently, an isoquant through C must lie to the NW and SE of C, and hence must have a negative slope at C.

Figure 9.2 also indicates the $V = 6$ isoquant for production function (2). This isoquant passes through the points $R_1 = 2, R_2 = 0$; $R_1 = 1, R_2 = 1$ and $R_1 = 0$, $R_2 = 2$. The $V = 6$ isoquant is a straight line parallel to the $V = 3$ isoquant. Notice that the $V - 6$ isoquant is further from the origin. If the production function is a montonically increasing function of both resources, it is obvious that isoquants further from the origin correspond to greater outputs.

Figure 9.3 illustrates the property that, if a production function is a monotonically increasing function in the resources, then the isoquants cannot intersect. In Figure 9.3 we have two isoquants intersecting at A, but this implies that there must be points such as B and C at which the same output is produced yet more of both resources are used at one point (that is, C) than the other (B). This cannot occur if the production function is a monotonically increasing function in both resources. To summarize these arguments: if a production function is a monotonically increasing function in the resources, the isoquants will have negative slopes; isoquants further from the origin will correspond to higher output levels, and isoquants cannot intersect.

The *marginal rate of substitution* between resources 1 and 2, denoted MRS_{12}, is the rate at which one resource can be substituted for the other so

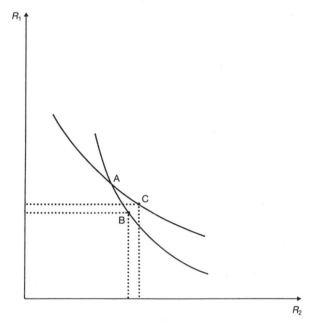

Figure 9.3. For a production function which is a monotonically increasing function of the resources, the isoquants cannot intersect

that the output level is exactly maintained. The marginal rate of substitution usually depends on the amounts of the resources 1 and 2 being used in production, and so will usually vary at the different points on the isoquant graph. Figure 9.4 is a graph of the $V = 3$ isoquant for production function (3). The marginal rate of substitution between resources 1 and 2 at A is given by the absolute value of the slope (or, more precisely, the slope of the tangent) to the isoquant at the point A (the tangent is represented by the dashed line in Figure 9.4).

An often observed empirical law is the *law of diminishing marginal rate of substitution*, which states that the more a resource is used in production relative to the others, the lesser its substitution value, so that more of it needs to be substituted to maintain the output level. In other words, the marginal product of the resource that is used more intensively declines relative to that of the other resources. The $V = 3$ isoquant in Figure 9.4 is strictly convex to the origin—that is, as we move downwards and to the right along the curve, the slope of the curve becomes flatter. Since the marginal rate of substitution between the resources is the absolute value of the slope, this implies a diminishing marginal rate of substitution between the resources. In contrast, the $V = 3$ isoquant for production function (2) in Figure 9.2 is convex to the origin, but not strictly convex. The slope of the isoquant is constant

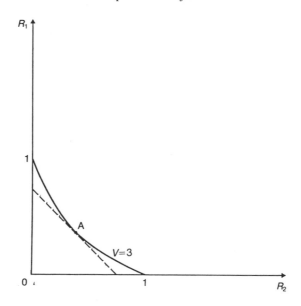

Figure 9.4. The production function $V = 3R_1 + 3R_2 + 2(R_1^{\frac{1}{2}} R_2^{\frac{1}{2}})$
The $V = 3$ isoquant

throughout its length, and so the production function does not admit the law of diminishing marginal rates of substitution.

Some of the arguments presented above can be made more rigorous by the following simple mathematics (which is not essential for the understanding of the remainder of the chapter). If we totally differentiate the general production function (1), we obtain

$$dV = V_1 \, dR_1 + V_2 \, dR_2 \qquad (4)$$

Along any isoquant $dV = 0$, so

$$0 = V_1 \, dR_1 + V_2 \, dR_2$$

or

$$\frac{dR_1}{dR_2} = \frac{-V_2}{V_1} \qquad (5)$$

dR_1/dR_2 can be interpreted as the slope of the isoquant (see Figure 9.5). The MRS_{12} is the absolute value of this slope, i.e. $|dR_1/dR_2|$, which from (5) is equal to the ratio $|-V_2/V_1| = |-MP_2/MP_1|$. If $MP_1 > 0$ and $MP_2 > 0$, then $MRS_{12} = MP_2/MP_1$, i.e. the ratio of the marginal products of the resources. Note that, if $MP_1 > 0$ and $MP_2 > 0$, then $dR_1/dR_2 < 0$, so the isoquants must have a negative slope. Also notice that, at a point on any smooth isoquant, the slope along the isoquant is the same in both directions, so that $MRS_{12} =$

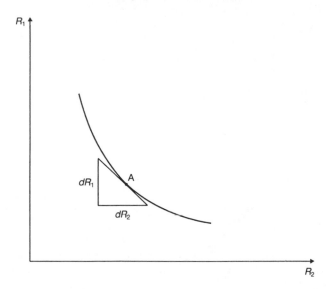

Figure 9.5. dR_1/dR_2 can be interpreted as the slope of the isoquant at the point A

MRS_{21}, i.e. the marginal rate of substitution of resource 1 for resource 2 = the marginal rate of substitution of resource 2 for resource 1. The slope (and hence the value of MRS_{12}) will, however, vary depending on the way in which the axes are labelled. (If R_2 appears on the vertical axis and R_1 on the horizontal, then the absolute value of the slope is $|dR_2/dR_1|$.) In the following sections we will maintain the convention that the slope is defined as in (5) and so, with positive marginal products, $MRS_{12} = V_2/V_1 = MP_2/MP_1$.

9.4   THE ELASTICITY OF SUBSTITUTION BETWEEN TWO RESOURCES

The marginal rate of substitution between two resources is a measure of the slope of an isoquant, and depends on the units in which the resources are measured. A measure of the curvature of an isoquant which is dimensionless is the *elasticity of substitution* between the resources. The elasticity of substitution between resources 1 and 2, denoted ES_{12}, is defined as the ratio of the proportional change in the relative resource levels, R_1/R_2, to the associated proportional change in the marginal rate of substitution between the resources as we move along an isoquant. In economic jargon, this is the elasticity of the relative resource levels, R_1/R_2, with respect to the MRS_{12} when moving along the isoquant. For a movement from a point on the isoquant along the isoquant, $d(R_1/R_2)$ measures the change in the use of R_1 as compared with R_2, and $dMRS_{12}$ measures the corresponding change in the marginal rate of substitution, so the elasticity of substitution can be expressed mathematically as

$$ES_{12} = \frac{d(R_1/R_2)}{R_1/R_2} \cdot \frac{MRS_{12}}{dMRS_{12}} \tag{6}$$

where R_1 and R_2 are allowed to vary so that output is constant.

The elasticity of substitution varies inversely with the curvature of the isoquant—the greater the curvature, the smaller the elasticity of substitution. If technology is such that resources must be used in fixed proportions in production, then there is no opportunity for substitution, and the elasticity of substitution is zero. A production function exhibiting this characteristic is not a monotonically increasing function of the resources, since, although output increases if more of both resources are used, it may not be possible to increase output if more of only one resource is used. Two isoquants for a fixed proportions production function are exhibited in Figure 9.6. In this Figure, we see that at least 2 units of resource 1 and 1 unit of resource 2 are required to produce 1 unit of output. If 4 units of resource 1 and 1 unit of resource 2 are available, then it is still only possible to produce 1 unit of output. More units of resource 2 are required to increase output. For example, with 4 units of resource 1 and 2 units of resource 2, 2 units of output can be produced.

Production function (2) lies at the other extreme of the substitutability spectrum. For production function (2) the resources are perfectly substitutable. This is easily seen since, at any R_1, R_2 level, if 1 unit of resource 1

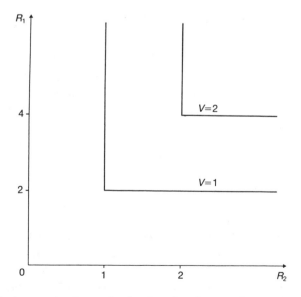

Figure 9.6. The isoquants of a production function that requires resources to be used in fixed proportions

is substituted for 1 unit of resource 2, output will remain unchanged. The elasticity of substitution at all values of R_1 and R_2 is infinite. This is always the case if the isoquants are downward-sloping straight lines, as in Figure 9.2.

An alternative expression for the elasticity of substitution is[1]

$$\text{ES}_{12} = \frac{V_1 V_2 (V_1 R_1 + V_2 R_2)}{R_1 R_2 (2 V_1 V_2 V_{12} - V_1^2 V_{22} - V_2^2 V_{11})} \tag{7}$$

Alternatively, it can be shown that[2]

$$\text{ES}_{12} = \frac{\text{MRS}_{12}(R_2 \text{MRS}_{12} + R_1)}{R_1 R_2 (\text{d}^2 R_1 / \text{d} R_2^2)}$$

$$= \frac{\text{MRS}_{12}(R_2 \text{MRS}_{12} + R_1)}{R_1 R_2 (\text{MRS}_{12}(\partial \text{MRS}_{12} / \partial R_1) - \partial \text{MRS}_{12} / \partial R_2)} \tag{8}$$

From (7), we can see that ES_{12} is symmetric in the two resources, so, unlike MRS_{12}, ES_{12} does not depend on the way the slope of the tangent to the isoquant is measured. From the first equality in (8), we see that ES_{12} is inversely related to the curvature of the isoquant because $\text{d}^2 R_1 / \text{d} R_2^2$ measures the rate of change of the slope of the isoquant. The larger the value of $\text{d}^2 R_1 / \text{d} R_2^2$, the more highly curved the isoquant and the smaller the value of ES_{12}. Also, if marginal productivities are positive and the isoquants strictly convex, we see that ES_{12} must be positive.

9.5 RETURNS TO SCALE, HOMOGENEITY, AND HOMOTHETICITY

The technical conditions of production can be described by the shape and position of the isoquants of the production function. In the previous two sections we have considered issues relating to the shape of the isoquants. Two production functions may have isoquants with exactly the same shape, but a different isoquant graph, because one is more efficient than the other, and hence the isoquants for the different output levels are positioned closer to the origin. This is the case for the production function $V = 6R_1 + 6R_2$ compared with production function (2), since, for example, when $R_1 = R_2 = 1$, $V = 12$ for this function, compared with $V = 6$ for production function (2).

Another question is the effect on output of doubling inputs or *the returns to scale*. For production functions (2) and (3), if the level of all resources is doubled, the output level is doubled. For example, for (2), if $R_1 = R_2 = 1$, $V = 6$ and if $R_1 = R_2 = 2$, $V = 12$. This phenomenon is known as *constant returns to scale*. Other production functions exhibit *increasing returns to scale*—that is, when all resource levels are doubled, output is more than doubled—and some *decreasing returns to scale*—that is, when all resource levels are doubled, output is less than doubled. An example of a production function exhibiting increasing returns to scale is

$$V = R_1 R_2 \tag{9}$$

If $R_1 = R_2 = 1$, $V = 1$, but if $R_1 = R_2 = 2$, $V = 4 > 2$. An example of a production function exhibiting decreasing returns to scale is

$$V = 1 + 3R_1 + 3R_2 \tag{10}$$

If $R_1 = R_2 = 1$, $V = 7$, but if $R_1 = R_2 = 2$, $V = 13 < 14$.

A useful concept relating to scale matters is *homogeneity*. A production function is said to be homogeneous of degree $\mu \geqslant 0$, if doubling all resources leads to output being increased by two to the power μ times the original output, or, more generally, if all resource levels are increased by some factor s, then output is increased by s to the power μ times the original output. Thus, if originally $V = f(R_1, R_2)$ and then all resources are increased by the factor s, the production function is homogeneous of degree μ, if $f(sR_1, sR_2) = s^\mu V$. If $\mu = 1$, then $f(sR_1, sR_2) = sV$ and the production function exhibits constant returns to scale. If $\mu > 1$, then the production function exhibits increasing returns to scale, and if $\mu < 1$, it exhibits decreasing returns to scale. As an illustration of these ideas, note that production function (9) is homogeneous of degree 2 and exhibits increasing returns to scale. Also, a production function need not be homogeneous to exhibit increasing or decreasing returns to scale; for example, production function (10) is inhomogeneous but exhibits decreasing returns to scale.

For an inhomogeneous production function, the returns to scale will vary depending on the resource values. A local measure of scale is given by the *elasticity of scale*. If there are two resources, the elasticity of scale is defined as

$$\text{ESC} = \sum_{i-1}^{2} \frac{\partial V}{\partial R_i} \cdot \frac{R_i}{V}$$

where the derivatives are evaluated at a particular set of resource values (say, $R_1 = 1$ and $R_2 = 1$) and V is the output value at these resource values. $(\partial V / \partial R_i)(R_i / V)$ is the *elasticity of output* with respect to the ith resource, so the elasticity of scale is the sum of the elasticities of output.

A production function homogeneous of degree 1 is sometimes said to be a linear homogeneous production function. This is a different concept from a linear production function. The production function (2) is an example of a linear production function and it is also a linear homogeneous production function; but a linear production function may not be a linear homogeneous production function (for example, $V = 1 + 3R_1 + 3R_2$ is a linear production function but not linear homogeneous). Also, a linear homogeneous production function may not be a linear production function (for example, $V = R_1^{\frac{1}{2}} R_2^{\frac{1}{2}}$ is linear homogeneous, since $(sR_1)^{\frac{1}{2}}(sR_2)^{\frac{1}{2}} = s^{\frac{1}{2} + \frac{1}{2}} R_1^{\frac{1}{2}} R_2^{\frac{1}{2}} = sV$, but is not a linear production function).

It can be shown that the isoquants of a production function homogeneous of degree 1 will all have the same general shape, in the sense that isoquants corresponding to higher output levels are blown up versions of those for lower output levels. The isoquants will also be equally spaced so that, for example, the $V = 2$ isoquant will be twice as far from the origin as the $V = 1$ isoquant. The isoquants of a production function homogeneous of degree μ will also have the same general shape, but will be positioned in a ratio depending on the value of μ. For example, for a production function homogeneous of degree 2 ((9) is an example), the $V = 4$ isoquant will be twice as far from the origin as the $V = 1$ isoquant.

The isoquants of a production function may all have the same general shape but the function may not be homogeneous of any degree. A *homothetic* function is any monotonically increasing function of a homogeneous function, so, if $V = f(R_1, R_2)$ is a homogeneous function, then $V^* = f^*(V)$ is homothetic if $\partial V^*/\partial V > 0$ for all R_1 and R_2 values. An example of a homothetic but not homogeneous production function is $V^* = 1 + 3R_1 + 3R_2$, because $V = 3R_1 + 3R_2$ is a homogeneous function and $\partial V^*/\partial V = 1$ for all R_1 and R_2 values.

9.6 THE COBB–DOUGLAS PRODUCTION FUNCTION

An often used production function in both theoretical and applied economic analysis is the *Cobb–Douglas production function* first mentioned by Wicksteed (1894) and popularized by Douglas and Cobb (1928). The Cobb–Douglas production function takes the form

$$V = AR_1^{\beta_1} R_2^{\beta_2} \tag{11}$$

where A, β_1, and β_2 are parameters which take positive values.

If we denote the logarithm of R_1 by $\ln R_1$, then, since $\ln R_1 R_2 = \ln R_1 + \ln R_2$ and $\ln R_1^{\beta_1} = \beta_1 \ln R_1$, (11) can be expressed

$$\ln V = \beta_0 + \beta_1 \ln R_1 + \beta_2 \ln R_2 \tag{12}$$

where $\beta_0 = \ln A$. The function has a simple linear form in the logarithms of output and the resource levels. From (12), $\partial \ln V/\partial \ln R_1 = \beta_1$, so β_1 can be identified as the elasticity of output with respect to the amount of resource 1 used, when R_2 is held constant. Notice that the value of this elasticity is the same at all R_1, R_2 values. One interpretation of the elasticity is that a 1 per cent increase in R_1, with R_2 held constant, adds (approximately) β_1 per cent to output.

The value of A will depend on the units of measurement of the resources and output and will also depend on the efficiency of production, since, once the units of measurement of the variables are determined, the larger the value of A then the larger output will be for given prescribed resource levels.

The marginal products of the two resources are obtained by taking first derivatives.

$$\text{MP}_1 = V_1 = A\beta_1 R_1^{\beta_1 - 1} R_2^{\beta_2} = \beta_1 A R_1^{\beta_1} R_2^{\beta_2} R_1^{-1} = \beta_1 V R_1^{-1}, \quad \text{and}$$

$$\text{MP}_2 = V_2 = \beta_2 V R_2^{-1}$$

The marginal products are positive for all R_1, R_2 values because $\beta_1 > 0$ and $\beta_2 > 0$.

The second order derivatives are

$$V_{11} = A\beta_1(\beta_1 - 1)R_1^{\beta_1 - 2} R_2^{\beta_1} = \beta_1(\beta_1 - 1)A R_1^{\beta_1} R_2^{\beta_2} R_1^{-2} = \beta_1(\beta_1 - 1)VR_1^{-2}$$

$$V_{22} = \beta_2(\beta_2 - 1)VR_2^{-2}, \quad \text{and}$$

$$V_{12} = V_{21} = A\beta_1 R_1^{\beta_1 - 1}\beta_2 R_2^{\beta_2 - 1} = \beta_1\beta_2 A R_1^{\beta_1} R_2^{\beta_2} R_1^{-1} R_2^{-1} = \beta_1\beta_2 VR_1^{-1}R_2^{-1}$$

The function admits diminishing returns to both resources if (eventually) $V_{11} < 0$ and $V_{22} < 0$. This will occur if $\beta_1 < 1$ and $\beta_2 < 1$. Notice that V_{12} is positive. This indicates that MP_1 increases as R_2 increases and MP_2 increases as R_1 increases.

Isoquants for particular output levels can be generated from (11). For example, the $V = 3$ isoquant is obtained by setting $V = 3$ and then solving for R_1 in terms of R_2, that is,

$$3 = A R_1^{\beta_1} R_2^{\beta_2}, \text{ so } R_1^{-\beta_1} = (A/3)R_2^{\beta_2} \quad \text{and} \quad R_1 = (A/3)^{-1/\beta_1} R_2^{-\beta_2/\beta_1}$$

The $V = 3$ isoquant is described by the R_1, R_2 values that satisfy this equation. The slope of an isoquant is given by

$$\frac{dR_1}{dR_2} = \frac{-V_2}{V_1} = \frac{-\beta_2 VR_2^{-1}}{\beta_1 VR_1^{-1}} = -\beta_2\beta_1^{-1}(R_1/R_2)$$

which is negative and varies with the resource level ratio R_1/R_2. The larger this ratio the more negative the slope. Consequently, the isoquants are strictly convex to the origin. The $V > 0$ isoquants do not touch the vertical or horizontal axes but are asymptotic to them.[3]

The marginal rate of substitution between the resources,

$$\text{MRS}_{11} = V_2/V_1 = (\beta_2 VR_2^{-1})/(\beta_1 VR_1^{-1}) = \beta_2\beta_1^{-1}(R_1/R_2)$$

The elasticity of substitution can be calculated from (7) using the first and second order derivatives obtained above. From (7)

$$E_{12} = \frac{V_1 V_2(V_1 R_1 + V_2 R_2)}{R_1 R_2(2V_1 V_2 V_{12} - V_1^2 V_{22} - V_2^2 V_{11})}$$

$$= \frac{\beta_1 VR_1^{-1}\beta_2 VR_2^{-1}(\beta_1 VR_1^{-1}R_1 + \beta_2 VR_2^{-1}R_2)}{R_1 R_2(2\beta_1 VR_1^{-1}\beta_2 VR_2^{-1}\beta_1\beta_2 VR_1^{-1}R_2^{-1} - \beta_1^2 V^2 R_1^{-2}\beta_2(\beta_2 - 1)VR_2^{-2}}{\qquad\qquad - \beta_2^2 V^2 R_2^{-2}\beta_1(\beta_1 - 1)VR_1^{-2})}$$

$$= \frac{\beta_1\beta_2 V^3 R_1^{-1} R_2^{-1}(\beta_1 + \beta_2)}{\beta_1\beta_2 V^3 R_1^{-1} R_2^{-1}(2\beta_1\beta_2 - \beta_1(\beta_2 - 1) - \beta_2(\beta_1 - 1))}$$

Since $2\beta_1\beta_2 - \beta_1(\beta_2 - 1) - \beta_2(\beta_1 - 1) = \beta_1 + \beta_2$, $E_{12} = 1$ at all R_1, R_2 values.

Finally, we look at the returns to scale properties of the Cobb–Douglas production function. If the resource levels are changed by a factor $s > 0$, the new level of output will be

$$V^* = A(sR_1)^{\beta_1}(sR_2)^{\beta_2} = AR_1^{\beta_1}R_2^{\beta_2}s^{\beta_1 + \beta_2} = Vs^{\beta_1 + \beta_2}$$

The new output level is $s^{\beta_1 + \beta_2}$ times the original level, so the production function is homogeneous of degree $\mu = \beta_1 + \beta_2$ for all R_1, R_2 values. If $\beta_1 + \beta_2 = 1$, then the production function exhibits constant returns to scale, if $\beta_1 + \beta_2 < 1$, the returns to scale will be decreasing and if $\beta_1 + \beta_2 > 1$, the returns will be increasing.

9.7 THE CONSTANT ELASTICITY OF SUBSTITUTION PRODUCTION FUNCTION[4]

The Cobb–Douglas production function is restrictive in the sense that the elasticity of substitution between the resources is equal to one for all R_1, R_2 values. *The Constant Elasticity of Substitution (CES) production function* was introduced by Arrow *et al.* (1961) as a generalization to allow the elasticity of substitution to be constant at values that may be different from one. The CES production function can be represented as

$$V = (\beta_1 R_1^\lambda + \beta_2 R_2^\lambda)^{\mu/\lambda} \tag{13}$$

where β_1, β_2, and μ are positive parameters and λ is a parameter taking a value less than or equal to one.[5]

The marginal products of the two resources are obtained by taking first derivatives.

$$\mathrm{MP}_1 = V_1 = (\mu/\lambda)(\beta_1 R_1^\lambda + \beta_2 R_2^\lambda)^{\mu/\lambda - 1}\beta_1 \lambda R_1^{\lambda - 1}$$

by the function of a function differentiation rule, so

$$\mathrm{MP}_1 = \mu\beta_1 R_1^{\lambda - 1}(\beta_1 R_1^\lambda + \beta_2 R_2^\lambda)^{\mu/\lambda}(\beta_1 R_1^\lambda + \beta_2 R_2^\lambda)^{-1}$$
$$= \mu\beta_1 R_1^{\lambda - 1}VV^{-\lambda/\mu}, \text{ because } (\beta_1 R_1^\lambda + \beta_2 R_2^\lambda) = V^{\lambda/\mu}$$
$$= \mu\beta_1 R_1^{\lambda - 1}V^{1 - \lambda/\mu}$$
$$\mathrm{MP}_2 = V_2 = \mu\beta_2 R_2^{\lambda - 1}V^{1 - \lambda/\mu}$$

For the admissible parameter values, the marginal products are positive for all R_1, R_2 values.

The second order derivatives are

$$V_{11} = \mu\beta_1((\lambda - 1)R_1^{\lambda - 2}V^{1 - \lambda/\mu} + R_1^{\lambda - 1}(1 - \lambda/\mu)V^{-\lambda/\mu}V_1)$$

by the product and function of a function differentiation rules, so

$$V_{11} = \mu\beta_1 R_1^{\lambda-1} V^{-\lambda/\mu}((\lambda-1)R_1^{-1}V - (\lambda/\mu - 1)V_1)$$

$$V_{22} = \mu\beta_2 R_2^{\lambda-1} V^{-\lambda/\mu}((\lambda-1)R_2^{-1}V - (\lambda/\mu - 1)V_2)$$

$$V_{12} = \mu\beta_1 R_1^{\lambda-1}(1 - \lambda/\mu)V^{-\lambda/\mu}V_2 = (1 - \lambda/\mu)V^{-1}V_1 V_2$$

The sign of V_{11} and V_{22} (and hence whether the CES function admits diminishing returns to these resources) depends on the signs of $(\lambda-1)R_1^{-1}V - (\lambda/\mu - 1)V_1$ and $(\lambda-1)R_2^{-1} - (\lambda/\mu - 1)V_2$, respectively, which, in general, depend on the values of R_1, R_2, and μ.[6] Nevertheless, when $\mu = 1$,

$$V_{11} = \beta_1 R_1^{\lambda-1} V^{-\lambda}(\lambda-1)(R_1^{-1}V - V_1) < 0 \text{ if } (R_1^{-1}V - V_1) > 0 \text{ and } \lambda \neq 1.$$

$$(R_1^{-1}V - V_1) = R_1^{-1}V - \beta_1 R_1^{\lambda-1} V^{1-\lambda} = R_1^{-1}V(1 - \beta_1 R_1^\lambda V^{-\lambda})$$

$$= R_1^{-1}V(1 - \beta_1 R_1^\lambda(\beta_1 R_1^\lambda + \beta_2 R_2^\lambda)^{-1}) > 0$$

because all terms are positive and $0 < \beta_1 R_1^\lambda(\beta_1 R_1^\lambda + \beta_2 R_2^\lambda)^{-1} < 1$. Hence if $\mu = 1$, $\lambda \neq 1$ the CES production function does admit diminishing returns to resource 1, and, by a similar argument, this is also true for resource 2.

$V_{12} > 0$ if $(1 - \lambda/\mu) > 0$, which is the case if $\mu \geq 1$, so when $\mu \geq 1$, MP_1 increases as R_2 increases and MP_2 increases as R_1 increases.

The isoquants for particular output levels can be generated from (13). For example, the $V = 3$ isoquant is given by $3 = (\beta_1 R_1^\lambda + \beta_2 R_2^\lambda)^{\mu/\lambda}$. Solving for R_1, we obtain

$$3^{\lambda/\mu} = \beta_1 R_1^\lambda + \beta_2 R_2^\lambda$$

$$R_1^\lambda = (3^{\lambda/\mu} - \beta_2 R_2^\lambda)\beta_1^{-1}$$

$$R_1 = (3^{\lambda/\mu} - \beta_2 R_2^\lambda)^{1/\lambda}\beta_1^{-1/\lambda}$$

The slope of the isoquant is given by

$$\frac{dR_1}{dR_2} = -\frac{V_2}{V_1} = -\frac{\mu\beta_2 R_2^{\lambda-1} V^{1-\lambda/\mu}}{\mu\beta_1 R_1^{\lambda-1} V^{1-\lambda/\mu}}$$

$$= -\beta_1^{-1}\beta_2(R_1/R_2)^{1-\lambda} \tag{14}$$

The slope is negative unless $(R_1/R_2)^{1-\lambda} = 0$, in which case it is zero. The slope varies with the resource level ratio R_1/R_2. If λ is finite and not equal to one, $1 - \lambda > 0$, hence the larger the R_1/R_2 ratio the more negative is the isoquant slope and the isoquants will be strictly convex. Three special cases are of interest. First, if $\lambda = 0$, $dR_1/dR_2 = -\beta_1^{-1}\beta_2(R_1/R_2)$, which is the same slope as for the Cobb–Douglas production function. Secondly, if $\lambda = 1$, $dR_1/dR_2 = -\beta_1^{-1}\beta_2$, so the slope does not depend on the resource level ratio but is constant. The isoquant is a straight line with slope $-\beta_1^{-1}\beta_2$, and so has the same shape as that of the linear production function, $V = \beta_1 R_1 + \beta_2 R_2$ (see Figure 9.2, p. 181). For this case the elasticity of substitution between the resources is infinite. Thirdly, the other extreme, zero elasticity of substitution, occurs when λ tends to minus infinity. For this case, if $R_1/R_2 > 1$, then $dR_1/dR_2 \to -\infty$, if $R_1/R_2 = 1$, then $dR_1/dR_2 \to -\beta_1^{-1}\beta_2$ and if $R_1/R_2 < 1$, $dR_1/dR_2 \to 0$. Hence when $\lambda \to -\infty$, the isoquants consist of horizontal and vertical line segments meeting in the SW corner similar to those in Figure 9.6 (p. 185). Consequently, they describe a production function which requires that the resources are used in fixed proportions. If $\lambda > 0$, then the isoquants are strictly convex to the origin and touch both axes. If $\lambda \leqslant 0$ and finite, the isoquants are strictly convex to the origin but do not touch either axis; they are asymptotic to both axes.[7]

The marginal rate of substitution between R_1 and R_2 is, from (14)

$$\mathrm{MRS}_{12} = \frac{V_2}{V_1} = \beta_1^{-1}\beta_2(R_1/R_2)^{1-\lambda} \tag{15}$$

Partial differentiation of MRS_{12} gives

$$\frac{\partial \mathrm{MRS}_{12}}{\partial R_1} = \beta_1^{-1}\beta_2 R_2^{\lambda-1}(1-\lambda)R_1^{-\lambda} = \beta_1^{-1}\beta_2(R_1/R_2)^{1-\lambda}R_1^{-1}(1-\lambda)$$

$$= \mathrm{MRS}_{12}(1-\lambda)R_1^{-1}$$

and $\qquad \dfrac{\partial \mathrm{MRS}_{12}}{\partial R_2} = \beta_1^{-1}\beta_2(\lambda-1)R_2^{\lambda-2}R_1^{-\lambda} = -\mathrm{MRS}_{12}(1-\lambda)R_2^{-1}$

The elasticity of substitution can be calculated from the second equality in (8)

$$E_{12} = \frac{\mathrm{MRS}_{12}(R_2\mathrm{MRS}_{12}+R_1)}{R_1R_2(\mathrm{MRS}_{12}(\partial \mathrm{MRS}_{12}/\partial R_1)-\partial \mathrm{MRS}_{12}/\partial R_2)}$$

$$= \frac{\mathrm{MRS}_{12}(R_2\mathrm{MRS}_{12}+R_1)}{R_1R_2(\mathrm{MRS}_{12}\mathrm{MRS}_{12}(1-\lambda)R_1^{-1}+\mathrm{MRS}_{12}(1-\lambda)R_2^{-1})}$$

$$= \frac{R_2\mathrm{MRS}_{12}+R_1}{\mathrm{MRS}_{12}(1-\lambda)R_2+(1-\lambda)R_1}$$

$$= \frac{R_2\mathrm{MRS}_{12}+R_1}{(1-\lambda)(R_2\mathrm{MRS}_{12}+R_1)} = \frac{1}{1-\lambda}$$

The elasticity of substitution only depends on λ, and so is constant for all R_1, R_2 values. This explains the name of the Constant Elasticity of Substitution production function.

Our analysis of the CES production function isoquants when $\lambda \to 0$ and $\lambda \to -\infty$ indicated similarities with the Cobb–Douglas and fixed proportions production functions, respectively. These are in fact the limiting cases of the CES function when λ approaches these values. As $\lambda \to 0$, the CES production function collapses to the Cobb–Douglas production function, which has an elasticity of substitution equal to one; and as $\lambda \to -\infty$, the CES function becomes the fixed proportions or fixed coefficients production function which has an elasticity of substitution equal to zero.[8] When $\lambda = 1$, the CES production function exhibits infinite elasticity of substitution, and if also $\mu = 1$, the function reduces to the linear production function, $V = \beta_1 R_1 + \beta_2 R_2$.

Returns to scale behaviour of the CES function can be examined by increasing the resource levels R_1 and R_2 by a factor s. The new output level is

$$(\beta_1(sR_1)^\lambda + \beta_2(sR_2)^\lambda)^{\mu/\lambda} = (s^\lambda(\beta_1 R_1^\lambda + \beta_2 R_2^\lambda))^{\mu/\lambda}$$
$$= s^\mu V$$

so the CES production function (13) is homogeneous of degree μ. If $\mu = 1$ there are constant returns to scale, if $\mu > 1$ increasing returns, and if $\mu < 1$ decreasing returns to scale. μ can be interpreted as the scale parameter. As with the Cobb–Douglas function, for given values of the parameters, the returns to scale behaviour is the same at all R_1, R_2 values.

The CES production function

$$V = (\beta_0 + \beta_1 R_1^\lambda + \beta_2 R_2^\lambda)^{\mu/\lambda} \tag{16}$$

is inhomogeneous. To see this, it is sufficient to consider the case when $\mu = \lambda = 1$, so $V = \beta_0 + \beta_1 R_1 + \beta_2 R_2$. If $R_1 = R_2 = 1$, then $V = \beta_0 + \beta_1 + \beta_2$, and if $R_1 = R_2 = 2$, then the output is $\beta_0 + 2\beta_1 + 2\beta_2 \neq 2^\mu(\beta_0 + \beta_1 + \beta_2) = 2^\mu V$, for any $\mu \geq 0$. The CES function (16) is, however, homothetic because it is a monotonically increasing function of the homogeneous CES production function (13).[9]

Finally, it is interesting that it can be shown that, if we impose the condition that technology exhibits homogeneity of degree μ and constant elasticity of substitution at all, R_1, R_2 values, then the production function can *only* be of the CES production form (13). If we also insist that $\mu = 1$, so that there are constant returns to scale, then the production function must be the CES function with $\mu = 1$. If we also insist that the elasticity of substitution is one, then the production function must be of the Cobb–Douglas form (11) with $\beta_1 + \beta_2 = 1$ (see Arrow *et al.* 1961).

9.8 GENERALIZING THE CES PRODUCTION FUNCTION TO ALLOW FOR MORE THAN TWO RESOURCES

The general form of a production function involving k resources can be represented as

$$V = f(R_1, R_2, \ldots, R_k) \tag{17}$$

Many of the concepts introduced in the previous sections can be readily applied to this production function, but there is no unique natural generalization of the two-resource production function definition of the elasticity of substitution. One way of defining the elasticity of substitution between pairs of resources is the *direct partial elasticity of substitution*, denoted DES_{ij}, which requires that all resource levels except R_i and R_j are kept constant, and R_i and R_j are varied so that output remains constant. To simplify matters, let $k = 3$ and set $i = 1$ and $j = 2$, then $DES_{ij} = DES_{12}$. DES_{12} measures the curvature, at a point, on an isoquant in $R_1 R_2$ space, when R_3 is fixed. The prescribed values of R_1, R_2, and R_3 determine the level at which resource 3 is fixed, and the point in $R_1 R_2$ space through which the isoquant passes. Mathematically,

$$DES_{12} = \frac{d(R_1/R_2)}{R_1/R_2} \cdot \frac{MRS_{12}}{dMRS_{12}} \tag{18}$$

when R_3 is fixed and R_1 and R_2 are allowed to vary so that output is constant. Alternative expressions for DES_{12} are[10]

$$DES_{12} = \frac{V_1 V_2 (V_1 R_1 + V_2 R_2)}{R_1 R_2 (2V_1 V_2 V_{12} - V_1^2 V_{22} - V_2^2 V_{11})} \tag{19}$$

and

$$DES_{12} = \frac{MRS_{12}(R_1 MRS_{12} + R_2)}{R_1 R_2 (d^2 R_1 / dR_2^2)}$$

$$= \frac{MRS_{12}(R_2 MRS_{12} + R_1)}{R_1 R_2 (MRS_{12}(\partial MRS_{12}/\partial R_1) - \partial MRS_{12}/\partial R_2)} \tag{20}$$

An alternative definition of the partial elasticity between resources i and j is the *Allen partial elasticity of substitution*,[11] AES_{ij}. We will focus attention on direct partial elasticities of substitution because they are easier to interpret in the context of manorial production functions.

When there are more than two productive resources, an important concept is that of *separability* of the production function. In economic terms, separability is concerned with whether the marginal rate of substitution between pairs of resources is affected by changes in a third resource level. For example, if $\partial MRS_{12}/\partial R_3 = 0$.

A production function is said to be *strongly separable* with respect to a partition of the k productive resources into k^* groups $\{G_1 G_2 \ldots G_k^*\}$ if $\partial MRS_{ij}/\partial R_p = 0$, for all resources i from some group, say G_r, all j from either G_r or some other group, say G_s, and all p from a group other than G_r and G_s.

A production function is said to be *weakly separable* with respect to the same partition if $\partial MRS_{ij}/\partial R_p = 0$, for all ij from some group, say G_r, and all p from any group other than G_r.

Clearly, a strongly separable production function is weakly separable.

In mathematical terms, if $k^* = 3$ and there are k_1 resources in group G_1 and $k_2 - k_1$ in G_2 and $k^* - k_2$ in G_3, a production function is strongly separable if it can be written

$$V = f(f_1(R_1, R_2, \ldots R_{k_1}) + f_2(R_{k_1+1}, \ldots R_{k_2}) + f_3(R_{k_2+1}, \ldots R_{k_*}))$$

where $V = f(\ )$ is a monotonically increasing function. The production function is weakly separable if

$$V = f(f_1(R_1, R_2, \ldots R_{k_1}), f_2(R_{k_1+1}, \ldots R_{k_2}), f_3(R_{k_2+1}, \ldots R_{k^*}))$$

An obvious way of generalizing the CES production function to allow for more than two resources is

$$V = (\beta_1 R_1^\lambda + \beta_2 R_2^\lambda + \beta_3 R_3^\lambda)^{\mu/\lambda} \qquad (21)$$

where, for simplicity, we set $k = 3$. $\beta_1, \beta_2, \beta_3$ and μ are positive parameters and λ is a parameter such that $\lambda \leqslant 1$.

Much of the analysis of this production function is almost identical to that for the two productive resource CES function (13), for example, the expressions for marginal products and second derivatives are the same, the slope of an isoquant in R_1, R_2 space, when R_3 is held constant, is given by (14) and the function is homogeneous of degree μ. The marginal rate of substitution between resources 1 and 2, MRS_{12}, is given by (15) and DES_{12}, calculated by using the second equality in (20), is equal to $1/(1 - \lambda)$. By similar calculations we find that $\mathrm{DES}_{13} = \mathrm{DES}_{23} = 1/(1 - \lambda)$. These elasticity of substitution results imply that the production function (21) forces the direct partial elasticities between all three pairs of resources to be equal to the same constant value.[12] Also, since $\mathrm{MRS}_{12} = \beta_1^{-1}\beta_2(R_1/R_2)^{1-\lambda}$, $\partial\mathrm{MRS}_{12}/\partial R_3 = 0$. Similarly, $\partial\mathrm{MRS}_{13}/\partial R_2 = \partial\mathrm{MRS}_{23}/\partial R_1 = 0$, so in terms of the partition of the resources into the groups $\{G_1 G_2 G_3\}$, where G_1 only contains the first resource, G_2 the second, and G_3 the third, (21) is a strongly separable production function.

The CES function (21) clearly imposes strong restrictions on production both in terms of direct elasticities of substitution between resources and in terms of separability. If an investigator is interested in the question of how resources can be substituted in production, an attractive empirical strategy is to make the simplifying assumption that partial elasticities of substitution for all pairs of resources are constant and then test for differences in these constant values. If we use the production function (21) to characterize production, it is clearly not possible to carry out this strategy, because the partial elasticities of substitution for all pairs of resources are forced to take the same value. It is of interest, then, to ask if there exists a CES function which does allow for different direct partial elasticities of substitution between different pairs of resources.

This question has been answered by McFadden. In (1963), he derived the general form of the production function homogeneous of degree 1 with constant direct partial elasticities of substitution. The function implies that the resources are partitioned into k^* groups, such that the direct elasticities of substitution for all pairs of resources from the same group are unity, and the direct partial elasticities for all pairs of resources from different groups are the same constant value. Clearly, the CES assumption imposes strong restrictions on the possible values the elasticities can take.[13]

9.9 THE MUKERJI PRODUCTION FUNCTION

Mukerji (1963) has investigated the obvious generalization of (21),

$$V = (\beta_1 R_1^{\lambda_1} + \beta_2 R_2^{\lambda_2} + \beta_3 R_3^{\lambda_3})^{1/\lambda} \tag{22}$$

where the parameters β_1, β_2, and β_3 take positive values and the parameters λ_1, λ_2, λ_3, and λ are less than or equal to 1.

The marginal products for resources 1 and 2 are

$$\mathrm{MP}_1 = V_1 = \lambda^{-1}(\beta_1 R_1^{\lambda_1} + \beta_2 R_2^{\lambda_2} + \beta_3 R_3^{\lambda_3})^{1/\lambda - 1}\beta_1\lambda_1 R_1^{\lambda_1 - 1}$$

$$= \lambda_1\lambda^{-1}\beta_1 V^{1-\lambda}R_1^{\lambda_1 - 1} > 0, \text{ and}$$

$$\mathrm{MP}_2 = V_2 = \lambda_2\lambda^{-1}\beta_2 V^{1-\lambda}R_2^{\lambda_2 - 1} > 0$$

Second-order derivatives are of the form,

$$V_{11} = \lambda_1\lambda^{-1}\beta_1(1-\lambda)V^{-\lambda}R_1^{\lambda_1 - 1}V_1 + \lambda_1\lambda^{-1}\beta_1 V^{1-\lambda}(\lambda_1 - 1)R_1^{\lambda_1 - 2}$$

$$= V_1(V_1(1-\lambda)V^{-1} - (1-\lambda_1)R_1^{-1}V_1)$$

$V_{11} > 0$, if $V_1(1-\lambda)V^{-1} > (1-\lambda_1)R_1^{-1}V_1$ and $V_{11} < 0$, if the inequality is reversed.[14]

$$V_{12} = \lambda_1\lambda^{-1}\beta_1(1-\lambda)V^{-\lambda}R_1^{\lambda_1 - 1}V_2 = V_1 V^{-1}(1-\lambda)V_2 > 0$$

The marginal rate of substitution between resources 1 and 2

$$\mathrm{MRS}_{12} = \frac{V_2}{V_1} = \frac{\lambda_2\lambda^{-1}\beta_2 V^{1-\lambda}R_2^{\lambda_2 - 1}}{\lambda_1\lambda^{-1}\beta_1 V^{1-\lambda}R_1^{\lambda_1 - 1}} = \lambda_2\lambda_1^{-1}\beta_2\beta_1^{-1}R_2^{\lambda_2 - 1}R_1^{1-\lambda_1}$$

$$\partial\mathrm{MRS}_{12}/\partial R_1 = \lambda_2\lambda_1^{-1}\beta_2\beta_1^{-1}R_2^{\lambda_2 - 1}(1-\lambda_1)R_1^{-\lambda_1} = \mathrm{MRS}_{12}(1-\lambda_1)R_1^{-1}, \text{ and}$$

$$\partial\mathrm{MRS}_{12}/\partial R_2 = -\mathrm{MRS}_{12}(1-\lambda_2)R_2^{-1}$$

Therefore, from the second equality in (20)

$$\mathrm{DES}_{12} = \frac{\mathrm{MRS}_{12}(R_2\mathrm{MRS}_{12} + R_1)}{R_1 R_2(\mathrm{MRS}_{12}(\partial\mathrm{MRS}_{12}/\partial R_1) - \partial\mathrm{MRS}_{12}/\partial R_2)}$$

$$= \frac{\mathrm{MRS}_{12}(R_2\mathrm{MRS}_{12} + R_1)}{R_1 R_2(\mathrm{MRS}_{12}\mathrm{MRS}_{12}(1-\lambda_1)R_1^{-1} + \mathrm{MRS}_{12}(1-\lambda_2)R_2^{-1})}$$

$$= \frac{R_2\mathrm{MRS}_{12} + R_1}{(1-\lambda_1)R_2\mathrm{MRS}_{12} + (1-\lambda_2)R_1}$$

which depends on the values of R_1 and R_2 and hence is not constant. Ratios of direct partial elasticities of substitution are not constant either. It can be shown that Allen partial elasticities of substitution are not constant, but that ratios of them are constant.[15] For example,

$$\frac{AES_{12}}{AES_{13}} = \frac{1 - \lambda_3}{1 - \lambda_2}$$

and more generally, when there are $k > 3$ resources,

$$\frac{AES_{ij}}{AES_{mn}} = \frac{(1 - \lambda_m)(1 - \lambda_n)}{(1 - \lambda_i)(1 - \lambda_j)}$$

The production function (22) is only homogeneous if $\lambda_1 = \lambda_2 = \lambda_3$ in which case it can be written in the form (21). It is only homogeneous of degree 1 when $\lambda_1 = \lambda_2 = \lambda_3 = \lambda$, corresponding to (21) with $\mu = 1$. Finally, as $\lambda_1, \lambda_2, \lambda_3$ and λ all tend to zero (at the same rate), the production function (22) converges to the Cobb–Douglas production function in three resources.

9.10 THE SATO PRODUCTION FUNCTION

In (1967), Sato introduced a more interesting generalization of (21); *the two-level CES production function*. An example of this function involving four resources is

$$V = (\alpha_r(\beta_1 R_1^\lambda + \beta_2 R_2^\lambda)^{\lambda/\lambda_r} + \alpha_s(\beta_3 R_3^\lambda + \beta_4 R_4^\lambda)^{\lambda/\lambda_s})^{\mu/\lambda} \qquad (23)$$

where the parameters $\alpha_r, \alpha_s, \beta_1, \beta_2, \beta_3, \beta_4$, and μ are positive and the parameters λ_r, λ_s, and λ less than or equal to 1.

The resources 1 and 2 are grouped together in group r, and resources 3 and 4 are in a second group, s. The Sato production function (23) can also be written

$$V = (\alpha_r Z_r^\lambda + \alpha_s Z_s^\lambda)^{\mu/\lambda} \qquad (24)$$

where, for example, $Z_r = (\beta_1 R_1^\lambda + \beta_2 R_2^\lambda)^{1/\lambda_r}$, or,

$$V = y^{\mu/\lambda} \qquad (25)$$

where $y = \alpha_r Z_r^\lambda + \alpha_s Z_s^\lambda$.

From (24), we see that V is a CES function in Z_r and Z_s, and that in turn, Z_r and Z_s are CES functions in R_1, R_2 and R_3, R_4, respectively. $\sigma_r = 1/(1 - \lambda_r)$ and $\sigma_s = 1/(1 - \lambda_s)$ can be thought of as the elasticities of substitution within the rth and sth groups (that is, intra-group elasticities), and $\sigma = 1/(1 - \lambda)$ can be thought of as the elasticity of substitution among the resource groups (that is, the inter-group elasticity). The inter-group and intra-group elasticities should not be confused with the partial elasticities of substitution for the R_i which, as we will see, may take different values.

If all intra-group elasticities are equal to the inter-group elasticity of substitution, that is, $\lambda_r = \lambda_s = \lambda$, then (23) reduces to

$$V = (\alpha_r \beta_1 R_1^\lambda + \alpha_r \beta_2 R_2^\lambda + \alpha_s \beta_3 R_3^\lambda + \alpha_s \beta_4 R_4^\lambda)^{\mu/\lambda} \tag{26}$$

This production function is of the same general form as (21) with four resources, although it is overparameterized. This is because, if we have data on output and the resource levels, we would be able to determine $\alpha_r \beta_1$ (say), but not α_r or β_1. If either α_r or β_1 are assigned a value, then the other parameter will be uniquely determined from the data. If α_r and α_s are set equal to 1, then (26) reduces to (21) with four resources. The same overparameterization problem occurs in the more general Sato function formulation (23), as can be seen by considering $\alpha_r Z_r^\lambda$.

$$\alpha_r Z_r^\lambda = \alpha_r (\beta_1 R_1^{\lambda_r} + \beta_2 R_2^{\lambda_r})^{\lambda/\lambda_r}$$

$$= (\alpha_r^{\lambda_r/\lambda}(\beta_1 R_1^{\lambda_r} + \beta_2 R_2^{\lambda_r}))^{\lambda/\lambda_r}$$

$$= (\alpha_r^{\lambda_r/\lambda}\beta_1 R_1^{\lambda_r} + \alpha_r^{\lambda_r/\lambda}\beta_2 R_2^{\lambda_r})^{\lambda/\lambda_r}$$

so it is clear that α_r and β_1 cannot be uniquely determined from the data. In view of this, we will set $\alpha_r = \alpha_s = 1$ in (23), (24), and (25), so that,

$$V = ((\beta_1 R_1^{\lambda_r} + \beta_2 R_2^{\lambda_r})^{\lambda/\lambda_r} + (\beta_3 R_3^{\lambda_s} + \beta_4 R_4^{\lambda_s})^{\lambda/\lambda_s})^{\mu/\lambda} \tag{27}$$

$$V = (Z_r^\lambda + Z_s^\lambda)^{\mu/\lambda} \tag{28}$$

$$V = y^{\mu/\lambda} \tag{29}$$

The resource marginal products are obtained from the first derivatives, for example

$$\mathrm{MP}_1 = V_1 = \mu\lambda^{-1}y^{\mu/\lambda - 1}\lambda\lambda_r^{-1}(\beta_1 R_1^{\lambda_r} + \beta_2 R_2^{\lambda_r})^{\lambda/\lambda_r - 1}\lambda_r\beta_1 R_1^{\lambda_r - 1}$$

$$= \mu V^{1 - \lambda/\mu}Z_r^{\lambda - \lambda_r}\beta_1 R_1^{\lambda_r - 1} > 0$$

$$\mathrm{MP}_2 = V_2 = \mu V^{1 - \lambda/\mu}Z_r^{\lambda - \lambda_r}\beta_2 R_2^{\lambda_r - 1} > 0$$

$$\mathrm{MP}_3 = V_3 = \mu V^{1 - \lambda/\mu}Z_s^{\lambda - \lambda_s}\beta_3 R_3^{\lambda_s - 1} > 0$$

Some second-order derivatives are

$$V_{11} = \mu(1 - \lambda/\mu)V^{-\lambda/\mu}V_1 Z_r^{\lambda - \lambda_r}\beta_1 R_1^{\lambda_r - 1}$$

$$+ \mu V^{1 - \lambda/\mu}(\lambda\lambda_r^{-1} - 1)Z_r^{\lambda - 2\lambda_r}\lambda_r\beta_1 R_1^{\lambda_r - 1}\beta_1 R_1^{\lambda_r - 1}$$

$$+ \mu V^{1 - \lambda/\mu}Z_r^{\lambda - \lambda_r}(\lambda_r - 1)\beta_1 R_1^{\lambda_r - 2}$$

$$= \mu V^{-\lambda/\mu}Z_r^{\lambda - \lambda_r}\beta_1 R_1^{\lambda_r - 1}((1 - \lambda/\mu)V_1 + V(\lambda\lambda_r^{-1} - 1)Z_r^{-\lambda_r}\lambda_r\beta_1 R_1^{\lambda_r - 1} + V(\lambda_r - 1)R_1^{-1})$$

which is not easy to sign without knowledge of the resource levels.

$$V_{12} = \mu(1 - \lambda/\mu)V^{-\lambda/\mu}V_2 Z_r^{\lambda - \lambda_r}\beta_1 R_1^{\lambda_r - 1}$$

$$+ \mu V^{1 - \lambda/\mu}(\lambda\lambda_r^{-1} - 1)Z_r^{\lambda - 2\lambda_r}\lambda_r\beta_2 R_2^{\lambda_r - 1}\beta_1 R_1^{\lambda_r - 1}$$

$$= \mu V^{-\lambda/\mu}Z_r^{\lambda - \lambda_r}\beta_1 R_1^{\lambda_r - 1}((1 - \lambda/\mu)V_2 + V(\lambda\lambda_r^{-1} - 1)Z_r^{-\lambda_r}\lambda_r\beta_2 R_2^{\lambda_r - 1})$$

$V_{12} > 0$ if $\mu \geqslant 1$ and $\lambda > \lambda_r$

$V_{13} = \mu(1 - \lambda/\mu)V^{-\lambda/\mu}V_3 Z_r^{\lambda-\lambda_r}\beta_1 R_1^{\lambda_r-1} > 0$ if $\mu \geqslant 1$.[16]

The marginal rate of substitution between resources 1 and 2 (which are from the same group) is

$$\text{MRS}_{12} = \frac{V_2}{V_1} = \frac{\mu V^{1-\lambda/\mu}Z_r^{\lambda-\lambda_r}\beta_2 R_2^{\lambda_r-1}}{\mu V^{1-\lambda/\mu}Z_r^{\lambda-\lambda_r}\beta_1 R_1^{\lambda_r-1}} = \beta_2\beta_1^{-1}(R_1/R_2)^{1-\lambda_r} \tag{30}$$

The MRS_{12} is of the same form as for the CES production function in two resources except that λ_r replaces λ—see (15). It follows that

$$\partial\text{MRS}_{12}/\partial R_1 = \text{MRS}_{12}(1 - \lambda_r)R_1^{-1}$$

$$\partial\text{MRS}_{12}/\partial R_2 = -\text{MRS}_{12}(1 - \lambda_r)R_2^{-1}$$

and from the second equality in (20), the direct partial elasticity between resources 1 and 2, $\text{DES}_{12} = 1/(1 - \lambda_r) = \sigma_r > 0$.

The marginal rate of substitution between resources 1 and 3 (which are from different groups) is

$$\text{MRS}_{13} = \frac{V_3}{V_1} = \frac{\mu V^{1-\lambda/\mu}Z_s^{\lambda-\lambda_s}\beta_3 R_3^{\lambda_s-1}}{\mu V^{1-\lambda/\mu}Z_r^{\lambda-\lambda_r}\beta_1 R_1^{\lambda_r-1}} = Z_s^{\lambda-\lambda_s}Z_r^{\lambda_r-\lambda}\beta_3\beta_1^{-1}R_3^{\lambda_s-1}R_1^{1-\lambda_r} \tag{31}$$

which is independent of μ. The second equality in (20) can be used to show that,

$$\text{DES}_{13} = \frac{x_{r1}^{-1} + x_{s3}^{-1}}{\sigma_r^{-1}(x_{r1}^{-1} - x_r^{-1}) + \sigma_s^{-1}(x_{s3}^{-1} - x_s^{-1}) + \sigma^{-1}(x_r^{-1} + x_s^{-1})} \tag{32}$$

where, for example, $x_r = Z_r(\partial V/\partial Z_r)V^{-1}$ and

$$x_{r1} = R_1(\partial V/\partial Z_r)V^{-1}(\partial Z_r/\partial R_1)$$

It can be shown that DES_{13} is greater than the smallest of the three numbers σ, σ_r, and σ_s and smaller than the largest of σ, σ_r, and σ_s, so $\text{DES}_{13} > 0$.

The appendix to Sato (1967), indicates that the Allen partial elasticities of substitution $\text{AES}_{13} = \text{AES}_{14} = \text{AES}_{23} = \text{AES}_{24} = \sigma$, the inter-group elasticity of substitution. Also, the intra-group Allen partial elasticities of substitution are

$$\text{AES}_{12} = x_r^{-1}(\sigma_r - \sigma) + \sigma, \text{ and}$$

$$\text{AES}_{34} = x_s^{-1}(\sigma_s - \sigma) + \sigma\,[17]$$

Notice that, as the inter-group direct partial elasticities of substitution and the intra-group Allen partial elasticities are not constant for all resource level values, strictly speaking the Sato function is not a CES function.

The Sato production function (27) is homogeneous of degree μ because

$$((\beta_1(sR_1)^{\lambda_r} + \beta_2(sR_2)^{\lambda_r})^{\lambda/\lambda_r} + (\beta_3(sR_3)^{\lambda_s} + \beta_4(sR_4)^{\lambda_s})^{\lambda/\lambda_s})^{\mu/\lambda}$$

$$= (s^\lambda(\beta_1 R_1^{\lambda_r} + \beta_2 R_2^{\lambda_r})^{\lambda/\lambda_r} + s^\lambda(\beta_3 R_3^{\lambda_s} + \beta_4 R_4^{\lambda_s})^{\lambda/\lambda_s})^{\mu/\lambda} = s^\mu V$$

With respect to the resource grouping $\{G_1 \ G_2 \ G_3 \ G_4\}$, where G_i contains the ith resource, the Sato function (27) is not strongly separable because, for example, from (31), MRS_{13} depends on R_2 through Z_r, and hence $\partial\mathrm{MRS}_{12}/\partial R_2 \neq 0$. Weak separability has no meaning when there is only one resource in each G_i group; however, if in (28) Z_r and Z_s are functions of four resources and there are two resources in each of the G_i groups, the Sato function will not be weakly separable. With respect to the partition $\{G_1 \ G_2\}$, where G_1 contains resources 1 and 2 and G_2 resources 3 and 4, the Sato function (27) is both strongly and weakly separable. This can be seen from the additive form of (28) or by noting that, for example, $\partial\mathrm{MRS}_{12}/\partial R_3 = 0$, because, from (30), MRS_{12} does not depend on R_3.

In (27) the resources 1 and 2 are grouped together in group r and the resources 3 and 4 form a second group s. Resources in the same group have a common intra-elasticity of substitution, and the marginal rate of substitution between two resources from the group is independent of any resource from outside the group. Resources within a group should be similar in their production characteristics and highly substitutable—perhaps, for example, different types of labour or land. We would usually expect the intra-elasticities of substitution to be greater than the inter-group elasticity. If the resources in group r are different types of labour and in group s different types of land, then Z_r and Z_s have an interesting interpretation in terms of 'higher level' factors (that is, aggregate land and aggregate labour) which are then combined with an elasticity of substitution of $\sigma = 1/(1 - \lambda)$ to produce output.

The two-level Sato production function can be generalized to allow for more than two groups of resources. For example, suppose we have three groups with two resources in each group, then (28) becomes

$$V = (Z_r^\lambda + Z_s^\lambda + Z_t^\lambda)^{\mu/\lambda} \tag{33}$$

where Z_r^λ *and* Z_s^λ are defined as before and

$$Z_t^\lambda = (\beta_5 R_5^{\lambda_t} + \beta_6 R_6^{\lambda_t})^{\lambda/\lambda_t}$$

In (33) the inter-group elasticities of substitution are the same[18] when considering a resource from the rth group and one from the sth group, one from the rth group and one from the tth group, or a resource from the sth group and one from the tth group. One way of allowing for differences in inter-group elasticities is to generalize (33) to a Mukerji-type function

$$V = (Z_r^{\lambda_1} + Z_s^{\lambda_2} + Z_t^{\lambda_3})^{1/\lambda} \tag{34}$$

(34) allows for differences in inter-group elasticities of substitution, but the function is only homogeneous if $\lambda_1 = \lambda_2 = \lambda_3$. The Mukerji function (22) is obtained from (34) as a special case when there is only one resource in each of the three groups, r, s, and t. An alternative way of allowing for differences in inter-group elasticities is to define a three-level CES production function such

as

$$V = ((Z_r^{\lambda_1} + Z_s^{\lambda_1})^{\lambda/\lambda_1} + Z_t^{\lambda})^{\mu/\lambda} \tag{35}$$

where Z_r and Z_s are grouped together in a higher-level group. Many of the properties of this production function can be derived by consideration of the properties of the two-level CES function. For example, the three-level function (35) is homogeneous of degree μ, and MRS_{12} is the same as for the two-level function (27), so $\mathrm{DES}_{12} = \sigma_r$ and $\partial \mathrm{MRS}_{12}/\partial R_3 = 0$. Similarly, $\mathrm{DES}_{34} = \sigma_s$, $\mathrm{DES}_{56} = \sigma_t$, $\partial \mathrm{MRS}_{34}/\partial R_1 = 0$ and $\partial \mathrm{MRS}_{56}/\partial R_1 = 0$.

9.11 FLEXIBLE FUNCTIONAL FORMS: THE GENERALIZED LINEAR (GL) PRODUCTION FUNCTION

Although there is no technical justification for restricting the elasticity of substitution to be constant, the empirical strategy of simplifying the analysis by assuming constant elasticities and then testing for different constant values may often work well. If, however, the elasticities are not approximately constant over the range of resource and output levels of interest, then the false maintained hypothesis may seriously affect the outcome of the tests. This kind of argument has led to the development of variable elasticity of substitution production functions (see, for example, Revankar 1971 and Vazquez 1971), and also variable returns to scale production functions (see Zellner and Revankar 1969). It has also led to the development of more flexible functional forms that impose weaker restrictions on production technology. With respect to this concept of flexibility, an interesting idea is to characterize the production technology by a production function which can be thought of as a second-order local approximation to any arbitrary, twice differentiable production function. It is advantageous if the functional form is linear in the parameters and hence easy to estimate. This concept of linear in parameters flexible functional forms which are second-order approximations at a point was suggested by Diewert. In (1971) he introduced the *Generalized Linear (GL) form* to illustrate the concept.[19] The GL production function in two resources can be represented

$$V = \beta_1 R_1 + \beta_2 R_2 + \alpha R_1^{\frac{1}{2}} R_2^{\frac{1}{2}} \tag{36}$$

where the parameters β_1, β_2, and α are positive. The function (3) is a special case of (36). The resource marginal products for the GL function (36) are

$$\mathrm{MP}_1 = V_1 = \beta_1 + \tfrac{1}{2}\alpha R_1^{-\frac{1}{2}} R_2^{\frac{1}{2}} > 0$$

$$\mathrm{MP}_2 = V_2 = \beta_2 + \tfrac{1}{2}\alpha R_1^{\frac{1}{2}} R_2^{-\frac{1}{2}} > 0$$

The second-order derivatives are

$$V_{11} = -\tfrac{1}{4}\alpha R_1^{-\frac{3}{2}}R_2^{\frac{1}{2}} < 0$$

$$V_{22} = -\tfrac{1}{4}\alpha R_1^{\frac{1}{2}}R_2^{-\frac{3}{2}} < 0, \text{ and}$$

$$V_{12} = \tfrac{1}{4}\alpha R_1^{-\frac{1}{2}}R_2^{-\frac{1}{2}} > 0$$

so the GL production function admits diminishing returns to both resources, MP_1 increases as R_2 increases and MP_2 increases as R_1 increases.

The slope of an isoquant is given by

$$dR_1/dR_2 = -V_2/V_1 = -(\beta_2 + \tfrac{1}{2}\alpha R_1^{\frac{1}{2}}R_2^{-\frac{1}{2}})(\beta_1 + \tfrac{1}{2}\alpha R_1^{-\frac{1}{2}}R_2^{\frac{1}{2}})^{-1} < 0$$

and since the GL function (36) is a concave function, the isoquants are convex to the origin.

The marginal rate of substitution between resources 1 and 2,

$$MRS_{12} = (\beta_2 + \tfrac{1}{2}\alpha R_1^{\frac{1}{2}}R_2^{-\frac{1}{2}})(\beta_1 + \tfrac{1}{2}\alpha R_1^{-\frac{1}{2}}R_2^{\frac{1}{2}})^{-1}$$

The GL function is homogeneous of degree 1, because,

$$\beta_1(sR_1) + \beta_2(sR_2) + \alpha(sR_1)^{\frac{1}{2}}(sR_2)^{\frac{1}{2}} = s(\beta_1 R_1 + \beta_2 R_2 + \alpha R_1^{\frac{1}{2}}R_2^{\frac{1}{2}}) = sV$$

The function can be generalized to be homogeneous of degree μ by redefining

$$V = (\beta_1 R_1 + \beta_2 R_2 + \alpha R_1^{\frac{1}{2}}R_2^{\frac{1}{2}})^{\mu} \tag{37}$$

The elasticity of substitution between resources 1 and 2 can be calculated from (7) or (8), or by using the theorem (see Vazquez 1971) that a production function involving two resources that is homogeneous of degree μ has

$$E_{12} = \frac{V_1 V_2}{(1-\mu)V_1 V_2 + \mu V V_{12}} \tag{38}$$

For the GL production function (36), this reduces to

$$E_{12} = \frac{V_1 V_2}{V V_{12}}$$

When the GL production function involves two productive resources, there are only three parameters in the function. However, because of the need for cross terms between each pair of resources, the number of parameters required increases rapidly as additional resources are introduced. With 4 resources there are 4 β but 6 α, one for each of the pairs $R_1 R_2, R_1 R_3, R_1 R_4, R_2 R_3, R_2 R_4, R_3 R_4$. With 10 resources there are 10 β and $9 + 8 + 7 + 6 + 5 + 4 + 3 + 2 + 1 = 45$ α. When there are more than three resources, the direct partial elasticities of substitution, in general, depend on the values of all the parameters and all resource levels, and the GL function is sufficiently flexible to allow for any set of direct partial elasticity values between the pairs of resources. If there are three resources, so

$$V = \beta_1 R_1 + \beta_2 R_2 + \beta_3 R_3 + \alpha_1 R_1^{\frac{1}{2}}R_2^{\frac{1}{2}} + \alpha_2 R_1^{\frac{1}{2}}R_3^{\frac{1}{2}} + \alpha_3 R_2^{\frac{1}{2}}R_3^{\frac{1}{2}} \tag{39}$$

the

$$\text{MRS}_{12} = (\beta_2 + \tfrac{1}{2}\alpha_1 R_1^{\frac{1}{2}} R_2^{-\frac{1}{2}} + \tfrac{1}{2}\alpha_3 R_2^{-\frac{1}{2}} R_3^{\frac{1}{2}})$$

$$\times (\beta_1 + \tfrac{1}{2}\alpha_1 R_1^{-\frac{1}{2}} R_2^{\frac{1}{2}} + \tfrac{1}{2}\alpha_2 R_1^{-\frac{1}{2}} R_3^{\frac{1}{2}})^{-1}$$

and hence $\partial \text{MRS}_{12}/\partial R_3 \neq 0$, unless $\alpha_2 = \alpha_3 = 0$. It follows that if $\alpha_2 \neq 0$ or $\alpha_3 \neq 0$, the GL function is neither strongly nor weakly separable with respect to the partition $\{G_1 \ G_2 \ G_3\}$, where G_i only contains the ith resource.

9.12 THE GENERALIZED QUADRATIC (GQ) PRODUCTION FUNCTION

The *Generalized Quadratic (GQ) production function*, discussed by Denny (1974), encompasses both the GL and the CES production functions. In two resources the GQ function can be represented as

$$V = (\beta_1 R_1^\lambda + \beta_2 R_2^\lambda + \alpha R_1^{\lambda/2} R_2^{\lambda/2})^{\mu/\lambda} \tag{40}$$

where the parameters β_1, β_2, α, and μ are positive and $\lambda \leqslant 1$.

If $\alpha = 0$, the GQ function reduces to the CES function (13). As λ tends to zero the GQ function converges to the Cobb–Douglas function (11) (whether or not $\alpha = 0$). When $\mu = \lambda = 1$, the GQ function reduces to the GL function (36). The GQ production function can be used to test for degree of homogeneity, separability, and the elasticity of substitution between pairs of resources.

The marginal products are

$$\text{MP}_1 = V_1 = \mu \lambda^{-1} V^{1-\lambda/\mu} (\lambda \beta_1 R_1^{\lambda-1} + \lambda/2 \alpha R_1^{\lambda/2-1} R_2^{\lambda/2})$$

$$= \mu \lambda^{-1} V^{1-\lambda/\mu} A_1, \quad \text{say}, > 0$$

$$\text{MP}_2 = V_2 = \mu \lambda^{-1} V^{1-\lambda/\mu} (\lambda \beta_2 R_2^{\lambda-1} + \lambda/2 \alpha R_1^{\lambda/2} R_2^{\lambda/2-1})$$

$$= \mu \lambda^{-1} V^{1-\lambda/\mu} A_2, \quad \text{say}, > 0$$

Some second derivatives are

$$V_{11} = V_1 A_1 ((\mu \lambda^{-1} - 1) V^{-\lambda/\mu} + A_1^{-2} ((\lambda-1)\lambda \beta_1 R_1^{\lambda-2} + (\lambda/2-1)\lambda/2 \alpha R_1^{\lambda/2-2} R_2^{\lambda/2})),$$

and

$$V_{12} = \mu \lambda^{-1} V^{-\lambda/\mu} A_1 ((1 - \lambda \mu^{-1}) V_2 + V A_1^{-1} \lambda^2 4^{-1} \alpha R_1^{\lambda/2-1} R_2^{\lambda/2-1})$$

The slope of the isoquants is given by $dR_1/dR_2 = -V_2 V_1^{-1} = A_2 A_1^{-1} < 0$, and since the GQ function (40) is a quasi-concave function, the isoquants are convex to the origin. The $\text{MRS}_{12} = V_2 V_1^{-1} = A_2 A_1^{-1}$.

The GQ production function is homogeneous of degree μ because

$$(\beta_1 (sR_1)^\lambda + \beta_2 (sR_2)^\lambda + \alpha (sR_1)^{\lambda/2} (sR_2)^{\lambda/2})^{\mu/\lambda} = s^\mu V$$

and the elasticity of substitution between the resources, E_{12}, is given by (38).

Finally, the GQ production function

$$V^* = (\beta_0 + \beta_1 R_1^\lambda + \beta_2 R_2^\lambda + \alpha R_1^{\lambda/2} R_2^{\lambda/2})^{\mu/\lambda} \tag{41}$$

is homothetic, but not homogeneous, with the same marginal rate of substitution, MRS_{12} and elasticity of substitution, E_{12}, between the resources as the homogeneous GQ production function (40).[20]

Notes

1. From (6), the elasticity of substitution is defined by

$$E_{12} = \frac{\mathrm{d}(R_1/R_2)}{R_1/R_2} \cdot \frac{\mathrm{MRS}_{12}}{\mathrm{dMRS}_{12}} = \frac{\mathrm{d}(R_1 R_2^{-1}) V_2 V_1^{-1}}{(R_1 R_2^{-1})\mathrm{d}(V_2 V_1^{-1})}.$$

$$\mathrm{d}(R_1 R_2^{-1}) = R_2^{-1}\mathrm{d}R_1 - R_1 R_2^{-2}\mathrm{d}R_2 = R_2^{-2}(R_2\mathrm{d}R_1 - R_1\mathrm{d}R_2).$$

From (5), $\mathrm{d}R_1 = -V_2 V_1^{-1}\mathrm{d}R_2$, so

$$\mathrm{d}(R_1 R_2^{-1}) = -R_2^{-2}(R_2 V_2 V_1^{-1} + R_1)\mathrm{d}R_2 = -R_2^2 V_1^{-1}(R_2 V_2 + R_1 V_1)\mathrm{d}R_2.$$

$$\mathrm{d}(V_2 V_1^{-1}) = (\partial(V_2 V_1^{-1})/\partial R_1)\mathrm{d}R_1 + (\partial(V_2 V_1^{-1})/\partial R_2)\mathrm{d}R_2$$

$$= (V_{12}V_1^{-1} - V_2 V_1^{-2}V_{11})\mathrm{d}R_1 + (V_{22}V_1^{-1} - V_2 V_1^{-2}V_{12})\mathrm{d}R_2,$$

but $\mathrm{d}R_1 = -V_2 V_1^{-1}\mathrm{d}R_2$, so

$$\mathrm{d}(V_2 V_1^{-1}) = -V_2 V_1^{-1}(V_{12}V_1^{-1} - V_2 V_1^{-2}V_{11} - V_2^{-1}V_{22} + V_1^{-1}V_{12})\mathrm{d}R_2$$

$$= -V_1^{-3}(2V_{12}V_1 V_2 - V_2^2 V_{11} - V_1^2 V_{22})\mathrm{d}R_2.$$

Hence
$$E_{12} = \frac{-R_2^{-2}V_1^{-1}(R_2 V_2 + R_1 V_1)\mathrm{d}R_2 V_2 V_1^{-1}}{-R_1 R_2^{-1}V_1^{-3}(2V_{12}V_1 V_2 - V_2^2 V_{11} - V_1^2 V_{22})\mathrm{d}R_2}$$

$$= \frac{V_1 V_2(R_1 V_1 + R_2 V_2)}{R_1 R_2(2V_1 V_2 V_{12} - V_1^2 V_{22} - V_2^2 V_{11})}.$$

2. From (5), $\mathrm{d}R_1/\mathrm{d}R_2 = -V_2 V_1^{-1}$, so

$$\mathrm{d}^2 R_1/\mathrm{d}R_2^2 = -V_{22}V_1^{-1} + V_2 V_1^{-2}V_{12} - (V_{12}V_1^{-1} - V_2 V_1^{-2}V_{11})\mathrm{d}R_1/\mathrm{d}R_2$$

$$= -V_{22}V_1^{-1} + V_2 V_1^{-2}V_{12} + V_{12}V_1^{-2}V_2 - V_2^2 V_1^{-3}V_{11}$$

$$= V_1^{-3}(2V_1 V_2 V_{12} - V_1^2 V_{22} - V_2^2 V_{11})$$

$$= V_1^{-3}z, \text{ say.}$$

$\mathrm{MRS}_{12} = V_2 V_1^{-1}$.

Hence

$$\frac{\mathrm{MRS}_{12}(R_2\mathrm{MRS}_{12} + R_1)}{R_1 R_2(\mathrm{d}^2 R_1/\mathrm{d}R_2^2)} = \frac{V_1^3 V_2 V_1^{-1}(R_2 V_2 V_1^{-1} + R_1)}{R_1 R_2 z}$$

$$= \frac{V_1^3(V_2^2 V_1^{-2}R_2 + V_2 V_1^{-1}R_1)}{R_1 R_2 z}$$

$$= \frac{V_1 V_2^2 R_2 + V_1^2 V_2 R_1}{R_1 R_2 z}$$

$$= \frac{V_1 V_2 (V_2 R_2 + V_1 R_1)}{R_1 R_2 z} = E_{12}.$$

The second equality in (8) holds because $\text{MRS}_{12} = V_2 V_1^{-1}$ so

$$\partial \text{MRS}_{12}/\partial R_1 = V_{12} V_1^{-1} - V_2 V_1^{-2} V_{11},$$

and $\quad \partial \text{MRS}_{12}/\partial R_2 = V_{22} V_1^{-1} - V_2 V_1^{-2} V_{12},$

hence

$$\text{MRS}_{12}(\partial \text{MRS}_{12}/\partial R_1) - \partial \text{MRS}_{12}/\partial R_2$$

$$= V_2 V_1^{-1}(V_{12} V_1^{-1} - V_2 V_1^{-2} V_{11}) - V_{22} V_1^{-1} + V_2 V_1^{-2} V_{12}$$

$$= V_2 V_1^{-2} V_{12} - V_2^2 V_1^{-3} V_{11} - V_{22} V_1^{-1} + V_2 V_1^{-2} V_{12}$$

$$= 2 V_2 V_1^{-2} V_{12} - V_2^2 V_1^{-3} V_{11} - V_{22} V_1^{-1}$$

$$= V_1^{-3}(2 V_1 V_2 V_{12} - V_2^2 V_{11} - V_1^2 V_{22})$$

$$= d R_1^2/d R_2^2.$$

3. An alternative proof that isoquants are convex is

$$d^2 R_1/d R_2^2 = z V_1^{-3}$$

$$= \beta_1 \beta_2 V^3 R_1^{-2} R_2^{-2}(2\beta_1 \beta_2 - \beta_1(\beta_2 - 1) - \beta_2(\beta_1 - 1)) V_1^{-3}$$

$$= \beta_1 \beta_2 V^3 R_1^{-2} R_2^{-2}(\beta_1 + \beta_2) V_1^{-3} > 0$$

The $V > 0$ isoquants cannot touch either axis because, for example, a point on the vertical axis implies that $R_1 = 0$, and from (11), $V = A 0^{\beta_1} R_2^{\beta_2} = 0$ for all R_2 values.
4. In this section the reader may find the following algebra useful. For $x > 0$, $(x^3)^2 = x^6$, $x^{-1} = 1/x$, $x^{\frac{1}{2}}$ — the square root of x, $x^2 x^{\frac{1}{2}} = x^{\frac{5}{2}} =$ the square root of x^5, $x^{-1} x = x^0 = 1$ and $(x^{\frac{1}{2}})^2 = x^1 = x$. These results can be easily illustrated by setting $x = 2$.
5. The CES production function is sometimes expressed in the form

$$V = \gamma[(1 - \delta) R_1^{-\rho} + \delta R_2^{-\rho}]^{-\mu/\rho}$$

and γ interpreted as an efficiency parameter and δ as a distribution parameter. (13) can be written in this form if we set $\beta_1 = \gamma^{-\rho/\mu}(1 - \delta)$, $\beta_2 = \gamma^{-\rho/\mu}\delta$ and $\lambda = -\rho$.
6.

$$(\lambda - 1) R_1^{-1} V - (\lambda/\mu - 1) V_1 = (\lambda - 1) R_1^{-1} V - (\lambda/\mu - 1)\mu\beta_1 R_1^{\lambda - 1} V^{1 - \lambda/\mu}$$

$$= \lambda(R_1^{-1} V - \beta_1 R_1^{\lambda - 1} V^{1 - \lambda/\mu}) - (R_1^{-1} V - \mu\beta_1 R_1^{\lambda - 1} V^{1 - \lambda/\mu})$$

$$= \lambda R_1^{-1} V(1 - \beta_1 R_1^{\lambda} V^{-\lambda/\mu}) - R_1^{-1} V(1 - \mu\beta_1 R_1^{\lambda} V^{-\lambda/\mu})$$

$$= R_1^{-1} V(\lambda(1 - Y) - (1 - \mu Y)), \text{ where } Y = \beta_1 R_1^{\lambda}(\beta_1 R_1^{\lambda} + \beta_2 R_2^{\lambda})^{-1}$$

and $0 < Y < 1$. If $\lambda > 0$ and $\mu Y > 1$ then $V_{11} > 0$, if $\lambda < 0$ and $\mu Y < 1$ then $V_{11} < 0$. The sign in the other cases will depend on the values of μ, λ, R_1, and R_2.

7. Convexity can also be proven by showing that $d^2R_1/dR_2^2 > 0$. The equation $V^{\lambda/\mu} = \beta_1 R_1^\lambda + \beta_2 R_2^\lambda$ indicates that positive outputs can be obtained when either R_1 or R_2 is zero and $\lambda > 0$, so the isoquants touch both axes. For the case $\lambda < 0$, consider the $V = 3$ isoquant. As $R_1 \to 0$, it is clear that R_2 must increase indefinitely for the equality $3^{\lambda/\mu} = \beta_1 R_1^\lambda + \beta_2 R_2^\lambda$ to be preserved. Consequently, the isoquants are asymptotic to the axes.

8. To show that the CES function

$$V = (\beta_1 R_1^\lambda + \beta_2 R_2^\lambda)^{\mu/\lambda}$$

collapses to the Cobb–Douglas function as $\lambda \to 0$, first redefine the parameters so that

$$V = \gamma((1-\delta)R_1^\lambda + \delta R_2^\lambda)^{\mu/\lambda}$$

where $\qquad\qquad \beta_1 = \gamma^{\lambda/\mu}(1-\delta)$ and $\beta_2 = \gamma^{\lambda/\mu}\delta$

Taking logarithms,

$$\ln V = \ln\gamma + (\mu/\lambda)\ln((1-\delta)R_1^\lambda + \delta R_2^\lambda) = \ln\gamma + g(\lambda)/h(\lambda)$$

where $\qquad g(\lambda) = \ln((1-\delta)R_1^\lambda + \delta R_2^\lambda)$ and $h(\lambda) = \lambda/\mu$

L'Hopital's rule states that

$$\operatorname*{Lim}_{\lambda \to 0} \frac{g(\lambda)}{h(\lambda)} = \frac{\partial g/\partial\lambda}{\partial h/\partial\lambda},$$

evaluated at $\lambda = 0$, providing $\partial h/\partial\lambda$, evaluated at $\lambda = 0$, is not zero.

$$\frac{\partial g}{\partial\lambda} = \frac{(1-\delta)R_1^\lambda \ln R_1 + \delta R^\lambda{}_2 \ln R_2}{(1-\delta)R_1^\lambda + \delta R_2^\lambda}$$

using the rule that

$$\frac{\partial R_1^\lambda}{\partial\lambda} = R_1^\lambda \ln R_1.$$

$$\frac{\partial h}{\partial\lambda} = \frac{1}{\mu},$$

so $\qquad\qquad \operatorname*{Lim}_{\lambda \to 0} \ln V = \ln\gamma + \mu(1-\delta)\ln R_1 + \mu\delta \ln R_2$

which from (12) is the Cobb–Douglas form.

9. If we denote the inhomogeneous CES function

$$V^* = (\beta_0 + \beta_1 R_1^\lambda + \beta_2 R_2^\lambda)^{\mu/\lambda}$$

and the homogeneous function

$$V = (\beta_1 R_1^\lambda + \beta_2 R_2^\lambda)^{\mu/\lambda}$$

then $\qquad (V^*)^{\lambda/\mu} = \beta_0 + \beta_1 R_1^\lambda + \beta_2 R_2^\lambda$, so $(V^*)^{\lambda/\mu} - \beta_0 = V^{\lambda/\mu}$,

and $\qquad\qquad\qquad V^* = (V^{\lambda/\mu} + \beta_0)^{\mu/\lambda}$.

Hence $\qquad \partial V^*/\partial V = \mu/\lambda(V^{\lambda/\mu} + \beta_0)^{\mu/\lambda - 1}\lambda/\mu V^{\lambda/\mu - 1} > 0$ for all R_1, R_2 values.

Notice that the inhomogeneous CES function has the unfortunate property that output is non-zero when $R_1 = R_2 = 0$. Also note that, since the MRS_{12} for the inhomogeneous CES function is also (15), from the second equality of (8), $ES_{12} = 1/(1 - \lambda)$.

10. This is the case because, if we totally differentiate (17) when $k = 3$, we obtain

$$dV = V_1 dR_1 + V_2 dR_2 + V_3 dR_3$$

so if R_3 and output are held constant, $dR_3 = dV = 0$, and $dR_1/dR_2 = -V_2/V_1$, which is the same result as (5). The results in notes 1 and 2 above can then be used to obtain (19) and (20).

11. For the case when there are k resources, the Allen partial elasticity of substitution

$$AES_{ij} = \frac{D_{ij}(R_1 V_1 + R_2 V_2 + \ldots + R_k V_k)}{D R_i R_j}$$

where D is the determinant of the matrix

$$\begin{bmatrix} 0 & V_1 V_2 & \cdots & V_k \\ V_1 & V_{11} V_{12} & \cdots & V_{1k} \\ \vdots & & & \\ V_k & V_{k1} V_{k2} & \cdots & V_{kk} \end{bmatrix}$$

and D_{ij} is the cofactor of V_{ij} in this matrix (see Henderson and Quandt 1980, for definitions of a matrix, a determinant, and a cofactor). A third partial elasticity of substitution in use is the Shaddow elasticity of substitution; see McFadden (1963). All three definitions reduce to ES_{12} when there are just two productive resources.

12. The Allen partial elasticities of substitution, AES_{ij} are also all equal to $1/(1 - \lambda)$.

13. McFadden has also characterized the production function homogeneous of degree 1 which has constant Shaddow partial elasticities of substitution, and Uzawa (1962) has characterized the production function homogeneous of degree 1 with constant Allen partial elasticities of substitution. The resulting functions also impose strong restrictions on the values that the elasticities can take.

14. When $\lambda_1 = \lambda$, $V_{11} = \beta_1 R^{\lambda-1} V^{-\lambda}(\lambda - 1)(R_1^{-1} V - V_1)$, which is equal to V_{11} for the CES function (13) with $\mu = 1$. Hence, using the argument presented in 9.7, $V_{11} < 0$, if $\lambda \neq 1$.

15. On this, see Mukerji (1963). Gorman (1965) proved that Allen partial elasticities of substitution stand in fixed proportions to each other if, and only if, the production function is of the Mukerji or Uzawa form.

16. The Sato function (27) is a quasi-concave function, and hence the isoquant surface is convex to the origin.

17. $AES_{12} = AES_{14} = AES_{23} = AES_{24} = \sigma > 0$, but in general AES_{12} and AES_{34} may be negative, however, if $\sigma_r \geqslant \sigma$ then $AES_{12} > 0$ and if $\sigma_s \geqslant \sigma$, then $AES_{34} > 0$.

18. The Allen partial elasticities of substitution for resources from different groups are also all the same, but this is not the case for direct partial elasticities of substitution; see (32).

19. One way of generating a parsimonious flexible function form is by making a

Taylor's expansion to second order about a point. The GL form

$$V = \gamma_0 + \gamma_1 R_1^{\frac{1}{2}} + \gamma_2 R_2^{\frac{1}{2}} + \gamma_3 R_1 + \gamma_4 R_2 + \gamma_5 R_1^{\frac{1}{2}} R_2^{\frac{1}{2}}$$

can be thought of as a second-order Taylor's expansion of V in powers of $R_i^{\frac{1}{2}}$. Many other production functions can be interpreted as Taylor's expansions about a point. In particular, the Cobb–Douglas function is a first-order expansion of the logarithm of V in powers of the logarithms of the resource levels, and the Translog production function of Christensen *et al.* (1971) is a second-order expansion. The CES function (homogeneous of degree μ) is a first order expansion of $V^{\lambda/\mu}$ in powers of R_i^{λ}, and the Generalized Quadratic production function of Lau (1974) is a second-order expansion of V in powers of R_i. The approximations are only of the stated order within a small neighbourhood about the point of expansion. It is possible that, in other regions of interest, the form may be a poor approximation to the true function, and may fail to satisfy basic properties of the true function such as monotonicity and convexity of isoquants. See Fuss and McFadden (1978) for further details.

20. See the lemma in Zellner and Revankar (1969).

10

Estimating stochastic production functions

10.1 INTRODUCTION

In Chapter 8 we reviewed some general statistical inferential procedures, and in Chapter 9 we introduced the subject of deterministic production functions. In this chapter we link these ideas together, and investigate the problem of estimating stochastic production relationships.

We begin by reviewing some aspects of the neoclassical theory of the firm. (The firm is a general name for the producing organization.) In 10.3 we discuss the traditional method (proposed by Marschak and Andrews in 1944) of specifying a stochastic relationship. An alternative specification of Zellner *et al.* (1966) is then discussed. In 10.5 Mundlak and Hoch's (1965) distinction between firm and non-systematic random effects is reviewed, and the problem of the existence of factors known to the producer but not to the analyst is reformulated as an omitted variables problem. Finally, in 10.6, 10.7, and 10.8 we analyse the problem of specifying and estimating a production function when it is assumed that the data are generated by the manorial model discussed in Chapter 6.

The neoclassical theory of the firm is discussed in greater detail in many texts, for example, Intriligator (1978), Varian (1984), and Henderson and Quandt (1980). The mathematical concepts are reviewed in Chiang (1974) and Henderson and Quandt (1980). Varian (1984) gives an introduction to the problem of estimating stochastic production functions. More advanced discussions are in Walters (1963), Bridge (1971), Intriligator (1978), and Fuss *et al.* (1978).

We focus throughout on direct production function estimation methods. Dual and indirect methods of estimation from cost, profit, conditional input demand functions, and reduced form equations cannot be employed because of the absence of price information in Domesday Book and other contemporary sources.

10.2 THE NEOCLASSICAL THEORY OF THE FIRM

The neoclassical theory of the firm assumes that the producer or entrepreneur chooses input and output levels in such a way that profit is maximized. To simplify matters, let us suppose that only one product is produced. If profit is denoted by $\prod$, total revenue by TR, and total cost by TC, then the producer attempts to

$$\text{maximize } \textstyle\prod = \text{TR} - \text{TC}$$

It is often useful to characterize the input and output market situations by perfect competition, which requires that there are several buyers and sellers and no one buyer or seller is able by his or her actions significantly to affect price. The total revenue obtained by the producer is equal to the price of the product, p, multiplied by the quantity produced, q. That is

$$\text{TR} = pq$$

If there are two variable inputs to the production process, let us suppose that

$$\text{TC} = p_1 R_1 + p_2 R_2 + k$$

where, for example, p_1 is the price and R_1 is the amount of input 1 used and k is a fixed cost. Hence the producer attempts to

$$\text{maximize } \textstyle\prod = pq - p_1 R_1 - p_2 R_2 - k$$

The assumptions of perfect competition in the input and output markets imply that the producer is a price-taker in these markets, so that p, p_1, and p_2 cannot be influenced by the producer's actions. The producer chooses q, R_1, and R_2 in order to maximize profits. In Chapter 9, we denoted pq by V, and the production function relationship between the value of output and the inputs by

$$V = f(R_1, R_2) \tag{1}$$

so profit

$$\textstyle\prod = V - p_1 R_1 - p_2 R_2 - k, \text{ or}$$

$$\textstyle\prod = f(R_1, R_2) - p_1 R_1 - p_2 R_2 - k$$

The first-order conditions for a local maximum of the profit function (see Henderson and Quandt 1980 and Chiang 1974) are

$$\textstyle\prod_1 = V_1 - p_1 = 0 \text{ and}$$

$$\textstyle\prod_2 = V_2 - p_2 = 0$$

where, for example, $\prod_1$ is the partial derivative of profit, and V_1 is the partial derivative of the value of output with respect to input 1. These conditions imply that R_1 and R_2 are such that $V_1 = p_1$ and $V_2 = p_2$, that is, that the values of the input marginal products equal their respective input prices. The first order conditions can be solved for R_1 and R_2 and the production function then used to solve for V. The second-order conditions for profit maximization are that, at the R_1, R_2 values satisfying the first order conditions,

$$V_{11} < 0, \; V_{22} < 0 \text{ and } V_{11} V_{22} > V_{12}^2$$

where, for example, V_{11} is the second partial derivative of V with respect to input 1.

The profit maximization conditions can be made more explicit if the production function (1) is given a particular form, such as, for example, the Cobb–Douglas form,

$$V = AR_1^{\beta_1}R_2^{\beta_2} \tag{2}$$

The first-order profit-maximizing conditions are

$$\beta_1 VR_1^{-1} = p_1, \text{ and}$$

$$\beta_2 VR_2^{-1} = p_2 \text{ (see section 9.6)}$$

Rearranging these equations, we obtain

$$R_1 = \beta_1 Vp_1^{-1} \tag{3}$$

$$R_2 = \beta_2 Vp_2^{-1} \tag{4}$$

(3), (4), and (2) can be solved for R_1, R_2, and V.

The second-order conditions are

$$\beta_1(\beta_1 - 1)VR_1^{-2} < 0$$

$$\beta_2(\beta_2 - 1)VR_2^{-2} < 0$$

and

$$\beta_1(\beta_1 - 1)VR_1^{-2}\beta_2(\beta_2 - 1)VR_2^{-2} > \beta_1^2\beta_2^2V^2R_1^{-2}R_2^{-2}$$

The first two conditions will be satisfied if β_1 and β_2 take positive values that are less than 1. The third condition implies that $(\beta_1 - 1)(\beta_2 - 1) > \beta_1\beta_2$ or $\beta_1 + \beta_2 < 1$, which will be the case if there are decreasing returns to scale. Decreasing returns to scale are a necessary condition for the existence of a local profit-maximizing output level. In addition, the equations (3) and (4) must be satisfied and, depending on the output and input prices, this may only occur when $R_1 = R_2 = V = 0$, that is, when no production occurs and profit is $-k$, so that the firm faces a loss if $k > 0$.

If the Cobb–Douglas production function exhibits constant returns to scale or increasing returns to scale, and there exist R_1, R_2 values such that profit is positive, then it always pays the producer to increase the scale of production. Clearly, however, at some point, as output increases, the assumption of fixed input and output prices becomes untenable.

Finally, notice that if some data on output and input levels of firms are generated by this deterministic model, and all firms have the same production function and face the same input and output prices, then all firms will produce the same output using the same input levels. Since there is no variation in the data, it is not possible to estimate the parameters of the production function.

10.3   THE STOCHASTIC SPECIFICATION OF MARSCHAK AND ANDREWS

Typically, all firms in an industry do not produce the same output and use the same input levels, so the deterministic model must be modified to allow for this observed behaviour. To see how this can be done, we first note that, if the second-order conditions are satisfied, the input and output levels are determined by the production function and the first-order conditions, that is, by

$$V = AR_1^{\beta_1}R_2^{\beta_2}$$

$$R_1 = \beta_1 V p_1^{-1}$$

$$R_2 = \beta_2 V p_2^{-1}$$

If we take the logarithms of the variables in these equations, we obtain

$$\ln V = \beta_0 + \beta_1 \ln R_1 + \beta_2 \ln R_2, \text{ where } \beta_0 = \ln A$$

$$\ln R_1 = \ln V + \ln \beta_1 p_1^{-1}$$

$$\ln R_2 = \ln V + \ln \beta_2 p_2^{-1}$$

Marschak and Andrews (1944) proposed modifying the deterministic model by introducing additive random disturbances ε, ε_1, and ε_2 into these equations to give

$$\ln V = \beta_0 + \beta_1 \ln R_1 + \beta_2 \ln R_2 + \varepsilon \tag{5}$$

$$\ln R_1 = \ln V + \ln \beta_1 p_1^{-1} + \varepsilon_1 \tag{6}$$

$$\ln R_2 = \ln V + \ln \beta_2 p_2^{-1} + \varepsilon_2 \tag{7}$$

The random disturbances ε_1 and ε_2 allow for random non-systematic errors to be made by the different producers when they attempt to adjust input levels in order to maximize profit. The different values that the ε_1 disturbance takes for the different firms are assumed to be uncorrelated drawings from a common probability distribution with zero mean and finite variance. The ε_2 disturbances are assumed to be generated in a similar way. Marschak and Andrews describe the random disturbance ε in the production function equation as reflecting 'technical efficiency' and depending on 'the technical knowledge, the will, effort and luck of a given entrepreneur'. Notice that the parameters β_1 and β_2 are the same for all firms, so that the production function for the firms are identical except for a neutral disembodied productivity differential. The values that ε takes for the different firms are also assumed to be uncorrelated drawings from a common distribution with zero mean and finite variance.

By solving (5), (6), and (7) for $\ln V$, $\ln R_1$, and $\ln R_2$ in terms of $\ln \beta_1 p_1^{-1}$, $\ln \beta_2 p_2^{-1}$ and the random disturbances, we can show that $\ln R_1$ and $\ln R_2$

depend on ε.[1] Specifically,

$$\ln R_1 = (1 - \beta_1 - \beta_2)^{-1}$$
$$\times (\beta_0 + \ln \beta_1 p_1^{-1} + \varepsilon + \varepsilon_1 + \beta_2 (\ln \beta_2 p_2^{-1} - \ln \beta_1 p_1^{-1} + \varepsilon_2 - \varepsilon_1)),$$

and

$$\ln R_2 = (1 - \beta_1 - \beta_2)^{-1}$$
$$\times (\beta_0 + \ln \beta_2 p_2^{-1} + \varepsilon + \varepsilon_2 + \beta_1 (\ln \beta_1 p_1^{-1} - \ln \beta_2 p_2^{-1} + \varepsilon_1 - \varepsilon_2))$$

This result has serious implications if we use the stochastic production function equation (5) to estimate the technology parameters β_0, β_1, and β_2 by ordinary least squares, because the explanatory variable values, $\ln R_1$ and $\ln R_2$, will be correlated with the equation disturbance ε.[21] Consequently, the ordinary least squares estimators will, in general, be biased and inconsistent. The problem arises because both the input and output levels are simultaneously determined by the profit maximization model.

10.4 THE STOCHASTIC SPECIFICATION OF ZELLNER, KMENTA, AND DREZE

A second problem with the Marschak–Andrews model is that the value of $\ln V$ is assumed to depend on luck, so that output and hence the profit function has a stochastic component. Consequently, the assumption of deterministic profit maximization by the entrepreneur does not appear sensible. Zellner *et al.* (1966) present an alternative stochastic specification which explicitly recognizes the stochastic nature of output. They assume that output is generated by the stochastic production function

$$V = A R_1^{\beta_1} R_2^{\beta_2} e^\varepsilon$$

where ε is a random disturbance 'representing factors such as weather, unpredictable variations in machine or labour performance, and so on'. The values that ε takes for the different firms are assumed to be uncorrelated drawings from a common probability distribution with zero mean and finite variance. It is assumed that the disturbance values only become apparent to the entrepreneur after the preselected quantities of inputs have been employed in production, so any given level of inputs will result in an uncertain quantity of output and hence uncertain profit. Consequently, Zellner *et al.* assume that the entrepreneur maximizes not profit itself but the expected value of profit — that is, the entrepreneur

$$\text{maximizes } E(\textstyle\prod) = E(V) - p_1 R_1 - p_2 R_2 - k$$

If the disturbance ε is normally distributed with zero mean and variance, σ^2, then

$$E(V) = A R_1^{\beta_1} R_2^{\beta_2} e^{\frac{1}{2}\sigma^2} \quad 3$$

The first-order conditions for profit maximization are

$$\partial E(\textstyle\prod)/\partial R_1 = 0, \text{ and}$$

$$\partial E(\textstyle\prod)/\partial R_2 = 0$$

where, for example, $\partial E(\textstyle\prod)/\partial R_1$ denotes the first partial derivative of the expected value of profit with respect to R_1.

$$\partial E(\textstyle\prod)/\partial R_1 = \beta_1 A R_1^{\beta_1-1} R_2 e^{\frac{1}{2}\sigma^2} - p_1 = \beta_1 E(V) R_1^{-1} - p_1$$

$$= \beta_1 V e^{\frac{1}{2}\sigma^2} e^{-\varepsilon} R_1^{-1} - p_1$$

hence the first-order conditions can be written:

$$R_1 = \beta_1 V p_1^{-1} e^{\frac{1}{2}\sigma^2} e^{-\varepsilon}, \text{ and}$$

$$R_2 = \beta_2 V p_2^{-1} e^{\frac{1}{2}\sigma^2} e^{-\varepsilon}$$

Taking logarithms of the production function and first-order conditions, we obtain:

$$\ln V = \beta_0 + \beta_1 \ln R_1 + \beta_2 \ln R_2 + \varepsilon \tag{8}$$

$$\ln R_1 = \ln V + \ln \beta_1 p_1^{-1} + \tfrac{1}{2}\sigma^2 - \varepsilon$$

$$\ln R_2 = \ln V + \ln \beta_2 p_2^{-1} + \tfrac{1}{2}\sigma^2 - \varepsilon$$

As before, we can introduce random disturbances ε_1 and ε_2, which allow for managerial errors, caused by inertia and ignorance, that result in input levels deviating from the profit-maximizing levels. These random disturbances are assumed to be uncorrelated drawings from common probability distributions, with zero mean and finite variance and uncorrelated with the ε random disturbance. Since ε results from 'acts of nature' such as weather and machine performance, and ε_1 and ε_2 result from 'human error', Zellner *et al.* argue that this assumption of uncorrelatedness is plausible. When the first-order equations are augmented by ε_1 and ε_2, we obtain

$$\ln R_1 = \ln V + \ln \beta_1 p_1^{-1} + \tfrac{1}{2}\sigma^2 - \varepsilon + \varepsilon_1, \text{ and} \tag{9}$$

$$\ln R_2 = \ln V + \ln \beta_2 p_2^{-1} + \tfrac{1}{2}\sigma^2 - \varepsilon + \varepsilon_2 \tag{10}$$

It is interesting that, although the input and output levels are simultaneously determined, in this model the explanatory variables $\ln R_1$ and $\ln R_2$ in (8) are uncorrelated with the equation disturbance ε, so that ordinary least squares estimation of the technology parameters β_0, β_1, and β_2 will result in consistent estimates. If ε is distributed independently of ε_1 and ε_2, then the ordinary least squares estimates of β_0, β_1, and β_2 will also be unbiased. To see that $\ln R_1$ and $\ln R_2$ do not depend on ε, we need to solve (8), (9), and (10) for $\ln R_1$, $\ln R_2$, and

$\ln V$ in terms of $\ln\beta_1 p_1^{-1} + \frac{1}{2}\sigma^2$, $\ln\beta_2 p_2^{-1} + \frac{1}{2}\sigma^2$, and the disturbances ε, ε_1, and ε_2.[4]

$$\ln R_1 = (1 - \beta_1 - \beta_2)^{-1}$$
$$\times (\beta_0 + \ln\beta_1 p_1^{-1} + \frac{1}{2}\sigma^2 + \varepsilon_1 + \beta_2(\ln\beta_2 p_2^{-1} - \ln\beta_1 p_1^{-1} + \varepsilon_2 - \varepsilon_1)),$$

and

$$\ln R_2 = (1 - \beta_1 - \beta_2)^{-1}$$
$$\times (\beta_0 + \ln\beta_2 p_2^{-1} + \frac{1}{2}\sigma^2 + \varepsilon_2 + \beta_1(\ln\beta_1 p_1^{-1} - \ln\beta_2 p_2^{-1} + \varepsilon_1 - \varepsilon_2))$$

so they are uncorrelated with ε.

10.5 FIRM EFFECTS AND NON-SYSTEMATIC RANDOM EFFECTS

The random disturbance ε in the production function relation of the Marschak–Andrews model includes random effects due to the particular environment of the firm, such as managerial efficiency and local input quality factors, which may be called firm effects, and also non-systematic errors such as weather, random variation in labour efficiency, breakdowns, and other factors resulting from 'bad luck'. In the Zellner *et al.* model, the random disturbance ε in the production function consists only of non-systematic errors or errors resulting from 'acts of nature'. Firm effects are known to the entrepreneur but not to the analyst (or not directly measured by him or her); however, the non-systematic effects are unknown both to the entrepreneur, at the time production decisions are made, and also to the analyst. Mundlak and Hoch (1965) emphasize the distinction between these random effects. They argue that effects known to the firm will be exploited in the profit maximization decision process, and hence that the chosen input and output levels will reflect these effects (the errors are said to be 'transmitted'), whereas this will not be the case for non-systematic random errors unknown at the time the production decisions were made. The input levels will therefore be uncorrelated with non-systematic errors and hence, in the Zellner *et al.* model, ordinary least squares estimates of the production function relationship have attractive properties. As we saw, in the Marschak–Andrews model, firm random effects do lead to estimation problems.

One way of seeing how factors known to the entrepreneur but not to the analyst lead to estimation problems is to formulate these factors as additional variables, the values of which are taken into account by the profit-maximizing behaviour of the firm but are not observed by the analyst. Suppose then that the stochastic production function relationship exploited by the firm is

$$V = AR_1^{\beta_1}R_2^{\beta_2}R_3^{\beta_3}e^\varepsilon \tag{11}$$

where the random disturbance ε consists of non-systematic errors and, for simplicity, we assume that ε is normally distributed with zero mean and finite variance, σ^2.

Also suppose that the analyst does not observe R_3 and hence assumes that

$$V = AR_1^{\beta_1}R_2^{\beta_2}e^u$$

where $e^u = R_3^{\beta_3}e^{\varepsilon}$, so that, $u = \beta_3 \ln R_3 + \varepsilon$. The first-order conditions for maximization of expected profit require that

$$R_1 = \beta_1 V p_1^{-1}e^{\frac{1}{2}\sigma^2}e^{-\varepsilon}, \text{ and}$$

$$R_2 = \beta_2 V p_2^{-1}e^{\frac{1}{2}\sigma^2}e^{-\varepsilon}$$

where, from (11), V depends on R_3, so that $\ln R_1$ and $\ln R_2$ are correlated with $\ln R_3$. Hence, when the analyst runs the regression

$$\ln V = \beta_0 + \beta_1 \ln R_1 + \beta_2 \ln R_2 + u$$

since $\ln R_1$ and $\ln R_2$ are correlated with u (through $\ln R_3$), the ordinary least squares estimates of the β-coefficients will, in general, be biased and inconsistent.

10.6 STOCHASTIC SPECIFICATION OF MANORIAL PRODUCTION FUNCTIONS

In Chapter 6, we characterized manorial production in Essex in 1086 in terms of the lords producing tradable goods using a common technology and a set of resources fixed in the short run. The manorial annual value was interpreted as a value-added measure of output. This model of production corresponds to the special case of the neoclassical theory of the firm, when the input levels are fixed exogenously.

The size and resources of the estates were regarded as being determined by the history and geography of the area, and by natural processes such as population growth. Generally speaking, labour was not brought in to work the estate; domiciled labour was used. Although there was an output market, there was little trading in inputs. In these circumstances, the lord was not able to vary input levels in the short run, but only to organize production so that it was technically efficient and the net value of goods produced was maximized.

To allow for non-systematic random effects on output, such as the weather, we introduced a random disturbance; and because of the uncertainty in production, we adopted the assumption of Zellner *et al.* (1966) that producers maximize expected profit. Since the input levels are fixed, this will occur when producers maximize the expected value added by the production process. The disturbance also allows for classical measurement errors in the annual values (see Schmidt 1976, ch. 3.4), the effect of a large number of minor omitted influences on output and random fluctuations in the value of output resulting from implicit output prices not being common to all producers (see Chapter 6 above).

Since the input levels are determined exogenously and not as part of the profit maximization process, the problem of transmitted errors does not arise, although there may be omitted variables problems (see 10.5). As the resource levels and disturbances are determined by different and unrelated influences, we assume that they are distributed independently of each other. We also assume that the disturbances are independently distributed across manors. Both these latter are simplifying assumptions. The first ignores some errors such as classical measurement errors in resource variables (see Schmidt 1976, ch. 3.4) and the second ignores effects, such as weather, that may jointly affect manors located in the same geographical area.

10.7 ESTIMATING MANORIAL PRODUCTION FUNCTIONS

In Chapter 8 we explained how the Box–Cox extended (BCE) method could be used to estimate the value–resources relationship for 682 lay manors in the county of Essex in 1086. The BCE form can be represented as

$$\frac{V_t^\lambda - 1}{\lambda} = \beta_0 + \sum_{i=1}^{8} \beta_i \left(\frac{R_{ti}^\lambda - 1}{\lambda} \right) + \varepsilon_t \tag{12}$$

where V_t is the annual value and R_{ti}, $i = 1, 2, \ldots 8$ are the resources of the tth manor, λ is the BCE transformation parameter, and ε_t is a random disturbance.[5] The estimates for this equation are given as regression 2 in Table 5.1 (p. 87) and regression 4 in Table 8.4 (p. 166).

Given that the data are generated by the manorial model, how can these estimates be interpreted? The BCE equation (12) can be rewritten

$$V_t = \left(\beta_0^* + \sum_{i=1}^{8} \beta_i^* R_{ti}^\lambda + \varepsilon_t^* \right)^{\mu/\lambda} \tag{13}$$

where $\quad \beta_0^* = 1 + \lambda\mu^{-1}\beta_0 - \mu^{-1}\sum_{i=1}^{8} \beta_i, \ \beta_i^* = \mu^{-1}\beta_i, \ i = 1, 2, \ldots 8$

$$\varepsilon_t^* = \lambda\mu^{-1}\varepsilon_t \text{ and } \mu = 1$$

Ignoring for the moment the disturbance, (13) can be interpreted as a CES function, homogeneous if $\beta_0^* = 0$, and if homogeneous, exhibiting constant returns to scale. The disturbance enters the BCE equation (12) additively, but in (13) the disturbance, although disembodied from the input levels, is neither additive nor multiplicative, as is often assumed. Apart from convenience, however, there seems to be no strong reason for preferring an additive or multiplicative disturbance in (13). An advantage of our specification is that it does appear to result in approximately homoskedastic and normally distributed disturbances.

An estimate of $\beta_0^* = 0.1159$ can be obtained from regression 2, Table 5.1 or regression 4, Table 8.4. A hypothesis test suggests this value is insignificant from zero.[6] In view of this, together with the fact that μ is set equal to unity (thus corresponding to constant returns to scale), it is not surprising that the sum of the elasticities in the regressions is almost unity. (The elasticities, $(\partial V_t/\partial R_{ti})/(R_{ti}/V_t)$, evaluated at the sample mean of the resource levels, can be interpreted as partial output elasticities. The sum is sometimes called the elasticity of scale and is a local measure of returns to scale—see 9.5). As we showed in 9.8, this particular CES form constrains all Allen and direct resource partial elasticities of substitution to be equal to $1/(1 - \lambda)$. The estimate for λ implies partial elasticities of substitution of 1.39. A value of this size implies that the isoquants eventually coincide with the axes, and consequently, as we might expect, output can be produced using only some of the resources (see 9.7, and Allen 1967, 54). To summarize: the estimates of equation (12) can be interpreted as defining a well-known production function exhibiting homogeneity of degree one, positive marginal products and diminishing returns for each resource, diminishing marginal rates of substitution between resources, and a sensible value for the partial elasticities of substitution.

The functional form (13) is, however, unnecessarily restrictive as a maintained hypothesis, as it imposes strong restrictions on such properties as separability, scale, and the partial elasticities of substitution. A much more general form is obtained if (13) is augmented by adding cross terms, one for each pair of resources, and μ is allowed to vary, so that, if there are three resources,

$$V_t = \left(\beta_0^* + \sum_{i=1}^{3} \beta_i^* R_{ti}^{\lambda} + \alpha_1 R_{t1}^{\lambda/2} R_{t2}^{\lambda/2} + \alpha_2 R_{t1}^{\lambda/2} R_{t3}^{\lambda/2} + \alpha_3 R_{t2}^{\lambda/2} R_{t3}^{\lambda/2} + \varepsilon_t^* \right)^{\mu/\lambda} \quad (14)$$

Equation (14) is a representation of the Generalized Quadratic (GQ) form discussed by Denny (1974) and in 9.12 above. The GQ form is a flexible functional form that allows different pairs of inputs to have different and variable elasticities of substitution and does not impose separability or homogeneity. If $\beta_0^* \neq 0$, then the function is homothetic but not homogeneous. If $\beta_0^* = 0$, then the function is homogeneous of degree μ. When $\lambda = \mu = 1$, the GQ function reduces to Diewert's parsimoniously parameterized Generalized Linear form (Diewert 1971). If all the $\alpha_i = 0$, we have the CES function (13) and as $\lambda \to 0$, the Cobb–Douglas function is the limiting form of the function.

Unfortunately, the number of parameters in the GQ function (14) increases rapidly as the number of resources increases (with 10 resource variables there are β_0 plus 10 β_i^* plus 46 α_i equals 56 parameters). Estimating a non-linear relationship involving so many parameters is hazardous, and was not possible with the computing facilities available to us. Moreover, the interpretation of the function in terms of scale and input substitution characteristics would be difficult. One way of dealing with the problem would be to aggregate the inputs into a small number of groups, using input prices as the weights. This price information is not, however, available to us.

An alternative way of generalizing the CES function (13) is in terms of a Sato two-level 'CES' production function (see Sato 1967, and 9.10 above), with capital, labour, and land resources in separate groups, so that, if there are two resources in each group,

$$V_t = (\beta_0^* + (\beta_1^* R_{t1}^\lambda + \beta_2^* R_{t2}^\lambda)^{\lambda/\lambda_r} + (\beta_3^* R_{t3}^\lambda + \beta_4^* R_{t4}^\lambda)^{\lambda/\lambda_s}$$
$$+ (\beta_5^* R_{t5}^{\lambda_T} + \beta_6^* R_{t6}^{\lambda_T})^{\lambda/\lambda_T} + \varepsilon^*)^{\mu/\lambda} \tag{15}$$

This function is homogeneous of degree μ if $\beta_0^* = 0$. Sato referred to $\sigma_r = (1 - \lambda_r)^{-1}$, $\sigma_s = (1 - \lambda_s)^{-1}$ and $\sigma_T = (1 - \lambda_T)^{-1}$ as intra-group elasticities of substitution and $(1 - \lambda)^{-1}$ as the inter-group elasticity of substitution.

Two advantages of this formulation as compared with the GQ function are that the lambdas have a direct interpretation in terms of the substitution of inputs in production and, secondly, there are far fewer parameters. A disadvantage is that the form places stronger restrictions on production behaviour. Nevertheless, it is less restrictive than the CES form (13) (the special case of (15) when $\lambda = \lambda_r = \lambda_s = \lambda_T$), in that it allows for different partial elasticities of substitution for different pairs of inputs, and for some non-separability of the inputs.

The Sato function can be further generalized by allowing value added to take the GQ form in the 'higher-level' inputs, capital, labour, and land, with the higher-level inputs themselves being CES in the original resources, so that if

$$Z_r = (\beta_1^* R_{t1}^\lambda + \beta_2^* R_{t2}^\lambda)^{1/\lambda_r}$$
$$Z_s = (\beta_3^* R_{t3}^\lambda + \beta_4^* R_{t4}^\lambda)^{1/\lambda_s}$$

and

$$Z_T = (\beta_5^* R_{t5}^{\lambda_T} + \beta_6^* R_{t6}^{\lambda_T})^{1/\lambda_T}$$
$$V_t = (\beta_0^* + Z_r^\lambda + Z_s^\lambda + Z_T^\lambda + \alpha_1 Z_r^{\lambda/2} Z_s^{\lambda/2} + \alpha_2 Z_r^{\lambda/2} Z_T^{\lambda/2} + \alpha_3 Z_s^{\lambda/2} Z_T^{\lambda/2} + \varepsilon^*)^{\mu/\lambda} \tag{16}$$

In the next section we give estimates of (16) for data that have been disaggregated, so that the variable, the number of plough-teams on the manor, is separated into its two components, the number of demesne and the number of peasants' plough-teams. While both categories of plough-teams were used on the demesne, the peasants' plough-teams were also employed for part of the time on the peasants' plots. Since the different categories of peasants had different contractual obligations with the lord, we also disaggregated the number of peasants on the manor into three groups: freemen and sokemen, villeins, and bordars.[7] First, however, we reanalyse the more aggregated resource variable data and re-estimate (13), treating the scale parameter μ as a parameter to be estimated, rather than setting it at unity, as the estimates in

Table 5.1 and 8.4 imply. We also give t-ratios which are not conditional on the value of λ. We then re-estimate (13) using the disaggregated data, estimate the more general Sato form (15), and finally the GQ function (16).

10.8   MORE SOPHISTICATED ESTIMATES

The t-ratios in Tables 5.1 and 8.4 are conditional on the estimate of λ. Unconditional t-ratios can be obtained by a non-linear least squares estimation. This is because the BCE maximum likelihood estimation problem can be converted to a non-linear least squares problem by dividing all the variables through by $\dot{V}^{\lambda/\mu-1}$, where $\dot{V}$ is the geometric mean of V_t, thereby reducing the Jacobian of the transformation to unity (see Box and Cox 1964, 216). Regression 1 in Table 10.1 gives the non-linear least squares estimates of the CES production function (13) with $\mu = 1$. These estimates can be compared with the estimates in regression 2, Table 5.1 and regression 4, Table 8.4. Comparing the estimates, we see that the t-ratio on the plough-teams variable falls from 17.8 to 8.9, but that the unconditional t-ratios for the other variables are similar to the conditional t-ratios. In regression 1, Table 10.1, the estimated standard error for λ is 0.031, so λ is significantly different from zero and unity. As before, $\beta_0^* = 0$ is not rejected at the 5 per cent significance level. The value of $\bar{R}^2$ is different in regression 1, Table 10.1 because the dependent variable and disturbance are different in the two regression (compare (12) with (13).)

Regression 2 of Table 10.1 gives non-linear least squares estimates when μ is treated as a parameter to be estimated. At the 5 per cent level, μ is significantly different from unity. Nevertheless, $\lambda/\mu = 0.279$, very similar to $\lambda/\mu = 0.281$ in regression 1. β_0^* is significantly different from zero, so the function is inhomogeneous. Since $\beta_0^* \neq 0$, the estimates suggest that manorial output is non-zero when there are no resources. However, since $\beta_0^{*\mu/\lambda} \simeq 0.5$ and the mean manorial output is 94.6 shillings, this represents only a minor misspecification. The main effect of β_0^* being non-zero is to alter the shape of the function at high resource values. Scale characteristics are now not independent of resource values, but substitution characteristics remain invariant.

The estimated coefficients are significantly positive, except for the beehives variable, which is negative but insignificant. The estimates indicate that, except for the beehives variable, the resources have positive marginal products, there are diminishing returns to resources, and the marginal product of a resource increases as the level of another resource increases.[8] The production function's isoquants are strictly convex, ensuring diminishing marginal rates of substitution between resources. The elasticity of substitution estimate is 1.59, a little higher than when μ is set at unity, and, as for that case, the function allows positive output if only some resources are used in production. The output elasticities, $(\partial V_t / \partial R_{ti})(R_{ti}/V_t)$, calculated at the mean resource levels, are very similar in regressions 1 and 2. The sum of the elasticities (the elasticity of scale) is very close to unity, which corresponds to constant returns to scale. The

Table 10.1. *CES production functions for Essex lay manors, 1086: non-linear least squares estimates using aggregated input data*

Explanatory variable	λ	μ	β^*_0	β^*_1 Pl	β^*_2 Li	β^*_3 N	β^*_4 S	β^*_5 W	β^*_6 Me	β^*_7 P	β^*_8 B	$\bar{R}^2$	F
regression 1: $\mu = 1$													
coefficient estimate	0.281	1	0.11	1.35	0.041	0.304	0.309	0.033	0.107	0.055	0.005	0.967	2246.5
t-ratio	9.0		1.9	8.9	6.3	5.8	5.2	2.7	3.9	4.0	0.1		$F(9,672)$
elasticity				0.55	0.07	0.17	0.11	0.03	0.06	0.04	0.00	$\Sigma = 1.01$	2.45
regression 2: μ, β^*_0 estimated													
coefficient estimate	0.370	1.326	0.83	0.90	0.023	0.194	0.220	0.016	0.074	0.032	−0.020	0.968	2076.1
t-ratio	9.6	15.4	5.8	6.2	5.0	4.6	4.5	2.2	3.8	3.7	−0.6		$F(10,672)$
elasticity				0.54	0.08	0.17	0.10	0.03	0.07	0.04	−0.01	$\Sigma = 1.02$	2.36
regression 3: $\beta^*_0 = 0$													
coefficient estimate	0.279	0.985	0	1.42	0.040	0.310	0.326	0.031	0.114	0.060	0.027	0.967	2236.3
t-ratio	8.8	53.1		9.3	5.5	5.7	5.4	2.4	4.1	4.3	0.5		$F(9,672)$
elasticity				0.54	0.06	0.16	0.10	0.03	0.06	0.04	0.01	$\Sigma = 0.99$	2.45

Notes: Pl is a variable measuring the number of plough-teams on the manor, Li the number of livestock, N the number of peasants, S the number of slaves, W the amount of woodland, Me the amount of meadow, P the amount of pasture, and B the number of beehives. The elasticities are partial output elasticities evaluated at the sample mean of the resources.

Σ is the sum of the output elasticities, that is, the elasticity of scale evaluated at the resource means. $\bar{R}^2$ is the coefficient of determination allowing for degrees of freedom. F is the F test statistic for the null hypothesis that $\beta^*_i = 0$, $i = 1, 2 \ldots 8$. Underneath are given the degrees of freedom under the null, and the 1 per cent critical value. For all equations, the hetero (a) and hetero (b) tests did not reveal significant heteroskedasticity in the disturbances. The estimates relate to the CES function, equation (13) in the text.

elasticities of scale calculated at low and high resource levels are also close to unity, and increase slightly as the resource values increase.[9]

Regression 3 of Table 10.1 gives estimates when β_0^* is set equal to zero but μ is estimated. This is the way CES functions have usually been estimated in the past. Notice that the estimate of μ is close to unity, and the other estimates are similar to the case when μ is set at unity. It is interesting that imposing the restriction $\beta_0^* = 0$, which is not supported by the data, forces μ towards unity. This may also have been the case for previous CES studies. However, perhaps the most remarkable feature of regressions 1, 2, and 3 is that, in most respects, the characteristics of the CES functions are very similar.

The disaggregated data results are reported in Table 10.2. Regression 1, Table 10.2 gives the CES function estimates when μ and β_0 are estimated and can be compared with regression 2, Table 10.1. The estimates of μ and λ are a little higher. The elasticity of substitution is also higher at 1.76. The other characteristics of the CES function are very similar. It is interesting that the coefficient on the demesne plough-teams variable is greater than that for the peasants' plough-teams. This is as a priori expected (see 6.5.1). For the labour variables, the villeins' coefficient is greater than that for bordars. This is also as we would a priori expect, since villeins generally worked more days on the demesne. The coefficient estimate and elasticity for freemen and sokemen is small, which is evidence supporting the hypothesis that they made only a minor contribution to manorial income (see note 7). Notice that the sum of the elasticities for the plough-teams variable in regression 1 of Table 10.2 is very similar to the elasticity for total plough-teams in regression 2, Table 10.1. The sum of the peasants' elasticities is a little higher than we might expect from regression 2, Table 10.1; but the other elasticities are very similar in the two regressions. Finally, we note that results analogous to those reported in Table 10.1 were obtained with the disaggregated data when μ was set at unity and β_0^* set at zero.

When the Sato function (15) was estimated, the estimates for λ_r, λ_s, and λ_T were very close to unity being 1.01, 1.11, and 0.99, respectively.[10] These estimates were neither individually nor jointly significantly different from unity at conventional significance levels; so in regression 2, Table 10.2 we give the estimates when $\lambda_r = \lambda_s = \lambda_T = 1$. These lambda values imply infinite intra-group elasticities of substitution. Whilst this is reasonable for some inputs, such as demesne and peasants' plough-teams, villeins and bordars, and meadow and pasture, it may not seem reasonable that, for example, plough-teams and livestock or woodland and meadowland are perfect substitutes in production. The estimates are more understandable if we recall that the production function does not relate inputs to a single output, but to the value added in the production of several outputs. Also, the Sato function (15) restricts the intra-group input elasticities of substitution to be common to all input pairs in a group. It would appear that in, for example, the capital group, the substitution relationship of the plough-teams inputs dominates that of plough-teams and livestock.

Table 10.2 CES production functions for Essex lay manors, 1086: non-linear least squares estimates using disaggregated input data

	λ	μ	β_0^* Explanatory variable	β_1^* Pld	β_2^* Plp	β_3^* Li	β_4^* FS	β_5^* V	β_6^* Bo	β_7^* S	β_8^* W	β_9^* Me	β_{10}^* P	β_{11}^* B	$\bar{R}^2$	F
regression 1: CES																
coefficient estimate	0.432	1.430	0.79	0.895	0.333	0.018	0.087	0.244	0.134	0.177	0.014	0.059	0.032	−0.042	0.969	1648.1
t-ratio	10.7	15.5	5.1	6.2	4.0	4.8	2.1	4.6	4.2	3.9	2.4	3.4	4.0	−1.2		$F(13,669)$
elasticity				0.41	0.16	0.09	0.03	0.15	0.11	0.08	0.03	0.06	0.04	−0.01	$\Sigma = 1.15$	2.15
regression 2: Sato																
coefficient estimate	0.320	1.265	0.38	1.207	0.746	0.0016	0.0029	0.0704	0.0229	0.0774	0.00003	0.0007	0.00016		0.972	1943.2
t-ratio	7.6	12.6	2.1	2.0	1.8	2.0	0.4	1.4	1.4	1.5	0.7	0.9	0.9			$F(12,670)$
elasticity				0.32	0.23	0.11	0.00	0.15	0.10	0.09	0.02	0.06	0.03		$\Sigma = 1.11$	2.22

	λ	μ	β_0	α_1	α_2	α_3									$\bar{R}^2$	F
regression 3: GQ																
coefficient estimate	0.311	1.341	0.47	−0.249	−0.227	0.136									0.972	4721.8
t-ratio	7.7	14.5	3.6	−1.0	−0.9	0.3										$F(5,667)$ 3.05

Notes: Pld is a variable measuring the number of demesne plough-teams on the manor, Plp the number of peasants' plough-teams, Li the number of livestock, FS the number of freemen and sokemen, V the number of villeins, Bo the number of bordars, S the number of slaves, W the amount of woodland, Me the amount of meadow, P the amount of pasture, and B the number of beehives. The elasticities are partial output elasticities evaluated at the sample mean of the resources.
Σ is the sum of the output elasticities, that is, the elasticity of scale evaluated at the resource means. $\bar{R}^2$ is the coefficient of determination allowing for degrees of freedom. F is the F test statistic for the null hypothesis that $\beta_i^* = 0$, $i = 1, 2 \ldots 11$. Underneath are given the degrees of freedom under the null, and the 1 per cent critical value. For all equations, the hetero (a) and hetero (b) tests did not reveal any significant heteroskedasticity in the disturbances. The CES estimates relate to equation (13) in the text, the Sato estimates to equation (15), and the GQ estimates to equation (16).

Although the Sato function estimates exhibit a very good overall fit, and μ and λ are highly significant, the β^*-coefficients appear much less significant than in the previous regressions. The t tests reported in Table 10.2 are based on the asymptotic distribution of the estimators. Alternatively, likelihood ratio tests (based on the optimization criterion) can be performed. In non-linear models (and the Sato function is highly non-linear), these tests are not asymptotically equivalent. On the basis of simulation evidence, Gallant and Jorgenson (1979, 276) conjecture that the likelihood ratio test possesses greater robustness of validity (i.e., the nominal significance level computed according to the asymptotic distribution will be more nearly correct in finite samples). Gallant (1975, 930) recommends using the likelihood ratio test when the hypothesis is an important aspect of the study. We found that t-ratios based on the likelihood ratio test were much higher than those reported in regression 2 of Table 10.2. For example, the t-ratios for demesne plough-teams, livestock, bordars, and slaves were 14.0, 7.9, 5.5, and 6.3 respectively. In addition, likelihood ratio tests that output is not explained by each of the three higher-level inputs, capital, labour, and land, are clearly rejected at all conventional significance levels.[11]

Generally speaking, the characteristics of the Sato function are similar to the CES results in regression 1, Table 10.2. The input marginal products are positive; they increase as the levels of inputs from other groups increase; and each one exhibits diminishing returns if an input from its own group is increased.[12] For inputs from different groups, the isoquants are strictly convex, so there are diminishing marginal rates of substitution between these resources. The individual output elasticities for demesne and peasants' plough-teams vary a little in the two regressions, but the sum of the plough-teams' elasticities is almost the same. The other output elasticities are very similar. The elasticity of scale is 1.11 and the inter-group elasticity of substitution 1.47. Finally, $\beta_0^{*\mu/\lambda} = 0.02$, which is very close to zero.

Regression 3 of Table 10.2 gives the GQ function estimates (see equation (16)). The higher-level inputs Z_r, Z_s, and Z_T were defined as in regression 2. Because of the complexity of the non-linear regression, the β_i^*, $i = 1, 2, \ldots 10$ were not estimated jointly with the other parameters. None of the α_i, $i = 1, 2, 3$ are individually significant, and the joint hypothesis that the α_i are all zero was not rejected at the 5 per cent level.[13] These are the results we would expect to obtain if the Sato function adequately characterized the production relationship.

To summarize: the preferred function is a Sato two-level CES function, with the capital, labour, and land resources in separate higher-level input groups; but in most respects the simpler CES function estimations give similar results.

10.9 WIDER APPLICATION OF THE QUANTITATIVE ANALYSIS

The economic and statistical approach outlined in Chapters 8, 9, and 10 explains the basis of the historical reconstruction in Part I. Yet it has a wider purpose. It is our hope that the approach developed and presented here will be of assistance to historians who wish to undertake quantitative work on the Domesday data, and to academics in a variety of disciplines who wish to conduct classroom exercises either in quantitative historical analysis or in applied econometrics based upon the remarkable wealth of detail in the Conqueror's Survey. The possibilities for exercises of this nature are expanding rapidly with the growing availability of mainframe and micro-computers. Of course this approach is not limited to Domesday Book, but can be applied to any source of detailed cross-sectional data.

Notes

1. Rewrite equations (5), (6), and (7) as

$$x_0 = \beta_0 + \beta_1 x_1 + \beta_2 x_2 + \varepsilon \qquad \text{(i)}$$

$$x_1 = x_0 + \lambda_1 + \varepsilon_1 \qquad \text{(ii)}$$

$$x_2 = x_0 + \lambda_2 + \varepsilon_2 \qquad \text{(iii)}$$

where, for example, $x_0 = \ln V$, $x_1 = \ln R_1$ and $\lambda_1 = \ln \beta_1 \, p_1^{-1}$. Substitute (i) into (ii) to give

$$x_1 = \beta_0 + \beta_1 x_1 + \beta_2 x_2 + \varepsilon + \lambda_1 + \varepsilon_1 \qquad \text{(iv)}$$

Subtracting (iii) from (ii),

$$x_1 - x_2 = \lambda_1 - \lambda_2 + \varepsilon_1 - \varepsilon_2 \qquad \text{(v)}$$

From (iv)

$$x_1 = \beta_2(x_2 - x_1) + (\beta_1 + \beta_2)x_1 + \beta_0 + \lambda_1 + \varepsilon + \varepsilon_1$$

Using (v)

$$x_1 = (1 - \beta_1 - \beta_2)^{-1}(\beta_0 + \lambda_1 + \varepsilon + \varepsilon_1 + \beta_2(\lambda_2 - \lambda_1 + \varepsilon_2 - \varepsilon_1))$$

Similarly

$$x_2 = (1 - \beta_1 - \beta_2)^{-1}(\beta_0 + \lambda_2 + \varepsilon + \varepsilon_2 + \beta_1(\lambda_1 - \lambda_2 + \varepsilon_1 - \varepsilon_2))$$

From (ii)

$$x_0 = (1 - \beta_1 - \beta_2)^{-1}(\beta_0 + \lambda_1 + \varepsilon + \varepsilon_1 + \beta_2(\lambda_2 - \lambda_1 + \varepsilon_2 - \varepsilon_1)) - \lambda_1 - \varepsilon_1$$

2. Identification of the production function equation requires some additional assumptions, for example, that ε is uncorrelated with ε_1 and ε_2 (see Zellner *et al.* 1966, 790; Walters 1963, 17; Bridge 1971, 340–2).

3. This follows because $E(AR_1^{\beta_1} R_2^{\beta_2} e^{\varepsilon}) = AR_1^{\beta_1} R_2^{\beta_2} E(e^{\varepsilon})$. To evaluate $E(e^{\varepsilon})$, note that if ε is normally distributed with mean zero and variance σ^2, then $E(\varepsilon) = 0$, $E(\varepsilon^2) = \sigma^2$, and $E(\varepsilon^4) = 3\sigma^4$. Using these results and also the fact that

$$e^{\varepsilon} = 1 + \varepsilon + \frac{\varepsilon^2}{2!} + \frac{\varepsilon^3}{3!} + \frac{\varepsilon^4}{4!} + \ldots,$$

$$E(e^{\varepsilon}) = 1 + 0 + \sigma^2/2 + 0 + 3\sigma^4/24 + \ldots$$

$$= 1 + \sigma^2/2 + (\sigma^2/2)^2/2 + \ldots$$

$$= e^{1/2\sigma^2}$$

4. Rewrite equations (8), (9), and (10) as

$$x_0 = \beta_0 + \beta_1 x_1 + \beta_2 x_2 + \varepsilon \qquad \text{(i)}$$

$$x_1 = x_0 + \delta_1 - \varepsilon + \varepsilon_1 \qquad \text{(ii)}$$

$$x_2 = x_0 + \delta_2 - \varepsilon + \varepsilon_2 \qquad \text{(iii)}$$

where, for example $\delta_1 = \ln \beta_1 p_1^{-1} + 1/2\sigma^2$.

Substitute (i) into (ii):

$$x_1 = \beta_0 + \beta_1 x_1 + \beta_2 x_2 + \delta_1 + \varepsilon_1 \qquad \text{(iv)}$$

Subtract (iii) from (ii):

$$x_1 - x_2 = \delta_1 - \delta_2 + \varepsilon_1 - \varepsilon_2$$

From (iv)

$$x_1 = \beta_2(x_2 - x_1) + (\beta_2 + \beta_1)x_1 + \beta_0 + \delta_1 + \varepsilon_1, \text{ so}$$

$$x_1 = (1 - \beta_1 - \beta_2)^{-1}(\beta_0 + \delta_1 + \varepsilon_1 + \beta_2(\delta_2 - \delta_1 + \varepsilon_2 - \varepsilon_1)), \text{ and}$$

$$x_2 = (1 - \beta_1 - \beta_2)^{-1}(\beta_0 + \delta_2 + \varepsilon_2 + \beta_1(\delta_1 - \delta_2 + \varepsilon_1 - \varepsilon_2)).$$

$$x_0 = (1 - \beta_1 - \beta_2)^{-1}(\beta_0 + \delta_1 + \varepsilon_1 + \beta_2(\delta_2 - \delta_1 + \varepsilon_2 - \varepsilon_1)) - \delta_1 + \varepsilon - \varepsilon_1.$$

5. We focus on the preferred relationship with the mills and horses explanatory variables omitted from the regression. The notation is consistent with that of Chapter 9 but slightly different from that of Chapter 8, in that the intercept is denoted β_0 and the resource variables, R_{ti}, are numbered from 1 to 8 rather than 2 to 9.

6. The test involves comparing the residual sum of squares from the BCE equation (12), denoted RSS_1, with the residual sum of squares from the regression of (V^λ/λ) on $(R_{t1}^\lambda/\lambda)\ldots(R_{t8}^\lambda/\lambda)$, with $\lambda=0.280$, denoted RSS_2, via the F statistic $(\text{RSS}_2 - \text{RSS}_1)/(\text{RSS}_1/(682-9))$, which, conditional on $\lambda=0.280$ and $\beta_0^*=0$, has an F distribution with 1 and 673 degrees of freedom. The null hypothesis is not rejected at the 5 per cent level.

7. There were relatively few freemen and sokemen, but their obligations to the lord were somewhat different from that of villeins and bordars in that they did not usually work on the demesne. While freemen and sokemen were closely attached to the manor after the Norman Conquest (only a very small minority were completely independent), the dues they paid are thought to have been relatively small (Harvey 1983, 49–50).

8. This follows because, denoting the partial derivative of V with respect to the ith resource by V_i, $V_i = \mu\beta_i^* R_i^{\lambda-1} V^{1-\lambda/\mu} > 0$ if $\beta_i^* > 0$ and $\mu = 1.326$. Denoting the second partial derivatives V_{ij}, $V_{ii} = \mu\beta_i^* R_i^{\lambda-1} V^{-\lambda/\mu}((\lambda - 1)R_i^{-1} V - (\lambda/\mu - 1)V_i) < 0$, if μ and $\beta_i^* > 0$ and $(\lambda - 1)R_i^{-1} V - (\lambda/\mu - 1)V_i < 0$. The second condition can be written $(\lambda - 1)(R_i^{-1} V - V_i) + (\lambda - \lambda/\mu)V_i < 0$ or, when $\lambda = 0.370$, $\mu = 1.326$, $-0.63(R_i^{-1} V - V_i) + (0.09)V_i < 0$. Now

$$R_i^{-1}V - V_i = R_i^{-1}V\left(1 - \mu\beta_i^* R_i^\lambda \left(\sum_{j=1}^{8} \beta_j^* R_j^\lambda\right)^{-1}\right) > 0$$

if all $\beta_i^* > 0$ and μ not much greater than 1. Given the regression 2 estimates of Table 10.1, for all sample values of the R_i,

$$-0.63(R_i^{-1}V - V_i) < 0 \text{ and } 0.63(R_i^{-1}V - V_i) > 0.09V_i, \text{ for } i = 1, 2, \ldots 7$$

thus proving diminishing returns. $V_{ij} = (1 - \lambda/\mu)V^{-1}V_iV_j > 0$, when $\mu = 1.326$ and $\lambda = 0.370$.

9. The elasticity of scale when resource levels are equal to their means minus half a standard deviation or zero (whichever is greater) is 0.91, and when resource levels are equal to their mean plus one standard deviation, 1.07.

10. The beehives variable was insignificant in all previous regressions, and was dropped for the more complex Sato and GQ estimations. As with the CES regression, the null hypothesis of homoskedasticity was accepted at the 5 per cent significance level in the hetero (*a*) and hetero (*b*) tests described in 8.12.

11. The likelihood ratio tests were based on the test statistic

$$F = (\text{RRSS} - \text{URSS})(682 - k)(\text{URSS} \cdot H)^{-1}$$

where RRSS is the restricted and URSS the unrestricted residual sum of squares, H the number of restrictions imposed under the null and k the number of parameters estimated under the alternative hypothesis. When the null hypothesis is true, in large samples, F is approximately distributed as an F distribution with H and $682 - k$ degrees of freedom, so if $H = 1$, the square root of F has a t distribution. For the test that output is not explained by capital (i.e., $H_0: \beta_1 = \beta_2 = \beta_3 = 0$), $F = 113.5$, for the test that output is not explained by labour, $F = 25.8$, and for the test that land does not help to explain output, $F = 11.6$. The 1 per cent critical values for these tests are less than 3.5.

12. These statements can be verified by noting that

$$V_1 = \mu\beta_1^* Z_r^{\lambda - 1} V^{1 - \lambda/\mu} > 0 \text{ if } \mu \text{ and } \beta_1^* > 0$$

$$V_{11} = \mu\beta_1^* Z_r^{\lambda - 1} V^{-\lambda/\mu}((\lambda - 1)Z_r^{-1}\beta_1^* V - (\lambda/\mu - 1)V_1)$$

Using an argument similar to that used in note 8 above, this is negative, given the Sato function estimates, for all sample values of the R_i. Also,

$$V_{12} = \mu\beta_1^* Z_r^{\lambda - 1} V^{-\lambda/\mu}((\lambda - 1)Z_r^{-1}\beta_2^* V - (\lambda/\mu - 1)V_2) < 0$$

given the Sato estimates, for all sample values of the R_i. Finally,

$$V_{14} = \mu\beta_1^* Z_r^{\lambda - 1} V^{-\lambda/\mu}(1 - \lambda/\mu)V_4 > 0$$

if μ, β_1^* and $\beta_4^* > 0$.

13. The likelihood ratio test statistic value was 0.42 as compared with the 5 per cent critical value of 2.61.

Bibliography

Scholarly works are identified in the text and Bibliography by the date of first publication; page references are to the first publication, unless a later reprint is mentioned here.

Abels, R., 1985, Bookland and fyrd service in later Saxon England, in *Proceedings of the Battle Conference on Anglo-Norman Studies*, vol. 7, ed. R. A. Brown, Woodbridge, Boydell Press

Allen, R. G. D., 1967, *Macro-economic Theory*, London, McMillan.

Arrow, K. J., H. B. Chenery, B. Minhas, and R. M. Solow, 1961, Capital–labour substitution and economic efficiency. *Review of Economic Studies* **43**, 225–50

Aston, T. H., 1958, The origins of the manor in England. *Transactions of the Royal Historical Society* **8**, 59–83

—— 1962, Domesday Book, *The Oxford Magazine*, 287–9

Ballard, A., 1906, *The Domesday Inquest*, London, Methuen

Baring, F. H., 1898, The Conqueror's footprints in Domesday, *English Historical Review* **13**, 17–25

Baumol, W. J., 1977, *Economic Theory and Operations Analysis*, London, Prentice-Hall

Booth, C. (ed.), 1889–1902, *Labour and Life of the People of London*, 17 vols., London, Macmillan

Bowley, A. L., and A. R. Burnett-Hurst, 1915, *Livelihood and Poverty: A Study in the Economic Conditions of Working-class Households in Northampton, Warrington, Stanley and Reading*, London, G. Bell

Box, G. E. P., and D. R. Cox, 1964, An analysis of transformations, *Journal of the Royal Statistical Society*, series **B 26**, 211–52

Bridge, J. L., 1971, *Applied Econometrics*, Amsterdam, North-Holland

Brown, R. A., 1984, *The Normans*, Woodbridge, Boydell Press

Campbell, B. M. S., 1983a, Agricultural progress in medieval England: some evidence from eastern Norfolk, *Economic History Review* **36**, 26–46

—— 1983b, Arable production in medieval England: some evidence from Norfolk, *Journal of Economic History* **43**, 379–404

Campbell, J., 1975, Observations on English government from the tenth to the twelfth century, *Transactions of the Royal Historical Society* **25**, 39–54

Chiang, A. C., 1974, *Fundamental Methods of Mathematical Economics*, New York, McGraw-Hill.

Christensen, L. R., D. W. Jorgensen, and L. J. Lau, 1971. Conjugate duality and the transcendental logarithmic functions. *Econometrica* **39**, 255–6 (abstract)

Clanchy, M. T., 1983, *England and its Rulers, 1066–1272*, Glasgow, Fontana

Darby, H. C., 1952, *The Domesday Geography of Eastern England*, reprinted 1971, Cambridge, Cambridge University Press

—— 1977, *Domesday England*, reprinted 1979, Cambridge, Cambridge University Press

Darby, H. C., and R. W. Finn, 1967, *The Domesday Geography of South West England*, Cambridge, Cambridge University Press

Darby, H. C., and I. S. Maxwell (eds.), 1962, *The Domesday Geography of Northern England*, Cambridge, Cambridge University Press

Darlington, R. R., 1955, Introduction to the Wiltshire Domesday, in *VCH Wiltshire*, vol. 2, London, Oxford University Press

David, P. A., 1982, Cooperative games for medieval warriors and peasants, Discussion paper, Department of Economics, Stanford University

Denny, M., 1974, The relationship between functional forms for the production system, *Canadian Journal of Economics* 7, 21–31

Diewert, W. E., 1971, An application of the Shepard duality theorem: a generalised Leontief production function, *Journal of Political Economy* 79, 481–507

Domar, E., 1970, The causes of slavery or serfdom: a hypothesis, *Journal of Economic History* 30, 18–32

Douglas, P. C., and C. W. Cobb, 1928, A theory of production. *American Economic Review* 18, 139–65

Dove, P. E. (ed.), 1888, *Domesday Studies*, vols. 1, 2, London, B. Franklin

Draper, N. R., and D. R. Cox, 1969, On distributions and their transformation to normality. *Journal of the Royal Statistical Society*, series **B 31**, 472–6

Duby, G., 1974, *The Early Growth of the European Economy: Warriors and Peasants for the 7th–12th Centuries*, English translation, Ithaca: Cornell University Press

Eyton, R. W., 1878, *Key to Domesday: An Analysis and Digest of the Dorset Survey*, London and Dorchester, Taylor.

Fenoaltea, S., 1975, Authority, efficiency and agricultural organisation in medieval England and beyond: a hypothesis. *Journal of Economic History* 35, 693–718

—— 1976, Risk, transaction costs, and the organisation of medieval agriculture, *Explorations in Economic History* 13, 129–51

Finn, R. W., 1963, *An Introduction to Domesday Book*, London, Longman

—— 1971, *The Norman Conquest and its Effects on the Economy*, London, Shoestring

Fleming, R., 1983, Domesday estates of the King and the Godwines: A study in late Saxon politics, *Speculum* 58, 987–1007

Frisch, R., 1929, Correlation and scatter in statistical variables, *Nordic Statistical Journal*, 36–103

Fuss, M., and D. McFadden (eds.), 1978, *Production Economics: A Dual Approach to Theory and Applications*, 2 vols., Amsterdam, North-Holland

Fuss, M., D. McFadden, and Y. Mundlak, 1978, A survey of functional forms in the economic analysis of production, in *Production Economics: A Dual Approach to Theory and Application*, ed. M. Fuss and D. McFadden, vol. 1, Amsterdam, North-Holland

Galbraith, V. H., 1942, The making of Domesday Book, *English Historical Review*, 57, 161–77

—— 1961, *The Making of Domesday Book*, Oxford, Clarendon Press

—— 1974, *Domesday Book: Its Place in Administrative History*, Oxford, Clarendon Press

Gallant, A. R., 1975, Testing a subset of the parameters of a nonlinear regression model, *Journal of the American Statistical Association* 70, 927–32

Gallant, A. R., and D. W. Jorgensen, 1979, Statistical inference for a system of simultaneous, non-linear, implicit equations in the context of instrumental variable estimation, *Journal of Econometrics* **11**, 275–302

Godfrey, L. G., and M. R. Wickens, 1981, Testing linear and log-linear regressions for functional form, *Review of Economic Studies* **48**, 487–96

Gorman, W. M., 1965, Production functions in which the elasticities of substitution stand in fixed proportion to each other, *Review of Economic Studies* **32**, 217–24

Green, J. A., 1981, The last century of danegeld, *English Historical Review* **96**, 241–58

Hallam, H. E., 1981, *Rural England, 1066–1348*, Brighton, Fontana

Hamilton, N. E. S. Á. (ed.), 1876, *Inquisitio Comitatus Cantabrigiensis*, London, Royal Society of Literature

Harvey, S. P. J., 1970, The knight and the knight's fee in England, *Past and Present* **49**, 3–43

—— 1971, Domesday Book and its predecessors, *English Historical Review* **86**, 753–73

—— 1975, Domesday Book and Anglo-Norman governance, *Transactions of the Royal Historical Society* **25**, 175–93

—— 1980, Recent Domesday studies, *English Historical Review* **95**, 121–33

—— 1983, The extent and profitability of demesne agriculture in England in the later eleventh century, in *Social Relations and Ideas: Essays in Honour of R. H. Hilton*, ed. T. H. Aston *et al.*, Cambridge, Cambridge University Press

Heathfield, D. F., 1971, *Production Functions*, London, Macmillan

Henderson, J. M., and R. E. Quandt, 1980, *Microeconomic Theory*, New York, McGraw-Hill

Hicks, J., 1969, *A Theory of Economic History*, Oxford, Clarendon Press

Hollister, C. W., 1965, *The Military Organisation of Norman England*, Oxford, Clarendon Press

Holt, J. C., 1972, Politics and property in early medieval England, *Past and Present* **57**, 3–52

—— 1982, Feudal society and family in early medieval England, I, The revolution of 1066, *Transactions of the Royal Historical Society* **32**, 193–212

—— 1984, The introduction of knight service in England, in *Proceedings of the Battle Conference on Anglo-Norman Studies*, vol. 6, ed. R. A. Brown, Woodbridge, Boydell Press

Huang, C. J., and B. W. Bolch, 1974, On the testing of regression disturbances for normality, *Journal of the American Statistical Association* **69**, 330–5

Intriligator, M. L., 1978, *Econometric Models, Techniques and Applications*, Englewood Cliffs, Prentice-Hall

John, E., 1960, *Land Tenure in Early England*, Leicester, Leicester University Press

Johnson, C. (ed.), 1950, *Dialogus de Scaccario*, London, Oxford University Press

Judge, G. G., W. E. Griffiths, R. C. Hill, and T. Lee, 1980, *The Theory and Practice of Econometrics*, New York, Wiley

Kmenta, J., 1971, *Elements of Econometrics*, New York, Macmillan

Lahiri, K., and D. Egy, 1981, Joint estimation and testing for functional form and heteroskedasticity, *Journal of Econometrics* **15**, 299–307

Langdon, J., 1982, The economics of horses and oxen in medieval England, *Agricultural History Review* **30**, 31–40

Lau, L. J., 1974, Comments on applications of duality theory, in *Frontiers of Quantitative Economics*, ed. M. D. Intriligator and D. A. Kandrick, vol. 2, Amsterdam, North-Holland

Lawson, M. K., 1984, The collection of danegeld and heregeld in the reigns of Aethelred II and Cnut, *English Historical Review* **99**, 721–38

Lemmon, C. H., 1966, Chapter in *The Norman Conquest*, Whitelock *et al.* 1966

Lennard, R., 1944, The origin of the fiscal carucate, *Economic History Review* **14**, 51–63

—— 1959, *Rural England, 1086–1135: A Study of Social and Agrarian Conditions*, Oxford, Clarendon Press

Levi, M., 1984*a*, The theory of predatory rule, Mimeo, Social Justice Project, Australian National University, Canberra

—— 1984*b*, Creating compliance to taxes, Mimeo, Social Justice Project, Australian National University, Canberra

Loyn, H. R., 1962, *Anglo-Saxon England and the Norman Conquest*, reprinted 1981, London, Longman

—— 1965, *The Norman Conquest*, London, Hillary House

—— 1979, Domesday Book, in *Proceedings of the Battle Conference on Anglo-Norman Studies*, vol. 1, ed. R. A. Brown, Ipswich, Boydell Press

—— 1983, *The Governance of Anglo-Saxon England, 500–1087*, London, Edward Arnold

McCloskey, D. N., 1972, The enclosure of open fields: preface to a study of its impact on the efficiency of English agriculture in the eighteenth century, *Journal of Economic History* **32**, 15–35

—— 1977, Fenoaltea on open fields: a comment, *Explorations in Economic History* **14**, 402–4

McDonald, J., and G. D. Snooks, 1984, *Flinders Domesday File: A Computerised Data Base for the Domesday Book Counties of Essex and Wiltshire*, Adelaide, Flinders University

—— 1985*a*, Were the tax assessments of Domesday England artificial? The case of Essex, *Economic History Review* **38**, 353–73

—— 1985*b*, The determinants of manorial income in Domesday England: evidence from Essex, *Journal of Economic History* **45**, 541–56

—— 1985*c*, Statistical analysis of Domesday Book (1086), *Journal of the Royal Statistical Society*, series **A 148**, 147–60

—— 1986, The economics of Domesday England, in *Great Domesday: The 1986 Facsimile*, London, Alecto Historical Editions

McFadden, D., 1963, Constant elasticity of substitution production functions, *Review of Economic Studies* **30**, 73–83

Mack, K., 1984, Changing thegns: Cnut's conquest and the English aristocracy, *Albion* **16**, 375–84

Maitland, F. W., 1897, *Domesday Book and Beyond*, reprinted 1921, Cambridge, Cambridge University Press

Marschak, J., and W. H. Andrews, 1944, Random simultaneous equations and the theory of production, *Econometrica* **12**, 143–205

Miller, E., and J. Hatcher, 1978, *Medieval England: Rural Society and Economic Change, 1086–1348*, London, Longman

Ministry of Agriculture Fisheries and Food, 1968, *A Century of Agricultural Statistics, Great Britain 1866–1966*, London, HMSO

Mitchell, S. K., 1914, *Studies in Taxation under John and Henry III*, New Haven, Yale University Press

Moser, C. A., 1958, *Survey Methods in Social Investigation*, London, Heinemann

Mosteller, F., and J. W. Tukey, 1977, *Data Analysis and Regression*, Reading, Mass.: Addison-Wesley

Mukerji, V., 1963, A generalised SMAC function with constant ratios of elasticities of substitution, *Review of Economic Studies* **30**, 233–36

Mundlak, Y., and I. Hoch, 1965, Consequence of alternative specifications in estimation of Cobb–Douglas production functions, *Econometrica* **33**, 814–28

Nicol, A., 1981, *Domesday Book*, Public Record Office Museum Pamphlets no. 10, London, HMSO

North, D., and R. P. Thomas, 1971, The rise and fall of the manorial system: a theoretical model, *Journal of Economic History* **31**, 777–803

Pagan, A. R., and A. D. Hall, 1983, Diagnostic tests as residual analysis, *Econometric Reviews* **2**, 159–218

Painter, S., 1943, *Studies in the History of the English Feudal Barony*, Baltimore, Johns Hopkins University Press

Pearson, C. H., 1867, *History of England during the Early and Middle Ages*, vol. 1, London, Bell and Daldy

Pindyck, R. S., and D. L. Rubinfeld, 1981, *Econometric Models and Econometric Forecasts*, Auckland, McGraw-Hill

Poole, R. L., 1912, *The Exchequer in the Twelfth Century*, Oxford, Clarendon Press

Postan, M. M., 1966, Medieval agrarian society in its prime, in *The Cambridge Economic History of Europe*, vol. 1, ed. M. M. Postan, Cambridge, Cambridge University Press

—— 1972, *The Medieval Economy and Society: An Economic History of Britain in the Middle Ages*, London, Weidenfeld & Nicolson

—— 1983, Feudalism and its decline: a semantic exercise, in *Social Relations and Ideas: Essays in Honour of R. H. Hilton*, ed. T. H. Aston *et al.*, Cambridge, Cambridge University Press

Prestwick, J. O., 1954, War and finance in the Anglo-Norman State, *Transactions of the Royal Historical Society* **4**, 19–43

Raftis, J. A., 1957, *The Estates of Ramsey Abbey: A Study in Economic Growth and Organisation*, Toronto, Pontifical Institute of Medieval Studies

Revankar, N., 1971, A class of variable elasticity of substitution production functions, *Econometrica* **39**, 61–72

Round, J. H., 1888, Notes on Domesday measures of land, in *Domesday Studies*, vol. 1, ed. P. E. Dove, London, B. Franklin

—— 1891, The introduction of knight service into England, *English Historical Review* **6**, 417–43, 625–45

—— 1892, The introduction of knight service into England, *English Historical Review* **7**, 11–24

—— 1895, *Feudal England: Historical Studies on the Eleventh and Twelfth Centuries*, reprinted 1964, London, Allen & Unwin

—— 1903, Essex survey, in *VCH Essex*, vol. 1, reprinted 1977, London, Dawson

Sato, K., 1967, A two level constant elasticity of substitution production function, *Review of Economic Studies* **34**, 201–18

Sawyer, P. H., 1955, The original returns and Domesday Book, *English Historical Review* **70**, 177–97

—— 1963, Review of Darby and Maxwell (1962) and Darby and Campbell, *The Domesday Geography of South-East England* (1962), *Economic History Review* **16**, 155–7

Schmidt, P., 1976, *Econometrics*, New York, Dekker

Shewhart, W. A., 1933, Annual survey of statistical developments in sampling theory, *Econometrica* **1**, 225–37

Stenton, D. M., 1951, *English Society in the Early Middle Ages*, reprinted 1983, Harmondsworth, Penguin

Stenton, F. M., 1932, *The First Century of English Feudalism, 1066–1166*, Oxford, Clarendon Press

—— 1943, *Anglo-Saxon England*, reprinted 1975, Oxford, Clarendon Press

Stephan, F. F., 1948, History of the uses of modern sampling procedures, *Journal of the American Statistical Association* **43**, 12–38

Stephenson, C., 1954, *Medieval Institutions: Selected Essays*, ed. B. D. Lyon, Ithaca, Peter Smith

Stubbs, W., 1874, *The Constitutional History of England*, vol. 1, reprinted 1903, Oxford, Clarendon Press

Tait, J., 1936, *The Medieval English Borough: Studies on its Origins and Constitutional History*, reprinted 1968, Manchester, Manchester University Press

Theil, H., 1971, *Principles of Econometrics*, Amsterdam, North-Holland

Thomas, J. J., 1973, *Introduction to Statistical Analysis for Economists*, London, Weidenfeld & Nicolson

Tinbergen, J., 1933, The notions of horizon and expectancy in dynamic economics, *Econometrica* **1**, 247–64

Uzawa, H., 1962, Production functions with constant elasticities of substitution, *Review of Economic Studies* **29**, 291–99

Varian, H. R., 1984, *Microeconomic Analysis*, New York, Norton

Vazquez, A., 1971, Homogeneous production functions with constant or variable elasticity of substitution, *Zeitschrift für die Gesamte Staatswissenschaft* **127**, 7–28

Vinogradoff, P., 1908, *English Society in the Eleventh Century*, reprinted 1968, Oxford, Clarendon Press

—— 1911, *The Growth of the Manor*, London, Allen & Unwin

Walters, A. A., 1963, Production and cost functions: an econometric survey, *Econometrica* **31**, 1–66

Warren, W. L., 1984, The myth of Norman administrative efficiency, *Transactions of the Royal Historical Society* **34**, 113–32

White, H., 1980, A heteroskedastic-consistent covariance matrix estimator and a direct test for heteroskedasticity, *Econometrica* **48**, 817–38

White, K. J., 1978, A general computer program for econometric methods—SHAZAM, *Econometrica* **46**, 239–40

Whitelock, D. *et al.* 1961, *The Anglo-Saxon Chronicle: A Revised Translation*, London, Eyre & Spottiswoode

Wicksteed, P., 1894, Coordination of the laws of distribution, *Economic Journal* **4**, 308–13

Zellner, A., J. Kmenta, and J. Dreze, 1966, Specification and estimation of Cobb–Douglas production function models, *Econometrica* **34**, 784–95

Zellner, A., and N. S. Revankar, 1969, Generalized production functions, *Review of Economic Studies* **36**, 241–50

Index